Joints in Buildings

Joints in Buildings

Bruce Martin

MA(Cantab), AADip(Hons), FRIBA, MSIA

GEORGE GODWIN LIMITED · LONDON

JOHN WILEY & SONS · NEW YORK

© Bruce Martin 1977

All drawings prepared by Barbara Martin

First published in Great Britain by
George Godwin Limited 1977

Reprinted 1979

ISBN 0 7114 4001 8

George Godwin Limited
The book publishing subsidiary
of the Builder Group
1-3 Pemberton Row
Red Lion Court, Fleet Street
London EC4

Published in the USA
by Halsted Press, a Division
of John Wiley & Sons, Inc
New York

ISBN 0-470-99106-2

**Library of Congress Cataloging in
Publication Data**

Martin, Bruce.
    Joints in buildings.

    Bibliography : p.
    Includes indexes.
    1. Buildings – Joints. I. Title.
TH2060.M37 1977   690   77-2288
ISBN 0-470-99106-2

Typeset by
Chapel River Press, Andover, Hampshire

Printed and bound in Great Britain by
Billing & Sons Limited,
Guildford, London and Worcester

Contents

Author's preface

This work is a serious attempt to bring order to a new field. By nature building tends to be empiric. It is a practical art in which the result springs directly from the operations. The practitioners are rarely literary enthusiasts and seldom academic philosophers in the best sense of those terms. Building is only changing slowly from a craft to an industry and the science of building is of recent origin.

Science, as an organised body of knowledge concerning a field of endeavour, is built on technology to provide a foundation for understanding and creative change. Its creation calls for hard work, persistence and obstinacy, driven perhaps by economic necessity, a thirst for knowledge, a need for security and order, and a horror of the inexact, the ill-defined and the uncertain. These are no longer generally admired attributes as they were in some earlier centuries. In an age of holidays with pay, leisure activities, ever-shortening working hours, a decline in craftsmanship, watching television and waiting for something to turn up, the explorer is very much on his own.

Jointing is the very essence of building because to joint is to put together and to put things together is to build. It has been carried out in practice as an integral part of a long tradition of workmanship and has received little conscious study. The field of joints and jointing is a central part of the larger field of building construction and has not been studied in its own right until recently. However, over the past ten years many theoretical and applied research projects have been undertaken with the result that the field has been surveyed, measured, defined and examined in detail. A proper terminology has been laid down and a reasonably comprehensive theory has been evolved.

I intend this book to be a source of sound reliable knowledge concerning the kernel of building construction. At the same time it may serve as a useful historical record of the state of the art in the middle of the second half of the twentieth century.

I should like to thank all those who have helped me in the preparation of this book: my wife Barbara Martin, for the preparation of all the drawings; George Atkinson, H. W. Harrison and R. B. Bonshor of the Building Research Establishment, for advice on the subject; Jan Bobrowski, David Dean, Roger D. Foster, R. Howard, Malcolm Johnson, Susan Martin, Anthony Williams and Philip Wykeham, who have all given valuable advice and assistance; Colette Moase for the typing of the texts; and Julia Burden and Kay King for their careful checking of the typescript.

I should like to thank all those companies who have kindly supplied technical information. The names of these firms, together with the associations who also kindly offered assistance, are listed on page 212.

In particular I should like to thank: A. H. Anderson; A. J. Aston; A. J. Brooks; A. R. Bruce; A. R. Burch; S. G. Clements; E. J. Collins; L. D'Eath; B. Dore; F. S. Drake; P. H. Dunstone; M. E. Ewer; R. F. Freemantle; G. M. Fullman; P. Gardiner; S. R. Gee; Tore Gjelsvik; D. A. Gomm; P. M. Gracie; J. W. Hamling; D. H. Helliwell; C. A. W. Horne; R. Howorth; E. J. Keeble; F. J. Keil; K. Lynch; N. Marson; J. McNeil; G. G. Phillips; J. Ritter; D. L. Sawtell; P. J. Schryver; T. Shelton; S. A. Roe; P. Toohey; N. Veacock; G. Wesson; R. Woolman.

Publisher's note

Whilst the principles discussed and the joint details shown in this book are the product of careful study, the author and publisher cannot in any way guarantee the suitability of any joint for any particular situation, and they shall not be under any legal liability of any kind in any respect of or arising out of the form or contents of this book or any error therein, or the reliance of any person thereon.

Manufacturers have co-operated with the author in supplying details of their products, and free use has been made to adapt the information supplied within a reasonable compass to make this book as useful as possible to architects and designers.

It should be carefully noted that the inclusion of any material, component, product or system in this book does not imply that any rights are available other than those of using the material, component, product or system in the design of a building.

It is in the nature of modern technology that products and processes are constantly changing. Frequently, however, some considerable time elapses before the most recent changes are adopted throughout the industry. Indeed, it sometimes happens that the latest innovation never gains wide acceptance.

This book is an attempt to show what is regarded as good current practice. Every effort has been made to ensure accuracy within the situation shown.

Part I
Aspects of theory

Chapter 1
Joints in building

1.1 EXTENT OF THE FIELD

We are faced today with methods of constructing buildings that range from traditional simple hand-craft methods to those based upon the most advanced industrial techniques. Between the two extremes lies every form of building from the completely traditional forms of building construction to the most highly developed forms of engineering.

Traditional building was characterized by the use of local materials, a definite style of design and a well-established method of construction. It was usually the work of a small society with its own set of rules, scarcely affected by foreign ideas and influences. The rules were passed on from father to son and were seldom written down. One learnt by doing.

If traditional forms of building had continued and had remained the only forms, then this book would have been largely unnecessary and certainly without its present content. For in local building, the simple use of one or two natural materials led to a few recognised methods of construction with a correspondingly limited number of ways of making the few joints that were needed. These methods were used, tried and tested over many generations so that they became proven and reliable. The joints could be depended upon.

Over a period of two hundred years scientific methods, the Industrial Revolution, and the social revolutions that followed, brought about the end of craftsmanship. New forms of building have appeared for the first time in recorded history. There has been an enormous increase in both the rate of production and the total stock of building. The introduction of factory-production of building components with new materials and methods of manufacture has changed the relationship between the architect and the man on the building site. The ability to construct effective joints in the traditional way has gradually been lost. New materials, new production methods and new needs have brought about new forms of construction, methods of assembly and ways of making joints.

When properly carried out, the design processes are founded upon a clear description of the requirements in terms of anticipated performance and are carried out methodically with the aid of specifications and large-scale drawings. The building is conceived as an articulate set of parts able to be arranged in predictable patterns. The parts are designed so that they may be made in a factory and later assembled on the building site. The details of the construction and, in particular, the joints between the parts, are few in number and are carefully worked out. Prototypes are made and tested in advance to ensure compliance with requirements before they are standardized for repetitive production. The factory production is based upon detailed know-how of production methods and on rigorous methods of quality control. The parts are made of high quality material with known and measured characteristics, whose performance can be calculated and future performance predicted with confidence. The material is generally man-made with many new properties often especially useful for building, such as lightness, thermal insulation, or strength. The material is formed by machines into parts that are made strictly in accordance with prescribed standards of all kinds and, in particular, to standard sizes with specified tolerances.

Many of the parts are relatively large, their size, however being limited by the form of transport used to take the parts from the factory to the site. Assembly on the building site is a rapid sequence of operations, being based upon the complete coordination of the sizes of all the parts with those of the building layout, and on the correct use of rules for measurement and the control of sizing and positioning. With this new way of building the joints between the parts become as important as the parts between the joints.

Relatively few buildings have been built fully in accordance with these principles of design, manufacture and erection. The best early examples, such as the Crystal Palace, and the great railway stations, were the products of a highly organised wealthy industrious society at the centre of an Empire. Two World Wars caused massive destruction, destroyed all traditional methods and led to improvisation and experiment on a vast scale. The building programme doubled and redoubled. Every possible way of constructing buildings by some means or other was sought and carried out. The real cost of building rose steadily. Many types of building, such as some of the American skyscrapers, were extravagant in the use of materials and energy both to construct the buildings and to maintain them. The provision of shelter accounted for an ever-increasing proportion of the national expenditure. Administrative economic measures to reduce cost led to cheeseparing and to construction having insufficient factors of safety to meet exceptional conditions and even in some cases, probable conditions of stress. Methods of construction became more and more complicated and diversified. Methods of jointing followed the same pattern and, in consequence, failures followed.

It is possible, certainly desirable, and probably necessary that joints in building construction should become few, simple and widely accepted. But at the present time and perhaps to be able to reach such a future condition, we need to record as many as possible of the different current methods of jointing so as to discover their range of application and the nature of their diversity. It is partly for these reasons that such a record has been made, and selected examples have been redrawn as illustrations for Part II of this book.

1

1.2 THE NAMING OF JOINTS

The naming of joints in traditional building construction

In traditional building, joints were not consciously studied. There was no theory of joints and no need for technical terms. The joints were not analysed and the parts were not named. On the other hand it was necessary, in each of the building crafts, to be able to designate a particular joint so as to distinguish it from others. The names given to joints that were used in traditional building construction reflect the different trades involved and the techniques employed. There were few trades and the joints used were well established and few in number. Many of these joints are still in use.

The carpenter and later the joiner, by that very description, have been particularly concerned with joining together pieces of wood and many names describe the shape of the cut as, for example, skew notch joint, birdsmouth joint, cogging joint, dovetail joint, indented joint, butt joint, scarfed joint, comb joint, hook joint, tongued joint, ploughed joint, mitre joint, V-joint. Some names describe the position of the timber members as, for example, the angle joint, lapped joint, corner locking joint, housed joint. Other names are derived from the method of doing the work as, for example, the halved joint, the scribed joint, the coped joint. Other names are based on the jointing component employed as, for example, the nailed joint, screwed joint, connectored joint, cottered joint, dowelled joint.

In the construction of masonry, some names of joints describe the position of the mortar between stones as, for example, bed joint, coursing joint, cross joint, straight joint, transverse joint. Other names refer to the shaping of the stone as, for example, interlocking joint, joggle joint, mason's joint, mason's mitre joint and secret key joint.

In brickwork some of the mortar joints are described according to the shape of the pointing on the face of the wall: flat joint, concave joint, recessed joint, V-joint.

In plumbing, some joints are named after the shape of the material, the pipe or fitting: spigot and socket, astragal joint, ball joint, cup-and-cone joint, flanged joint, hollow roll, screwed joint, capillary joint, swivel joint. Other joints are named after the material used: brazed joint (brass), lead-welded joint (lead), solvent joint (solvent), soldered joint (solder). Other joints are named after a component used to make the joint: gland joint, O-ring joint. Others are described by the method used to make the joint: compression joint, fusion joint, lead-welded joint, welded joint, manipulative joint. Yet others are named by the position of the pipework: branched joint, upright joint, underhand joint, knuckle joint. One joint is named by its function: flexible joint.

The naming of joints in new building construction

With the development of science and technology, new materials, forms and methods of building construction have given rise to new ways of jointing and to the introduction of additional names that usually describe a single attribute of the joint. There are only a few of these. *Open joint* (or open drained joint) (or drained joint) is named after character of its gap. *Sealed joint* is named after the jointing material that is used (a sealant). *Glued joint* is similarly named (glue). *Labyrinth* joint is named after the general form of the joint profile.

A number of joints in engineering work are named according to their purpose: movement joint (to permit movement); expansion joint (to permit expansion); sliding joint (to permit relative sliding action); contraction joint (to permit contraction such as shrinkage); induced contraction joint; partial contraction joint. One is named after the jointing component used: riveted joint (rivet).

In general, however, it may be said that joints are no longer given a name. Thus, for example, there are many ways of glazing a window, but the different joints that result are not distinguished by name. The materials, jointing products, functions and performance characteristics are named, but the joints as such are not identified by name. A joint is therefore described in terms of the building element of which it forms a part, or its situation in the element, or the profile of the joint face, or a particular attribute, or by some other descriptive means. As there is no orderly description, a rigorous classification of joints is not possible.

1.3 JOINTS IN TIMBER

LAP JOINT also SHEAR JOINT or LAPPED JOINT
A joint between two pieces of timber formed by placing
the end of one piece over the end of the other and
fastening the two with through bolts, straps or U-bolts.

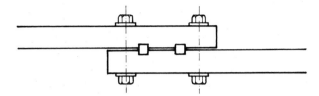

HALVED JOINT
A joint between the ends of two pieces of wood of the
same thickness formed by cutting away half the end of
each timber and placing the cut surfaces together. The
joint is glued or glued and bolted, or nailed, or screwed.

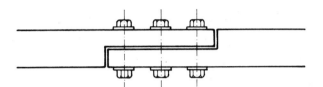

BEVEL HALVING also BEVELLED HALVING
A halved joint in which the meeting surfaces are cut at
an angle to the plane of the pieces so as to give resistance to longitudinal force.

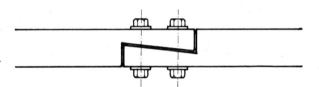

SCARFED JOINT also SCARF JOINT or SCARF
A joint between the ends of two pieces of timber formed
with a bevel on one piece that matches a similar bevel
on the other. The joint may be glued, bolted, or strapped,
and may incorporate joggles, wedges or keys.

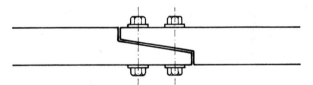

INDENTED JOINT
A joint between the ends of two pieces of timber formed
by cutting notches in the timbers and the fishplates that
correspond. The joint is bolted and may incorporate
wedges.

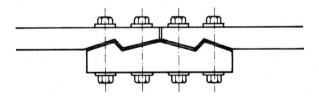

FINGER JOINT
A joint between the ends of two pieces of timber
formed by cutting V-shaped notches in the end of
one timber and corresponding notches in the end of
the other. The joint is cut with great accuracy on special
machines and is glued.

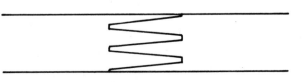

BUTT JOINT also SQUARE JOINT
A joint between the ends of two pieces of wood that meet without overlapping. The pieces may be end-to-end, edge-to-edge or at right angles and are normally glued.

REBATED JOINT
A joint between two pieces of wood that has a rebate in one piece that matches a similar rebate in the other.

TONGUE-AND-GROOVE JOINT
A joint that is formed between the edges of two boards by cutting a groove along the centre of one edge and a corresponding projecting tongue along the centre of the other edge, or nearer the lower edge as, for example, in floorboards.

CROSS-TONGUED JOINT also PLOUGHED-AND-TONGUED JOINT
A joint between the edges of two boards that is formed by fitting a spline or cross tongue into grooves cut along the length of both edges.

V JOINT
A V-shaped joint that is formed between the edges of two tongued-and-grooved boards that have been chamfered along their edges on the same side.

HOOK JOINT also HOOKED JOINT
A joint between the meeting edges of pairs of doors or casements that is formed by cutting an S-shaped rebate in one stile and a corresponding rebate in the other.

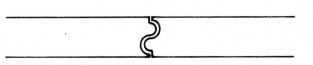

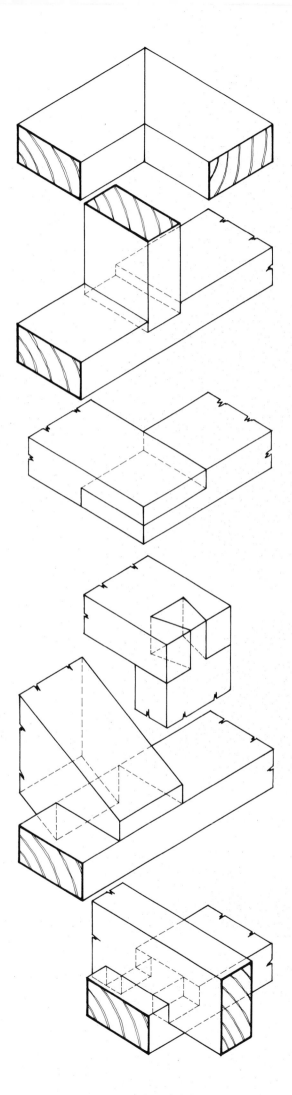

MITRE JOINT also MITRE

A joint between two pieces of timber of similar cross-section that meet at an angle. Each piece is cut to the same angle and the ends are butted and glued.

HOUSED JOINT also HOUSING JOINT or HOUSING

A joint between two pieces of timber formed by cutting a shallow rectangular or dovetailed groove in one piece and fitting the end of the other piece into it.

END-LAP JOINT

A joint between two pieces of timber at an angle in the form of a halved joint.

DOVETAIL JOINT also DOVETAIL

A mortise-and-tenon joint with a tenon that tapers towards its root. The angle of splay is usually 1 : 8 for hardwoods and 1 : 7 for softwoods. The joint is glued.

BIRDSMOUTH JOINT

A joint between two pieces of timber that is formed by cutting a notch in the end of one piece to fit over the other piece usually at right angles, as to fit a rafter over a wall plate.

COCKING JOINT also COGGING or CORKING

A joint between a beam and a wall plate that is formed by cutting a notch under the end of the beam and a notch on both sides of the wall plate so that the beam fits across it.

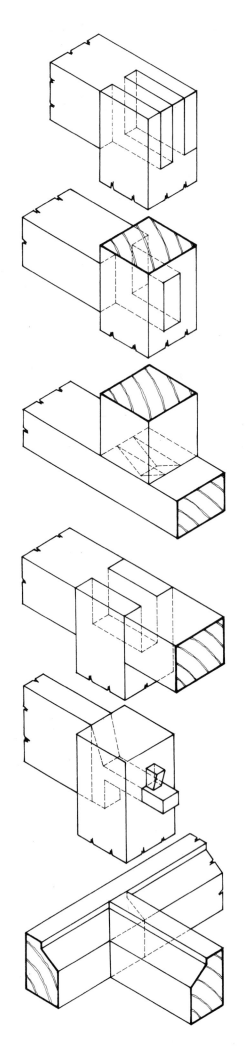

COMBED JOINT also **CORNERLOCKED JOINT FINGER-JOINTED JOINT** or **LAMINATED JOINT**
A joint between two pieces of timber at an angle formed by cutting a set of parallel tenons in one piece to match a set of slots cut in the other piece.

MORTISE-AND-TENON JOINT also **MORTISE JOINT**
A joint between two pieces of timber usually at right angles formed by cutting a rectangular slot in one piece, called the mortise, and cutting a corresponding projection on the other piece, called a tenon. The joint is glued and pinned or wedged.

BRIDLE JOINT
A mortise-and-tenon joint that is used to connect a timber beam to a post by forming a mortise or mortises in the beam and a tenon or tenons at the end of the post.

FORKED TENON
A joint between two pieces of timber that is formed by cutting an open mortise at the end of one piece that fits a tenon cut across the middle of the other piece.

TUSK TENON also **KEYED MORTISE AND TENON JOINT**
A mortise-and-tenon joint with a specially shaped tenon that passes through the mortise and itself has a mortise on the far side that takes a wedge.

SCRIBED JOINT also **COPED JOINT**
A joint between two wood mouldings that is formed by cutting away the end of one moulding to match the other that is usually at right angles.

1.4 JOINTS IN MASONRY

REBATED JOINT
A joint that has a rebate cut in the opposite sides of the two mating stones.

DRY BUTT JOINT
A joint in ashlar without any jointing material.

DOWELLED JOINT
A joint that is connected with a slate or non-ferrous metal dowel, or a stone pin, used horizontally as between coping stones or vertically as between two stones of a column.

FILLED JOINT
A joint between stones that is filled with jointing material.

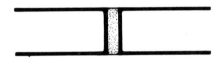

DOVETAIL KEY JOINT also CRAMP JOINT
A joint that has a dovetail shaped groove cut in adjoining stones so that a cramp in slate, lead or non-ferrous metal can be fitted to form a key.

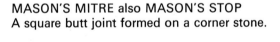

MASON'S MITRE also MASON'S STOP
A square butt joint formed on a corner stone.

SADDLE JOINT also SADDLED JOINT or WATER JOINT
A joint between two stones in a cornice or coping with the stones cut so as to form a slope to throw the water away from the joint.

INTERLOCKING JOINT also SECRET KEY JOINT or JOGGLE JOINT
A joint in ashlar that has a projection on one stone that is shaped to match a groove in the adjacent stone.

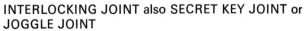

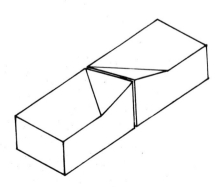

BED JOINT also COURSING JOINT (1)
A horizontal joint or a radiating joint between the voussoirs of an arch.

CROSS JOINT also HEADING JOINT (2)
A vertical mortar joint between bricks or stones. A *face joint* is that part of the joint seen on the face of the wall.

BREAK JOINT also BREAKING JOINT or STAGGERING JOINTS (3)
An arrangement of stones so that the vertical joints in one course do not align with those in the course above or the one below.

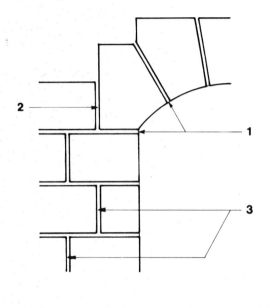

1.5 JOINTS IN BRICKWORK

FLATJOINT also FLUSHJOINT or FLUSHED JOINT
A mortar joint that has its surface flush with the face of the brickwork. The joint is finished or pointed as the work proceeds, the pointing being called *flat pointing.* The mortar is pressed flat with a trowel that leaves a smooth polished appearance. A sandy surface texture is achieved by rubbing the face of the mortar with a piece of wood or polystyrene.

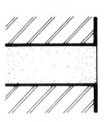

FLATJOINT JOINTED
A *flat joint* that has a narrow groove cut along its centre with the edge of a trowel or with a special tool, called a jointer, drawn against a straightedge. The resulting shadow gives the wall an added appearance of regularity.

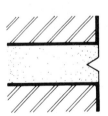

KEYED JOINT also CONCAVE JOINT
A mortar joint with a surface that follows a curved shallow depression. It may be formed by pressing a 13 mm diameter steel bar into the mortar while it is still green. The joint is pointed as the work proceeds and is very durable.

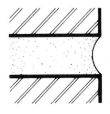

WEATHER-STRUCK JOINT also WEATHERED JOINT or STRUCK JOINT

A mortar joint pointed so that the mortar slopes inwards towards the top. The pointing, known as *weathered pointing* or *struck-joint pointing*, is done normally as work proceeds. When the colour of the pointing differs from that of the mortar, pointing is necessarily a separate operation.

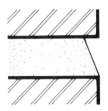

OVERHAND STRUCK JOINT also STRUCK JOINT

A mortar joint pointed so that the mortar slopes inwards towards the bottom. The ledge formed along the top of each brick course is liable to collect water so the joint should be used only when the wall is well protected. It is to be noted that the term Struck joint applies both to a weather-struck joint and to an overhand struck joint, despite their very different characteristics.

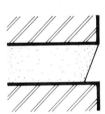

RECESSED JOINT

A mortar joint that is raked out to form a rectangular recess about 6 mm deep and the full thickness of the mortar. It gives to the wall a sculptural quality, but should not be used with soft bricks or on unprotected walls as the ledges formed along the top of the brick courses are liable to collect water and chemicals in solution. However, peeling off of mortar is lessened.

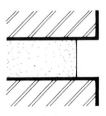

TUCK POINTING

A form of pointing a mortar joint that consists of a narrow squarebead of white lime putty that projects along the centre of the joint. The joint is raked out and filled flush with coloured mortar to match the brickwork. A tuck or narrow groove is cut in the centre of the joint face and the mortar allowed to set. The groove is thin pointed with putty that is cut to shape. In *bastard pointing*, also called *half-tuck pointing*, the bead is of the same material as the filling.

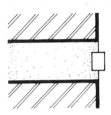

WEATHER JOINT also V-JOINT POINTING

A mortar joint that is pointed in the form of a V. Horizontal joints have asymmetrical slopes. Vertical joints are in the form of a symmetrical V.

1.6 JOINTS IN PLUMBING

WELDED JOINT
A joint for metals or plastics in which the parts are fused together by being heated to a critical temperature with or without the addition of molten or softened material from a filler rod.

AUTOGENOUS WELDED JOINT
A *welded joint* between two parts of the same metal with or without a filler rod made of the same metal.

LEAD WELDED JOINT
An *autogenous welded joint* for lead pipe or sheet made by butting together or lapping the parts to be joined and using a blowpipe to fuse them. Where necessary more lead from a filler rod is added to provide the requisite strength.

BRONZE WELDED JOINT
A *welded joint* that is made with molten bronze.

SOLDERED JOINT
A joint that is made with molten solder.

TAFT JOINT also FINGER-WIPED JOINT
A *soldered joint* for lead or lead alloy pipe that is made by shaping and fitting the pipe ends to form a taper and wiping in plumber's solder.

BLOCK TAFT JOINT
A *taft joint* that incorporates a lead flange that rests on a timber block and supports the pipe in a vertical chase.

BLOWN JOINT also CUP-AND-CONE JOINT or CUP JOINT or COPPER-BIT JOINT
A *soldered joint* for lead or lead alloy that is made by shaping and fitting the pipe ends to form a taper entering a bell mouth and melting in fine solder.

BRAZED JOINT
A joint that is made with molten brass.

WIPED SOLDERED JOINT also FUSED JOINT or BURNED JOINT
A joint, for lead or lead alloy pipe, in which the parts are prepared, shaped and fitted together. Molten plumber's solder is then poured on and manipulated with the aid of a pad of special cloth with which the cooling solder is wiped around the pipe to give the shape and volume required for the strength of the joint.

KNUCKLE JOINT
A *wiped soldered joint* that is used for joining a brass fitting at right angles to the end of a lead pipe where there is not enough room to form the normal branch joint.

UNDERHAND JOINT
A *wiped soldered joint* that is used to join two horizontal pipes in situ.

UPRIGHT JOINT
A *wiped soldered joint* that is used to join together two vertical pipes in situ.

SOLVENT-WELDED JOINT
A closely fitting *spigot and socket joint* of plastic tube, such as PVC, that is made by smearing both spigot and socket with a solvent before assembly.

FUSION JOINT
A joint made on certain types of plastic piping eg polythene, in which the surfaces that are to be in contact in a closely fitting spigot and socket joint are separately heated and assembled while still hot. On cooling the two pipes fuse together.

COMPRESSION JOINT
A joint that is usually made between light-gauge copper tubes by means of brass screwed fittings that grip the ends of the tubes.

MANIPULATIVE JOINT
A *compression joint* that does require the ends of the tubes slightly belled out so that a gland is not normally needed.

NON-MANIPULATIVE JOINT
A *compression joint* that does not require the ends of the tubes to be shaped before assembly as they are gripped by means of a compression ring contained within the pipe fittings.

EXPANSION JOINT
A joint that permits relative movement of the jointed parts caused by expansion and contraction due to temperature change.

FLANGED JOINT
A joint made by the connection of two flanges by bolts or studs, and nuts.

FLEXIBLE JOINT
A joint that permits some movement of the jointed parts out of their original alignment or that permits the jointing of parts that are not truly aligned.

SCREWED JOINT
A joint between two concentric cylindrical surfaces upon which have been formed matching screw threads. The joint is made by engaging the threads and rotating one or both parts.

SPIGOT and SOCKET JOINT
A joint for pipes or channels in which the plain end or *spigot* of one pipe is inserted into the enlarged end, or *socket*, of the other. The gap is filled with jointing material or with a ring of rubber or other material. For cast iron the caulking is with lead wool or molten lead. For glazed ware it is done with cement mortar plugged with old rope at the lower end.

ASTRAGAL JOINT
A *spigot and socket joint* that has ornamental mouldings on the outside of the socket called astragals.

CAPILLARY JOINT
A *spigot and socket joint* with a fine clearance that is filled with molten solder by capillary action during the application of heat.

CAULKED JOINT
A *spigot and socket joint* that is made tight by driving in lead wool or other similar material and compacting it with a caulking tool and hammer.

O-RING JOINT
A *spigot and socket joint* in which a rubber ring of circular cross section is used as the jointing material.

INTERNAL SPIGOT JOINT
A form of joint in an eaves gutter that has no projecting external socket.

BALL JOINT
A *movable joint* between two parts that have joint faces that correspond with part of the surface of a sphere.

SWIVEL JOINT
A joint between a fixed part and a movable part, which permits rotary movement about the common axis of the parts.

HOLLOW ROLL also SEAM ROLL
A joint between the edges of two lead sheets on the flat, made by turning up each edge at right angles to the flat surface, bringing the two turned-up parts together and shaping them over to form a roll.

LOCK JOINT also LOCK SEAM
A joint formed between the edges of metal sheets by folding the edges, engaging the folded portions and dressing down flat. Either single or double folds may be made, the completed joint being termed a single, or double welt respectively.

GLAND JOINT
A joint on a copper hot water or soil pipe that permits thermal movement.

1.7 JOINTS IN ENGINEERING STRUCTURES

CONSTRUCTION JOINT
A joint, especially in concrete work, which is formed where construction work has to be interrupted. Concreting operations should be planned where possible to end at an expansion or contraction joint, but where not possible a construction joint is used. It is not designed to accommodate movement but since it is a plane of weakness, it is a potential source of cracks.

CONTRACTION JOINT
A joint which is formed to accommodate shrinkage movements, especially contraction of concrete due to loss of moisture and thermal contraction associated with loss of heat or hydration, the latter causing most shrinkage. Shrinkage movements can be considered as irreversible although the joint will always be subjected to cyclic movement due to variations in moisture content and temperature.

EXPANSION JOINT
A joint which is formed to accommodate both expansion and contraction movements of the structure caused by cyclic variations in temperature and moisture content. In concrete work the expansion joint provides a discontinuity in both the concrete and the reinforcement. A gap is formed between adjacent parts of the structure with a clearance designed to accommodate the maximum closing movement.

GLUED JOINT
A joint, especially between timber components, in which fixing is by means of a layer of glue.

INDUCED CONTRACTION JOINT
A *contraction joint* which is formed to induce a crack by means of a top sealing slot and a middle or bottom fillet.

KICKER JOINT
A horizontal *construction joint* between a continuous upstand section of an in situ concrete slab cast integrally with the base slab and an in situ concrete wall.

LABYRINTH JOINT
An *open joint* in which overlapping planes provide a tortuous path so that rain penetration is resisted.

MOVEMENT JOINT
A joint which is formed to accommodate relative movement between adjoining parts of a structure.

OPEN JOINT also OPEN DRAINED JOINT or DRAINED JOINT
A joint between two building components, especially concrete panels, in which the gap is designed to be left open and may be bridged by a baffle.

PARTIAL CONTRACTION JOINT
A *contraction joint* in which deliberate discontinuity is provided in the concrete but the reinforcement is continuous across the gap.

RIVETED JOINT
A joint, especially between metal sheets, which is fastened by means of rivets.

SEALED JOINT
A joint which is sealed by means of a sealant.

SETTLEMENT JOINT
A *movement joint* which is used where unequal foundation pressures occur.

SLIDING JOINT
A *movement joint* which is designed especially to permit relative movement in the plane of the joint.

1.8 TERMS AND DEFINITIONS

It is only in recent years that the subject of joints in building has been studied sufficiently to produce a clear idea of the main parts of the field of study and to establish a consistent use for the few terms that are needed to encompass the field.

The word *join* is derived from the old French word *joindre,* that in turn comes from the latin verb *jungere, junctum,* to join. It means to connect, to unite, to associate, to add. It implies two or more things that are to be joined, the act of joining, a method of doing so, and a meeting place.

The word *joint* is derived directly from the word join and in ordinary language refers to the place where two separate things are joined or to the mode of joining parts in a structure.

In traditional masonry the word came to mean the surface of contact between two stones held together by means of cement or mortar or by a superincumbent weight. In brickwork the term referred to the mortar itself as used between two adjacent bricks. The word was used in carpentry to refer to the method of connecting timber sections as, for example, a lap joint or to the place of meeting of one piece of timber with another as, for example, an angle joint.

Joint

In building technology today the term joint refers to the way building products meet and where they meet. Two separate definitions are given in the international standard:

1 The construction formed by the adjacent parts of two or more building products, components or materials, when these are put together, fixed or united with or without the use of a jointing product.

2 A position in the building where a joint (1) is situated.

The joint may be formed without a jointing product, as between stones in a dry stone wall, or with one or more jointing products that are used to seal the joint, provide a fixing, or meet some other requirement.

Jointing product

Any product that is used in building to form a joint is termed a jointing product.

A jointing product therefore includes materials, sections and components. When these are used to form joints they are known collectively as jointing materials, jointing sections and jointing components.

Jointing materials include adhesives and sealing compounds. Jointing sections include strips, gaskets and flashings. Jointing components include connectors and fastenings.

The position and arrangement of building components in a building determines the position and kind of junctions. The junctions determine the positions and kinds of joints. In spite of the great variety of situations in a building, the geometry of space and the arrangement of the construction leads to a limited number of junctions which in turn limit the positioning and sizing of the joints.

The generic building joint may be represented for purpose of analysis and definition as the edge profile of two components with a jointing product in between.

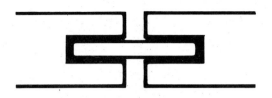

JOINT PROFILE
The part of a component profile designed to relate to the joint is defined as the *joint profile.*

JOINT FACE
The part of a joint profile that is considered in the calculation of the work size of a component is defined as the *joint face*.

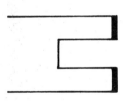

INTERFACE
The meeting face of a jointing product and a building component is defined as the *interface*.

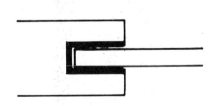

GAP
The space between the two components at the joint is defined as the *gap*.

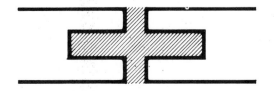

JOINT REFERENCE PLANE
The measurement and position of the joint profiles of adjacent building components and/or jointing products may be determined by means of a plane of a reference system that is normally taken as a plane placed centrally between the two joint faces, and defined as the *joint reference plane.*

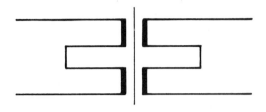

CLEARANCE
The distance between the joint faces of adjacent components is defined as the *clearance*.

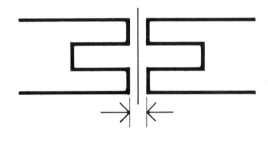

MARGIN
The distance between the joint face of a building component and the joint reference plane is defined as the *margin*.

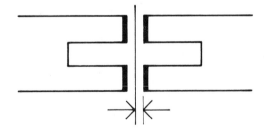

JOINTING
The process of forming a joint is called *jointing.* Analysis of the process reveals a set of operations that are closely related to the building and jointing products and through them to the performance requirements of the design. The geometry of the design can affect the sequence of assembly of the parts. The parts are determined by the functions that the joint is required to fulfil.

1.9 THE NATURE OF JOINTS IN BUILDING

Assembly

The basis of the building process is the putting together of constituent parts to form a total structure and it is in this sense we refer to the assembly of a building. (Fr *assembler: ensemble* — together ; from the Latin *simul* — at once, together, at the same time.) But assembly is not enough. The parts must also be joined. Jointing is required to bring about stability, weather tightness, fire resistance, and many other characteristics that may be required.

Jointing

Jointing includes positioning, fixing and protection. The process of jointing begins after the components have been *delivered* to the site, *placed* in the building and *located* in their allocated space.

Positioning, the first jointing operation, implies the accurate locating of components, that is to say location within the specified positional tolerance and in relation to the setting out lines.

Fixing, usually the second jointing operation, consists in joining one component to another with a suitable jointing product. The type of product and the method of jointing should depend on the performance requirements of the joint.

Protection, normally the final jointing operation, consists in completing the joint with one or more jointing products to ensure that the finished joint fully complies with the joint performance requirements. The gap is filled, pointed, sealed or otherwise treated to resist external forces and afford protection.

Positioning

The place of a joint and its components can be described with reference to the building as a whole, with reference to the location of building elements or with reference to a particular reference plane. From another standpoint the place of the joint may be said to be described in terms of successive degrees of exactitude. For a description of this kind the first requirement is a system of reference. In the context of building, as in engineering, the concept of the plane as a basis of reference is fundamental. Joseph Whitworth, who sought accuracy in the manufacture of engineering parts, said 'I cannot impress too strongly . . . the vast importance of possessing a true plane as a standard of reference. All excellence in workmanship depends on it.'

Joint reference plane

In the context of joints in building and their positioning in the building, the *joint reference plane* must be regarded as the essential basis for both theory and practice.

The adoption of a joint reference plane enables the position of components to be described and to be shown on drawings. It also enables building components in the course of construction to be positioned within the specified limits. Much of the craft of a traditional craftsman, such as a bricklayer, consists in achieving accurate positioning with horizontal beds, vertical perpends and regular widths of joints between bricks. In relation to adjacent components, the joint reference plane is the plane that bounds the space occupied by each component.

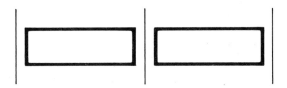

Adjacent components are placed in their respective spaces and are spaced apart to preserve a uniform pattern, to avoid the necessity of cutting and fitting material on site, to allow components to be assembled separately and not in an interdependent sequence, to provide for thermal expansion, effects of humidity and structural movement. The space between adjacent components is defined as the *gap* and the distance between the components is known as the *clearance*.

Fixing

When the two components have been positioned fixing may then be provided. The degree of fixing depends upon the performance requirements of the given joint.

Fixing is achieved by reliance upon natural forces amongst which must be included gravitational, magnetic, chemical and mechanical. When a simple component like a brick is positioned on a horizontal surface, such as a slab, a horizontal joint is formed. Gravitational force acting vertically and frictional forces acting horizontally keep the brick in contact with the slab and, if no other forces are applied, the brick can be said to be joined to the slab but it is not fixed. The space between the brick and the slab is unfilled and there is no jointing product. Such a method of construction and jointing is used to build dry stone walls that are heavy and wide enough to resist wind pressure and do not need to have joints sealed for other purposes. In a building, on the other hand, the building as a whole, the components and the joints between them are subject to movement as a result of applied forces. In a joint the clearance between adjoining components may vary due to changes in the state of the materials that result from shrinkage, contraction, creep, expansion, elastic deformation, vibration, and other consequences of applied forces. To accommodate, minimise, or prevent such movements, the components must be fixed. The type of fixing is dependent on the forces that act and on their relationship to the joint reference plane. The principal forces to be considered are tensile and torsional. They may act at right angles to the joint reference plane or parallel to it. A degree of fixity or fixing is achieved by producing forces to counteract the applied forces. When two components meet at right angles to the joint reference plane the arrangement is the simple case of a butt joint.

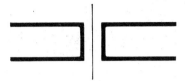

If the components are not fixed and a tensile force is applied perpendicularly to the reference plane, there is nothing to prevent the parting of the components and the failure of the joint.

When the components meet paralled to the joint reference plane, the arrangement is the simple lap joint.

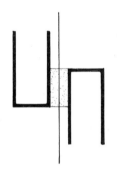

If the components are not fixed and are subjected to a tensile force applied parallel to the joint reference plane, the joint will again fail.

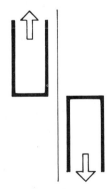

In the same way, torsional forces, whether applied at right angles or parallel to the joint reference plane, will produce failure of the joint provided it is not fixed so as to resist such applied forces.

Adhesion

The first principal method of fixing is *adhesion*. The gap between the components is filled with a special jointing material such as mortar, glue, or adhesive. The behaviour of a joint fixed with adhesive depends on the quality of the interface between the surface of the components and the adhesive. It depends also on the direction of the applied load in relation to the joint reference plane and on the area of the surface to which the adhesive is applied. It is probable that the face of the adhesive layer forms a jagged interface with the face of the component and that an adhesive bond is essentially mechanical. Chemical and mechanical forces produce the adhesion and, at the same time, may improve the performance of the joint in several other respects. Wet mortar, for example, permits accurate positioning of the component, such as with a brick, and when dry forms a durable hard bond that resists movement and weather.

With a butt joint and with tensile forces applied perpendicularly to the joint reference plane, the adhesive bond is weak and there is a tendency to failure of the joint. Such is especially the case if the applied forces are not uniformly distributed over the area of the adhesive or if the load is slightly offset. Stress distribution then becomes very uneven leading to a possible failure.

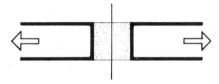

Torsional forces applied perpendicularly to the joint reference plane produce a moment tending to open the joint on one side that leads to cleavage due to the concentration of stress along one side of the adhesive.

With a lap joint and with tensile forces applied parallel to the joint reference plane, the adhesive bond is in shear and the tensile stresses are distributed across the whole area of the adhesive. The distribution is not normally entirely uniform; there is an increase of stress around the edges.

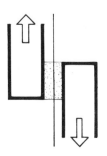

When torsional forces are applied parallel to the joint reference plane, torsional shear stresses are produced in the plane of the adhesive and the adhesive has to prevent relative rotation of the components.

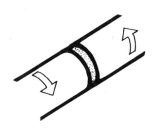

Torsional forces applied perpendicularly to the joint reference plane will tend to bend the dowel.

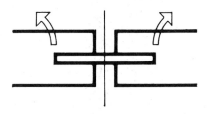

When applied parallel to the joint reference plane the components are likely to rotate and the resistance of the dowel is dependent on frictional forces and the elasticity of the materials.

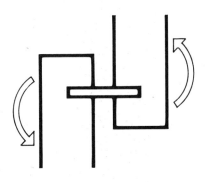

Connection

The second principal method of fixing is *connection*. The two components that are to be joined are connected by means of a jointing section or component such as a dowel, nail or pin. A hole is drilled in both the components and the dowel is driven into both holes to give a tight fit. Frictional forces between the dowel and the sides of the holes in the components combined with the elasticity of the materials produce the fixing.

With a butt joint and tensile forces applied perpendicularly to the joint reference plane, the surface of the dowel and the sides of the hole are subjected to shear forces that have to be resisted by two sets of forces: friction around the dowel and the elasticity of the material that contains the holes. It is important that the dowel fits the hole as tightly as possible. A loose fit, in this case, obviously means immediate failure.

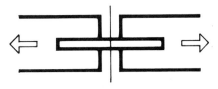

With a lap joint and tensile forces applied parallel to the joint reference plane, the dowel is in shear so that the cross-sectional area of the material and its strength become the significant factors in this case. Displacement of the dowel due to these applied forces is not likely, but a tight fit is still desirable.

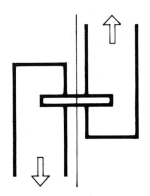

Fastening

The third principal method of fixing is *fastening*. The two components to be joined are fastened by a jointing component such as a screw, bolt, rivet or other fastener. When the screw is tightened the two components are brought together and subjected to mechanical pressure due to the bearing of the screw head on the face of one component and the bearing of the screw threads on the material of the other component. Applied loads have to overcome the bearing resistance of these surfaces.

With a butt joint and the tensile forces applied perpendicularly to the joint reference plane, the shape of the screw threads and the screwed hole formed in the components produces bearing surfaces that take shear stress to resist the applied forces.

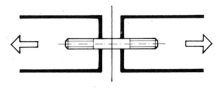

With a lap joint and tensile forces applied parallel to the joint reference plane, the screw is in shear and in bearing. It acts in the same way as a dowel, but with the added advantage that the screw thread combined with the head of the screw render withdrawal very unlikely.

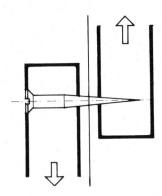

Torsional forces applied perpendicularly to the joint reference plane tend to subject the screw to bending.

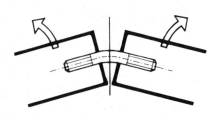

When applied parallel to the joint reference plane there is a tendency for the components to rotate and the only resistance to rotation is the frictional stress exerted by the screw and the elasticity of the material of the components.

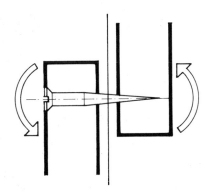

stresses are set up on some of the interfaces and resist the applied forces.

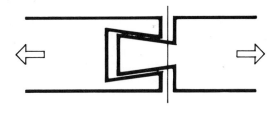

Tensile forces applied parallel to the joint reference plane produce similar resistance.

Locking

The fourth principal method of fixing is *locking*. The two components to be joined are locked together by forming a lock or hook or joggle in one component that fits a corresponding and mating profile on the other component. The two components are fitted together and fixed without the intervention of a jointing component.

With a lock joint when the tensile forces are applied perpendicularly to the joint reference plane shear

1.10 FIXING METHODS

There are four main methods of fixing. To fix is to adhere, to connect, to fasten and to lock. These are not just synonyms for a common process. They are distinct fixing operations that produce the same result. They are all related to the behaviour of a fixed joint that basically depends upon the formation of a mechanical bond between the components brought about by the bearing of one surface upon another. Adhesion, connection, fastening and locking are alternative methods of producing jagged interfaces that provide bearing surfaces able to resist applied forces. It is the relative size of the interfaces that tends to conceal the common characteristic.

ADHESION

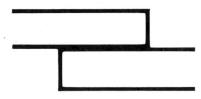

CONNECTION

FASTENING

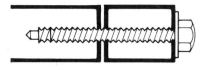

LOCKING

Adhesion includes sticking, glueing, gumming, welding and soldering.

Connecting includes anchoring, attaching, dowelling, nailing, pinning, spiking, tenoning and clipping.

Fastening includes bolting, clamping, hooking, riveting, screwing and linking.

Locking is the result of shaping the components to be joined and does not require the use of jointing products in addition.

The fixing process and the product used to provide the fixing are a mirror of each other to such an extent that in the English language the word for the fixing operation is always almost matched by a corresponding word for the product. Securing and notching seem to be exceptions to this general rule.

Protection

The final jointing operation of protection is intended to deal with the environmental conditions surrounding the joint as distinct from those of dimensional positioning and structural stability.

The protection of the joint against the effects of external forces and agencies is achieved in practice by the use of fillers, sealants, and sectional jointing material such as strips, gaskets and flashings.

Chapter 2
The performance of joints

2.1 INTRODUCTION

> . . . for want of a nail the shoe was lost;
> for want of a shoe, the horse was lost;
> and for want of a horse the rider was lost.

The maxim of Benjamin Franklin published in 1758 sums up the essential importance of a joint and the way it performs.

Joints between building parts are no less important, for without a joint which performs properly, the building element which contains it may fail and so lead in due course to the failure of the building.

The performance of a joint in building is the way it behaves under stress. Such behaviour depends on the material and form of the joint, its location, and the external forces to which it is subject. These three principal factors are all inter-related. The materials and their form are sometimes referred to as the inherent or intrinsic characteristics of the joint and must be designed to suit the location and its required performance. The location of the joint in the building largely determines the forces which it is called upon to withstand, and so its design. The forces which operate at a given location determine the functions of the joint at that location and should determine its design.

2.2 THE FUNCTION OF JOINTS

Joints may be affected by living organisms and by energy of all kinds. As essential parts of a building process they must facilitate the fixing and the positioning of the components. As part of the architectural design, they must be visually acceptable.

An analysis of the many functions of a joint in building construction has been made in recent years and is contained in the International Standard, ISO 3447.

The list is reproduced here:

A1   To control passage of insects and vermin
A2   To control passage of plants, leaves, roots, seeds and pollen
A3   To control passage of dust and inorganic particles
A4   To control passage of heat
A5   To control passage of sound
A6   To control passage of light
A7   To control passage of radiation
A8   To control passage of air and other gases
A9   To control passage of odours
A10 To control passage of water, snow and ice
A11 To control passage of water vapour
A12 To control condensation
A13 To control generation of sound
A14 To control generation of odours

To resist stress in one or more directions due to:

B1   compression
B2   tension
B3   bending
B4   shear
B5   torsion
B6   vibrations (or any other type of stress which may induce fatigue)
B7   impact
B8   abrasion (indicate, for each particular case, the type of wear)
B9   shrinkage or expansion
B10   creep
B11   dilation or contraction due to temperature variations

C1   To control passage of fire, smoke, gases, radiation and radioactive materials
C2   To control sudden positive or negative pressures due to explosion or atmospheric factors
C3   To avoid generation of toxic gases and fumes in case of fire
C4   To avoid harbouring or proliferation of dangerous micro-organisms

D1   To accommodate variations in the sizes of the joint at assembly due to deviations in the sizes and positions of the joined components (induced deviations)

D2 To accommodate continuing changes in the sizes of the joint due to thermal, moisture and structural movement, vibration and creep (inherent deviations)

E1 To support joined components in one or more directions
E2 To resist differential deformation of joined components
E3 To permit operation of movable components

F1 To have acceptable appearance
F2 To avoid promotion of plant growth
F3 To avoid discoloration due to biological, physical or chemical action
F4 To avoid all or part of the internal structure showing
F5 To avoid dust collection

G1 To have known first cost
G2 To have known depreciation
G3 To have known maintenance and/or replacement costs

H1 To have specified minimum life, taking into account cyclic factors
H2 To resist damage or unauthorized dismantling by man
H3 To resist action of animals and insects
H4 To resist action of plants and micro-organisms
H5 To resist action of water, water vapour or aqueous solutions or suspensions
H6 To resist action of polluted air
H7 To resist action of light
H8 To resist action of radiation (other than radiation of light)
H9 To resist action of freezing of water
H10 To resist action of extremes of temperatures
H11 To resist action of airborne or structure-borne vibrations, shock waves or high-intensity sound
H12 To resist action of acids, alkalis, oils, fats and solvents
H13 To resist abrasive action

J1 To permit partial or complete dismantling and reassembly
J2 To permit replacement of decayed jointing products

K1 To perform required functions over a specified range of temperatures
K2 To perform required functions over a specified range of atmospheric humidity
K3 To perform required functions over a specified range of air or liquid pressure differentials
K4 To perform required functions over a specified range of joint clearance variations
K5 To exclude from the joint if performance would be impaired:
  a) insects
  b) plants
  c) micro-organisms
  d) water
  e) ice
  f) snow
  g) polluted air
  h) solid matter
K6 To perform required functions over a specified range of driving rain volume

2.3 THE LOCATION OF JOINTS

The particular functions of a particular joint are to a large extent determined by its location in the building. It is evident that in any element made up of components joints are present, but the functions of a particular joint are not necessarily the same as the functions of the components being joined. Components are juxtaposed to form the construction and gaps occur between them.

The gaps bring about a break in the continuity of the construction which will influence its performance. The performance of the element depends on the performance of its components and that of its joints *taken together*. The gaps may be left open, as between the tiles on a pitched roof, or may need to be filled, as between floor tiles. When structural continuity is required, fixings between components must transmit the forces across the joint.

The performance of a joint will depend therefore primarily upon its place in the building. A joint between the same two components will have to perform in different ways if the location is changed. A joint between two tiles on a steeply pitched roof will not behave in the same way as between the same two tiles placed in a low pitched roof. The location affects the behaviour of the joint. The location also determines the functions required of the joint. When the location is known, the performance requirements may be specified based upon the functions which it has to perform, and taking into account the functions of the joined components and the functions required of the element as a whole. The type of nail depends upon the shoe and the actions of the rider.

2.4 INTRINSIC CHARACTERISTICS

The chief intrinsic characteristics of a joint, which determine the functions it can perform, are its gap, the joint profiles of the building components, and its jointing products.

In relation to the spread of fire, for example, the dimensions of an open joint gap regulate the passage of heat, smoke and flame. Heat, in the form of hot gas, will exploit gaps in a similar way to water under pressure. A wide short gap will facilitate immediate transmission of fire through it. A narrower or longer gap will delay the passage of fire. A very narrow and long gap will cause additional resistance due to lack of oxygen and heat in the gap to sustain the fire.

The material of the building components which form the joint profiles may be either combustible, in which case the gap will increase in size and so increase the rate of transmission of the fire, or non-combustible, in which case the size of the gap and the rate of transmission remain unaltered. The thermal expansion of the material of adjacent components, due to the fire, may damage or destroy the jointing products and lead to the collapse of the element.

The materials of the jointing products also may assist in the propagation of the fire or resist its transmission. Alternatively, the sealing material itself may burn or melt and leave a gap through which the fire is able to penetrate and spread.

In relation to the passage of sound, the existence of an open gap will have an adverse effect on the acoustic performance of the element. Direct air paths, such as exist in cracks, allow a significant passage of sound. The traditional wet plastering was very helpful in this respect insofar as it sealed efficiently all joints and cracks. Where finely finished concrete surfaces exist without plaster, residual settlement, shrinkage and vibration may open up fine cracks at the junctions of wall and ceiling which permit the passage of sound and are difficult to trace. Jointing products, such as cornices are essential in such conditions. Cracks having an area no larger than that of an open keyhole in the door between two rooms will permit the passage of sound to such an extent that it will materially affect the sound reduction of the partition of which the door forms a part.

Chapter 3
The design of joints

3.1 THE POSITION OF JOINTS

Joints are situated in every part of a building. They are located between elements or within elements. Between elements, they are positioned between building components, while within elements they are positioned between building components or within components.

Two types of position

As a general principle it is convenient to distinguish those joints which occur between building components from those which occur between the parts of a component. Normally joints between components are made on site, whereas those within a component are made in the factory or workshop.

A pane of glass bedded in an opening frame contained within a metal frame seated on a timber surround set in a brickwork opening has four joints, one of which requires to be made on site.

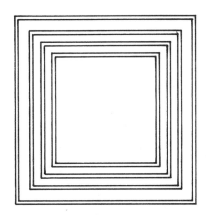

The joint between the outer window frame and the surrounding wall construction is made on site. The other joints, being contained within the window component, are usually part of the window construction, although in this particular example it is traditional practice to fix the glass on site after the joint between the window and its surrounding construction has been made.

Joints between building components

The position of a joint between components may be described with reference to the location of one of its components or, alternatively, with reference to its reference plane.

But although a joint is made between components, it occurs necessarily within the element of which the component forms a part, or between that element and another of a different kind.

The reference plane of the component will usually coincide with the joint reference plane so that the final position of adjacent components will determine the final position of the joint.

Conversely, the final position of a joint depends on the location of the adjacent components and the placing of the elements of which they form a part.

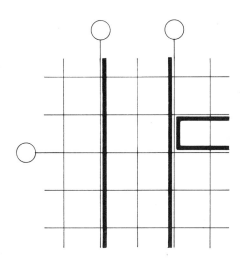

Joints between the parts of a component

Joints between the parts of a component are necessarily positioned within the component so that their location is known although the situation in the building will be determined by the component's location.

Classification based upon position

The close and necessary relationship between the position of a joint, its building components and the elements that contain them provides a reliable and convenient method of classification. It is this classification that is used in Part II of this book.

A given joint is classified firstly by its element, secondly by its component, and thirdly by an attribute such as material, form or function. Where a joint lies between two elements, it is classified under the element that contains the last component to be assembled.

Junctions

A junction is not a joint. A junction is a place where things meet. A joint may therefore occur at a junction or several joints may occur at a junction. A particular junction may be named and the name may be transferred to the joint or joints that occur there. Thus, for example, strictly speaking, a verge, an abutment or an eaves is a junction, and is therefore a location for a joint or joints.

3.2 GAPS, GAP WIDTHS, AND CLEARANCES

Gaps

The construction of buildings appears to involve two distinct methods of assembly. In one method the components are positioned closely together so that the gap between adjacent components is virtually zero. The gap may be filled with adhesive as for a glued joint or may be left unfilled as between two components joined by a nail or bolt. The adjacent parts may be fitted by cutting and matching as for a mortice and tenon joint or by placing components tightly against one another during assembly as with tongued and grooved boards or as with the components of a structural steelframe.

In the other method of assembly the components are positioned deliberately so that there is a gap between adjacent components. The gap may be filled with mortar as for a mortar joint in brickwork or may be left unfilled as for the joint between a door and door frame. The components are spaced apart to present a uniform pattern, to avoid the necessity of cutting and fitting material on site, to permit components to be assembled independently of one another and not in sequence, to provide for thermal expansion and moisture changes, and to permit the use of different materials adjacent to one another.

Gap widths

In the first method of assembly, the gap width is small and, in any given position, is fixed and invariable. The size of the gap width rarely exceeds 3 mm.

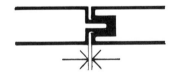

In the second method of assembly, the gap width is relatively large and it is recognised that it will vary in size between permissible limits.

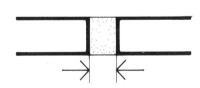

The maximum and minimum gap width are determined by the performance requirements of the joint, taking into account the size and position of adjacent components, and the dimensional capabilities of the jointing products. The gap width may be intended to vary during its working life and the joint must be designed to accommodate the changes in size. The size of the gap width varies from zero to about 30 mm.

Clearance

The lower limit or the minimum permissible clear distance between adjacent joint faces is termed the minimum clearance and is the width of the minimum gap required to take the jointing products and form the joint. The upper limit or the maximum permissible clear distance between adjacent joint faces is termed the maximum clearance and is the width of the maximum gap required to take the jointing products and form the joint. The size of the clearance is determined by the position of the two adjacent building components. The adjacent building components must be positioned so as to bring about a clearance that lies between the permissible limits. Furthermore, when building components are assembled in runs to fit a given distance, such as a coordinating dimension, the actual size of the clearances will depend upon the actual sizes of the components used as well as upon their positions. For two components of the same kind the clearance is theoretically and mathematically equal to the difference between the coordinating size and the work size.

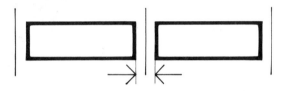

In practice, the actual sizes of the components will differ from their work sizes. Also, the components will deviate from their specified position.

When the two smallest components are placed apart as far as is permissible, the *maximum* clearance occurs.

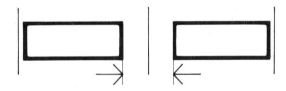

When the two *largest* components are placed as close together as is permissible, the *minimum* clearance occurs.

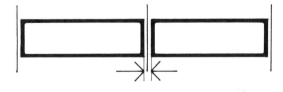

Consequently the clearance will vary over a range that must be within the capacity of the joint design.

Components that are made smaller or larger than the specified limits for the manufacturing sizes will have to be rejected, for either they will not go into position or the clearance will not permit an acceptable joint to be made.

Jointing products will require to be shaped and positioned so that all clearances from the maximum to the minimum are possible.

3.3 STANDARDS

British Standards for jointing products

The need to standardize jointing products was first recognised in the field of engineering. Joseph Whitworth, a mechanical engineer, read a paper before the Institution of Civil Engineers in 1841 in which he urged the necessity for an agreement upon a uniform system of screw threads which could be used to replace the wide range of different types and sizes then in existence. A unified system was designed and introduced during the following twenty years.

However, it was not until 1901 that an Engineering Standards Committee was formed to draw up standard specifications for certain engineering products, including structural steel sections. The first building standard was published in 1903 followed by several standards which covered the sizes of pipes, pipe fittings and pipe threads. In the early years of standardization, the following British Standard specifications for jointing products were prepared:

BS 1204 : 1964	Synthetic resin adhesives
BS 1210 : 1963	Wood screws
BS 1243 : 1964	Metal ties for cavity wall construction
BS 1494 : Part 1 : 1964	Fixings for sheet, roof and wall coverings
BS 1494 : Part 2 : 1967	Sundry fixings
BS 1579 : 1960	Connectors for timber
BS 2494 : Part 2 : 1967	Rubber joint rings for drainage purposes

The dates of the standards are, according to customary practice, the years of the latest issues and not necessarily the dates when the standards were first published.

In 1906 a Report on Limits and Fits for Engineering (Report No 27) provided the theoretical basis for the manufacture of interchangeable parts. A Standard Specification was subsequently prepared:

BS 164 : 1924 Limits and fits for engineering, now superseded by:
BS 1916 : 1953 and BS 4500 : 1969 ISO Limits and fits (ISO/R 286).

However, it was not until 1972 that a Draft for Development was issued on tolerances and fits for building which was concerned with the calculation of work sizes and joint clearances for building components. The proposals made in this draft have been the subject of practical tests and measurements taken on building sites, and it is hoped to revise the draft and issue a definitive standard.

International Standards for joints

The preparation of standards to cover the theory of joints in building construction started about 1968 under the auspices of the International Standards Organisation. Since then the following international standards have been published:

ISO 2444	Joints in building: Vocabulary
ISO 2445	Joints in building: Fundamental principles of design
ISO 3447 : 1975	Joints in building: General checklist of joint functions

Sub-committees are currently engaged in the preparation of international standards to cover the following additional aspects of joints in building:

SC 8   Jointing products
SC 4   Joint clearances
SC 5   Performance of joints

A technical committee of the British Standards Institution BLCP/65: Joints and Jointing in Building, is responsible for the preparation of a new Code of Practice on the design of joints and jointing in the construction industry.

3.4 JOINT PROFILES

A joint profile is defined as that part of the surface of a building component which is designed to relate to a joint. It forms part of the joint and for this reason the shape of the joint profile is determined primarily by the form of the jointing products used with the building component to make the particular joint that is required.

Adhesives, such as mortars and glues, will normally require plane, but not necessarily smooth, surfaces parallel to the joint reference plane. The joint profile is simple and usually rectilinear, as is the case with the common brick.

Connectors and fastenings require, in the corresponding adjoining joint faces of the building components, holes or grooves which are designed to fit and suit the particular jointing components or jointing sections to be used.

Direct locking between building components depends upon the correct shaping of corresponding joint faces, as for example with the edges of tongued and grooved boards.

From a theoretical standpoint, these three examples represent three basic geometric configurations: a neutral joint profile, a negative or recessed joint profile, and a positive or projecting joint profile.

Interface

When part of the joint profile of a building component is in contact with a jointing product the surface between the two materials is termed the interface. Thus the face between a screw thread and the matching face formed by the screw in the material of the building component is an interface which serves to transmit the load between the two parts.

The distance between the adjacent joint profiles of two building components at a joint is termed the gap width, the space being known as the gap. The size of the gap width may be measured at any point across the joint reference plane and will therefore vary from one point to another depending on the form of the joint profiles.

Joint face

The part of the joint profile of a building component which is nearest to the joint reference plane determines the clear space which is left available to make the joint and is termed the joint face. For an effective joint, the clear distance between adjacent joint faces must be maintained within specified limits.

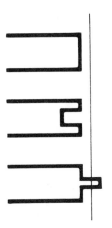

3.5 JOINT DRAWINGS

It has been traditional practice in the construction industry to regard information on joints as part of the constructional details of a building. When an unusual joint has been required, a special drawing has been prepared as part of the component details or as a separate assembly drawing. Joints have not often been the subject of much individual study and drawings of them have rarely been recognised in their own right.

The main types of working drawing in current use are location, assembly and component drawings. Location drawings are intended to give the overall layout of a design. They are usually to a small scale and do not often indicate joints. Assembly drawings are intended primarily to show the materials and location of building components. The position of their joints may be shown, but not large-scale details of the joints themselves. Component drawings are essentially concerned either with the ranges of a component or with the details required for its manufacture, but not with the representation of how the component is joined to other components of the same kind or of different kinds.

With the increasing use of different forms of construction and the attention being given to detail in construction, there is, on the evidence now available, a case for the recognition of a unique category of drawings intended primarily to convey information particular to the joints between building components.

A joint drawing identifies and shows, in relation to the joint reference plane, the joint profiles of the building components with the form and position of the jointing products. Such drawings are to a large scale: 1 : 1, 1 : 2, 1 : 5 or 1 : 10. Other information shown on the joint drawing is the following:

1 reference planes
2 material of the components
3 material and location of the jointing products
4 sequence of assembly
5 size of clearance.

The drawings which are included in Part II are examples of such joint drawings.

Chapter 4
Jointing products

4.1 INTRODUCTION

In the simplest forms of building there are no jointing products. A dry stone wall is built without mortar or fixings of any kind. A primitive timber frame is jointed without nails. A wickerwork roof is covered with interwoven leaves of date palm. But during the development of building construction fixing materials such as mortar and connections such as wooden pegs are introduced to strengthen the work or improve it in some other way. During the industrial revolution, new methods of production, and the introduction of improved and synthetic materials have led to new forms of construction in which jointing products become essential constituents of almost all forms of building.

Jointing products may be defined as building products that are used to make joints in building. Jointing products of all kinds now exist and may for convenience be classified morphologically into three main groups. These groups are defined in the international standard (ISO 2444) as jointing materials, jointing sections, and jointing components.

Jointing materials are unformed jointing products such as mortar, glue, adhesive, and sealing compounds.

Jointing sections are jointing products formed to a definite cross-section but of unspecified length and may be simple or complex in form, such as beads, gaskets and flashings.

Jointing components are jointing products consisting of a part or complex of parts formed as a distinct unit, as, for example, nails, anchors, screws and bolts.

A comprehensive list of jointing products arranged into the main groups and sub-groups is shown in the Table of Jointing Products on pages 28, 29.

4.2 JOINTING MATERIALS

Jointing materials may be divided into Adhesives that are used for fixing, and Sealing Compounds that are used to give protection.

Adhesives

Adhesives may, for convenience, be divided into mortars, glues, thermoplastic adhesives, thermosetting adhesives, elastomeric adhesives, two-polymer composition adhesives, weld metals and solders.

Sealing compounds may be divided, for convenience, into putties, mastics, bedding compounds, glazing compounds, caulking compounds and sealants.

MORTARS
The term mortar refers to a mixture of cement or lime or both, with sand and water, that is used as a jointing material between bricks, stones, tiles or blocks, and as a rendering. It may also be used for pointing. Before the manufacture of Portland cement, mortar was composed of a mixture of lime, sand and water, and was used both for brickwork and masonry. Such a mixture is sometimes called lime mortar.

- A mixture of Portland cement, sand and water is referred to as cement mortar, but may also include a proportion of lime. The use of Portland cement increases the strength of the mortar and its resistance to action by frost but it is less easy to lay and more liable to crack than one made with lime.

- A mixture of one part of Portland cement, one part of sand, and water is used as a grout to fill the joints between floor tiles.

- A mixture of one part of Portland cement, three parts of sand, and water is used to joint and point clay or concrete pipes.

- A mixture of one part of Portland cement, one of lime, six parts of sand, and water is used for laying bricks, concrete blocks or stone used for load-bearing walls or partitions.

- A mixture in the proportion of 1 : 2 : 8 and water is suitable for non-loadbearing walls or partitions.

- Mortar compositions, known as cement based adhesives (thin bed), are jointing materials in the form of a dry powder that is normally mixed with water before application. They comprise an hydraulic cement with additives and are most commonly used for fixing ceramic wall tiles that do not have deep keys or frogs. Mortar compositions known as mastic adhesives may also be used. They are jointing materials that include an organic material as the principal bonding agent. They are supplied ready for use and require no water or other substance to be added.

JOINTING MATERIALS   **Adhesives**   mortars
                                                                   glues
                                                                    thermoplastic adhesives
                                                                   thermosetting adhesives
                                                                   elastomeric adhesives
                                                                   two-polymer adhesives
                                                                   weld metal solders

                                  Joint sealing   putties
                                  compounds   mastics
                                                                   bedding compounds
                                                                   glazing compounds
                                                                   caulking compounds
                                                                   sealants

JOINTING SECTIONS   **Strips**   baffles
                                                                   battens
                                                                   beads
                                                                   cement fillets
                                                                   channels
                                                                   damp-proof courses
                                                                   expansion strips
                                                                   flashings
                                                                   gaskets
                                                                   glazing channels
                                                                   joint tapes
                                                                   rolls
                                                                   scrim
                                                                   separating strips
                                                                   splines
                                                                   trim
                                                                   water bars
                                                                   water stops
                                                                   weather strips

JOINTING COMPONENTS   **Anchors**   anchors
                                                                   expansion anchors
                                                                   screw anchors
                                                                   socket anchors

                                  Blocks   distance pieces
                                                                   fixing blocks
                                                                   fixing fillets
                                                                   folding wedges
                                                                   location blocks
                                                                   pellets
                                                                   pipe rollers
                                                                   plugs
                                                                   screw cups
                                                                   setting blocks
                                                                   shims
                                                                   washers
                                                                   wedges

JOINTING COMPONENTS (continued)

Bolts
bolts
coach bolts
foundation bolts
gutter bolts
handrail bolts
high strength friction grip bolts
hook bolts
roofing bolts
seam bolts
studs

Connectors
dowels
gang-nail connector plates
gussets
lead plugs
longscrews
oakley clips
shear plate connectors
splice bars
split-ring connectors
tie bars
timber connectors
toothed plate connectors
turnbuckles
wall ties

Fastenings
buttons
floor clips
gravity toggles
hangers
holderbats
holdfasts
joist hangers
latches
lugs
rivets
spring toggles
straps
three-way straps
toggles

Fittings
capillary fittings
compression fittings
collars
couplings
glands
jointing rings
nipples
sleeve pieces
sockets
spigots
tubulars
unions

Hinges
back-flap hinges
butt hinges
counter-flap hinges
H-hinges

Hinges
(continued)
lift-off butts
loose-pin butts
rising butt hinges
strap hinges

Hooks
bitches
cabin hooks
cramps
dogs
gate hooks
glazing cleats
pipe clamps
pipe hooks
screw hooks
shouldered screw hooks
wall hooks

Nails
annular nails
cedar shake nails
clout nails
convex head roofing nails
cut clasp nails
cut floor brads
cut lath nails
cut sharp point canada clasp nails
dowells
duplex head nails
extra large clout head nails
gimp nails
glazing sprigs
hardboard panel pins
lath nails
lost head nails
masonry nails
oval brad head nails
panel pins
pipe nails
plasterboard nails
round plain head nails
sleeved nails
square twisted shank flat head nails
staples
tacks
tenterhooks
tile pegs
tram nails
washer head slab nails
wiggle nails

Screws
screws
coach screws
dowel screws
grub screws
machine screws
roofing screws
self-tapping screws
wood screws

GLUES

Glue is a jointing material that is used mainly between timber surfaces. There are many kinds of glue that are derived from different source materials.

- *Animal glue,* which is also called Scotch glue, is made from the bones, hide, horn or skin of animals and formed into cakes or granules. It has been used over the centuries. It is strong but not resistant to the action of water.
- *Fish glue,* that is prepared from fish bladders and fish skins, is similar to animal glue being strong and durable in dry conditions.
- *Casein glue* is made from soured milk. It is more resistant to water than animal or fish glue. It is supplied as a powder, mixed with water and applied cold. It will fill gaps with a clearance of up to 1 mm.
- *Vegetable glues* include cassava and soya glue. Cassava glue is a starch glue that is made from the tapioca plant. Soya glue is a protein glue that is made from soya bean meal. It has properties that are similar to those of casein glue.
- *Natural resin glues* are made from gum resins such as asafoetida, frankincense and myrrh, and are soluble in water.

The use of most glues is diminishing since they are being superseded by the synthetic resin adhesives that are insoluble in water and not subject to attack by moulds or bacteria.

THERMOPLASTIC ADHESIVES

Thermoplastic adhesives are made from oleo-resins or synthetic resins. Oleo-resins are natural resins such as Canada balsam and true lacquer. Synthetic resins are substances that resemble natural resins and are prepared by chemical reaction from single compounds.

Thermoplastic adhesives are stronger than natural resin glues and are practically resistant to moisture or to attack by moulds or bacteria. However, they soften with heat and are liable to creep under stress. Adhesives based on polyvinyl acetal are used for interior jointing of timber. Acrylic polyester resin adhesives are used to make pipe joints and for filling gaps.

THERMOSETTING ADHESIVES

Thermosetting adhesives give stronger joints than in the other groups of adhesives and are not liable to creep. However, the bonds are brittle, of low resilience and subject to fracture under impact.

Thermosetting adhesives are based upon amino, phenolic, epoxy, and polyester resins, and incorporate additives. Phenolic formaldehyde and resorcinol formaldehyde adhesives are used for plywood and for the bonding of timber. Epoxy polysulphide adhesive is used for movement joints.

ELASTOMERIC ADHESIVES

Elastomeric adhesives are based upon natural and synthetic rubbers, prepared in the form of solvent solutions or solvent based viscous liquids. They have very low strength. Polychloroprene (Neoprene) adhesive is used to fit foam weather strip. Acrylo-nitrile butandiene adhesive is used to bond polychloroprene gaskets to metal. Styrene butadiene adhesive is used to fix floor and wall coverings. Silicone adhesive is used to stick silicone rubber gaskets.

TWO-POLYMER ADHESIVES

Two-polymer adhesives are compositions made by combining thermosetting resins with elastomers or thermoplastics. Phenolic-nitrile adhesives are used to bond metal to metal. Phenolic-polyvinyl acetal adhesives are used to bond honeycomb cores to laminate facings and metals. Epoxy-polyamide and phenolic-epoxy adhesives are used for bonding structures required to resist high temperatures. All two-polymer adhesives are highly resistant to oils and solvents.

Joint sealing compounds

The expression joint sealing compound refers to a jointing material that is used to seal the gap at the joint. Joint sealing compounds include putties, mastics, bedding compounds, glazing compounds, caulking compounds and sealants. Sometimes the term is used in a restricted sense to refer only to a sealant and at other times it is used to refer only to a jointing material that is waterproof. The purpose of a sealing compound is to seal a joint so as to prevent the passage of dust, moisture, wind and other external agencies. It must maintain close contact at the interface and, under certain conditions, be sufficiently elastic to take up movement at the joint during the life of the construction.

PUTTIES

Putty was the name given to a powder used by polishers or jewellers and known as polishers' or jewellers' putty-powder. Subsequently a mixture of whiting and linseed oil, sometimes with an addition of white lead, was used to secure window panes and stop up crevices in woodwork prior to painting. It came to be known as glazier's or painter's putty, or linseed oil putty, and it is this putty that is still in use today for retaining glass in primed softwood window frames. The putty has to be protected with paint as soon as the surface is hard enough to take it. This putty must not be confused with plasterer's putty, also called lime putty, that is a form of quicklime used to make plaster, or with mason's putty, a lime putty mixed with stone dust and Portland cement, used to joint ashlar: square cut stone. Glazier's putty is used both to form a bed in the frame rebate to support the glass when it is called bed putty or bedding putty, and to provide a triangular filler around the exposed outside edge of the glass when it is called face putty.

Putty known as metal casement putty, that is used to bed and front glass panes in metal window frames, is a synthetic glazing compound with characteristics similar to those of glazier's putty. It needs to be properly protected with paint. Mica metal casement putty is a metal casement putty with a much longer life and able to be left unpainted after application to the window frame.

MASTICS

Mastic is a traditional type of joint sealing compound and is also known as bituminous mastic. The term mastic has been applied rather indiscrimately to sealing compounds, bedding compounds and putties. Mastic consists of a mixture of selected bitumens, protective oils, solvents, asbestos fibres and special fillers. It provides a durable and resilient waterproof seal and filler that adheres well to clean surfaces. It is moisture proof, waterproof and acid-resistant and can be applied by trowel, putty knife, pressure gun or by hand. It is also available in a strip form that is usually plastic at the time of application. Bituminous mastic may also be poured while hot.

BEDDING COMPOUNDS

A bedding compound is a joint sealing compound that is used in the joints between window frames and their openings, between door frames and their openings, and between window subframes and frames, or connecting mullions or transoms. The material is not weatherproof or waterproof and when exposed requires protection by means of painting or by the application of a sealant. The principal bedding compounds are based on oil or butyl and they are generally applied by hand.

GLAZING COMPOUNDS

A glazing compound is a joint sealing compound that is used in the joints between glass and frame surrounds. It may also be used between infill panels and frame surrounds. The material is intended to provide a bedding for the glass and a weathertight joint between the glass and the surround. It may be a setting or non-setting material and may be applied by hand, knife, gun or as a preformed strip. The principal glazing compounds are based on synthetic rubbers or on elastomeric polymers, including in particular, polysulphides. The former, sometimes called non-setting glazing compounds, do not set although they normally have a surface skin that is produced by an additive agent. The latter, sometimes called flexible glazing compounds, cure to form a material of a tough rubbery consistency. They are intended to be used as alternatives to linseed oil putty and require protection with a suitable paint within a short period following application.

CAULKING COMPOUNDS

A caulking compound is a joint sealing compound that is used to fill tightly the gap between a pipe spigot and socket or to fill some similar joint. The material is usually hammered into position. It should be used on joints that are not subject to movement. A traditional caulking compound consists of equal parts of red and white lead mixed with hempen spun yarn to give a stiff mixture. Other caulking compounds may be oil-based or butyl-based.

SEALANTS

A sealant is a joint sealing compound which is intended to provide an effective seal so as to prevent the passage of dust, moisture, wind and other external agencies. It must be able to accept subsequent variations in the width of the gap that it fills. The material is both adhesive and elastomeric, but is not intended to be loadbearing. It may be applied by means of a trowel, knife, gun or in the form of a preformed strip or tape. A number of different materials are used as sealants, which may be divided into two broad categories: elastomeric and non-elastomeric or plastic.

Elastomeric sealants, such as those based on polysulphide, polyurethane or silicone rubber, are intended to cure after application and to form a rubber-like solid. They show some recovery and tend to be the higher performance materials. They are of two kinds. A one-part chemically curing sealant is cured by release of solvent and/or by absorption of moisture from the air after application to the joint. A two-part chemically curing sealant is cured by chemical reaction between the two different materials after their application to the joint.

The main types of elastomeric sealant classified by basic chemical ingredient are:

    One-part Polysulphide
    Two-part Polysulphide
    Acrylic Resin
    Silicone
    Polybutadiene
    Neoprene and Hypalon
    Hybrid Polymer

Plastic or non-elastomeric sealants, that are based on oil, bitumen/rubber, or butyl, are not intended to form a rubber-like solid whether or not curing takes place. They have no recovery properties and are the lower performance materials. They may be applied hot or cold. A hot applied sealant is a non-elastomeric sealant that is intended to be applied in a softened or liquified condition at a temperature above its recommended maximum service temperature. A cold applied sealant is a non-elastomeric sealant that is intended to be applied at normal service temperatures and that sets to form a plastic solid or that remains plastic but with the formation of a surface skin.

The main types of plastic sealant classified by basic chemical ingredients are:

    Bitumen based
    Oil based
    Polybutene
    Butyl
    Acrylic emulsion
    Acrylic resin

4.3 JOINTING SECTIONS

A jointing section is defined in British Standard 4663 as a jointing product formed to a definite cross-section but of unspecified length. As most sectional material is, by its nature, produced in continuous lengths in the form of strips, the continuity thereby provided is well suited for the protection of many types of joint.

In practice, the gap is normally afforded protection by a strip which is positioned across the joint face to act as a cover or in the gap itself to act as a filler.

The arrangement of strips at corners, T junctions and intersections requires particular attention and careful design. At these junctions continuity may cease and so may lead to lack of protection. The strips may be suitably lapped or mitred and may also be joined by adhesive.

Strips are fixed by adhesives or fastenings, or may be held in position by being compressed between the joint faces or located in the joint profiles.

When in use a jointing section consists of a type of strip selected for its material and cross-section to suit its position. Strips are made in most materials and the traditional name is usually a term that is descriptive of the form or the function of the particular strip that has been designed to meet a common situation.

The principal kinds of strip, arranged in alphabetical sequence, are as follows:

Baffles
Battens
Beads
Cement fillets
Channels
Damp-proof courses
Expansion strips
Flashings
Gaskets
Glazing channels
Joint tapes
Laths
Rolls
Scrim
Separating strips
Splines
Trim
Water bars
Water stops
Weather strips

Strips

BAFFLE
A strip of rubber, synthetic rubber or plastic with a special cross-section designed to be positioned in grooves in the vertical joint faces of wall panels to reduce the amount of rain entering the open joint.

BATTEN
A strip of timber, usually measuring about 50 mm x 20 mm, which is used to take fixings for roofing tiles, slates, ceiling tiles, floor boarding and internal linings.

BEAD also GLAZING BEAD or GLASS STOP or BEADING
A small strip of timber or metal which is used to retain a pane of glass in a rebate in a window frame.

CEMENT FILLET also WEATHER FILLET or CEMENTED JOINT or FILLET
A strip of cement mortar which is used to form the joint between a chimney stack and the roofing tiles or slates. It is a cheap substitute for a metal flashing.

CHANNEL
A U-shaped or dovetail section, sometimes with specially shaped flanges, which is cast into a concrete slab so as to provide a continuous slot for special fastenings.

DAMP-PROOF COURSE also DAMP COURSE or DPC
A strip of bituminous sheet, metal or other impervious material which is laid in a joint in a wall to prevent the passage of moisture across the joint.

EXPANSION STRIP also EXPANSION TAPE or ISOLATION STRIP or INSULATING STRIP or EDGE ISOLATION STRIP
A strip of cork, rubber, plastic or similar resilient material that is used to fill the gap in a wall or between a wall and a structural member so as to provide for movement.

FLASHING
A strip of sheet lead, zinc, copper, aluminium, roofing felt or similar impervious material which is used to protect the joint between a roof covering and another surface. Flashings for particular situations have special names such as apron flashing, cover flashing, raking flashing, stepped flashing.

GASKET
A strip of extruded rubber, rubber composition, polychloroprene, foamed butyl, polyethylene, polyurethane or other similar materials which may be in solid, tubular, fir-cone, cellular or other form and in a wide range of cross-sections. A gasket can form a continuous seal when compressed. The term gasket is used also to describe hemp fibres which are wound round the threads of a screw on the spigot end of a pipe to make a watertight joint.

GLAZING CHANNEL
A U-shaped extrusion made of plastic which is used to retain glass in a frame and is held in compression by glazing beads.

JOINT TAPE
A strip of paper, gummed brown paper, or similar material which is used to cover the joint between wallboard or plasterboard sheets. Tapes of pile or similar material are used to fill the joint around aluminium sliding windows or doors.

ROLL also WOOD ROLL or COMMON ROLL
A timber section which is shaped to form the joint between two metal roofing sheets. A *ridge roll* and a *hip roll* are cut to fit the ridge and hip respectively of a roof.

SCRIM
A strip of jute, cotton or metal mesh which is used to cover the joint between plasterboard sheets before plastering. Jute or cotton scrim is used also as reinforcement for fibrous plaster.

SEPARATING STRIP

A strip of foamed plastic or similar material which is fitted into the gap to give support to a joint sealing compound and to prevent an elastomeric sealant adhering to the material at the back of sealant. The separating strip should not be confused with back-up material or a backing strip which is intended mainly to limit the depth and hence the shape and quantity of the sealant.

SPLINE also TONGUE or FEATHER

A strip of hardwood, hardboard or similar material which is fitted into a groove in the joint face of a component.

TRIM or COVER STRIP

A strip of timber, metal or plastic made to a wide range of cross-sections. Traditionally, in joinery, the term covers architraves, skirtings, dados, picture rails, cover mouldings and the like which are used to form cover strips.

WATER BAR also WEATHER BAR

A bar of galvanized steel, normally measuring 25 mm x 6 mm, which is bedded in a groove in the top of a sill to prevent the entry of water.

WATER STOP

A rubber or plastic section which is positioned across the gap between two concrete slabs, especially in foundations, to prevent the passage of water.

WEATHER STRIP also WIND STOP or DOOR STRIP or DRAUGHT EXCLUDER

A strip of metal, wood, rubber or other material which is used to close the gap between a door or window casement and its surround frame. Strips of spring steel, particularly stainless steel, are used to retain glass in patent glazing bars.

4.4 JOINTING COMPONENTS

Anchors

ANCHOR

A fastening which is used to provide a secure fixing to masonry or concrete. There are a number of alternative devices which operate in different ways.

EXPANSION ANCHOR also EXPANDING BOLT

An anchor which is fitted into a hole in the masonry or concrete and is made secure by the expanding action of shields, cores, sleeves or wedges.

SCREW ANCHOR

A small sleeve made of metal or plastic which is inserted into a hole in masonry or concrete to provide a fastening for a screw.

SOCKET ANCHOR also CAST IN SOCKET

An anchor or an expansion anchor with a threaded socket into which a bolt or a stud may be fastened.

Blocks

DISTANCE PIECE

A small block of resilient material which is positioned between the face of a pane of glass and the frame rebate or between the face and a bead to prevent lateral movement of the glass.

FIXING BLOCK also FIXING BRICK or NAILING BRICK or NOG.

A block in the form of a brick made of wood or light-weight concrete, or other similar material to which fastenings can be made. When made of wood, it is also called a WOOD BRICK.

FIXING FILLET also FIXING SLIP or PAD or PALLET or PALLET SLIP

A small piece of wood with the thickness of a mortar joint that is positioned between bricks so that a fastening can be made.

FOLDING WEDGES also EASING WEDGES or STRIKING WEDGES or LOWERING WEDGES

A pair of wedges positioned in the gap between two components and used together so as to vary the gap width.

LOCATION BLOCK

A small block of resilient material which is positioned between the edge of a pane of glass and its surround frame so as to ensure a minimum clearance. It is not intended to take any stress.

PELLET

A small flat disc of wood or plastic that is used to fill the countersunk hole and cover the head of a countersunk screw.

PIPE ROLLER

A small cylindrical steel drum mounted on a spindle which is free to rotate and support a pipe. It allows the pipe to move longitudinally.

PLUG also WALL PLUG

A small peg of wood, fibre, metal or plastic which is pushed into a pre-drilled hole in a wall so as to provide a material to which fastenings can be made.

SCREW CUP

A specially formed washer for use with a countersunk wood screw to provide a seating in the countersinking. It is used to provide a neat finish when the screws are exposed and made a feature.

SETTING BLOCK

A small block of polychloroprene, lead, or similar material that is positioned to support the bottom edge of a pane of glass in its surround frame.

SHIM also SPACER

A small block used in the gap, as between a base plate and a concrete slab to maintain a predetermined gap width.

WASHER

A ring, usually flat, made of metal or rubber or plastic or other suitable material which is used between surfaces to distribute load and form a tight joint.

WEDGE

A tapered block of wood or strips of lead or copper folded into a wedge shape.

Bolts

BOLT

A cylindrical bar with a head at one end and a screw thread at the other end which is fitted with a nut.

COACH BOLT

A bolt with a convex head and a square section below it which fits into a corresponding recess in the material thus preventing the bolt from turning when the nut is screwed on.

FOUNDATION BOLT also HOLDING-DOWN BOLT or ANCHOR BOLT

A bolt used with a large plate washer which is cast into the concrete or masonry to provide a fastening in the form of a threaded bolt that projects.

GUTTER BOLT

A bolt which is used to fasten the socket to the spigot at a joint in a gutter.

HANDRAIL BOLT also JOINT BOLT

A rod with a thread at both ends which is used to draw together and fasten two lengths of handrail.

HIGH STRENGTH FRICTION GRIP BOLT also HSFG BOLT

A high strength friction grip bolt which is used with a hardened circular washer to fasten structural steel members to one another.

HOOK BOLT

A galvanized iron rod with a U-shaped hook at one end and a screw thread at the other end which is fitted with a washer and nut. The bolt is used to fasten corrugated sheeting to steel purlins.

ROOFING BOLT

A bolt which is used to stitch side laps of corrugated sheeting and to fix fittings to roofing or cladding sheets.

SEAM BOLT

A steel bolt used with a nut and a plastic washer to fasten corrugated sheets to one another.

STUD

A rod with one end threaded and one end plain or a rod threaded both ends. The plain end is usually welded to the supporting structure so as to provide a threaded projection to which a fastening can be made.

Connectors

DOWEL also TRENAIL or TREENAIL or TRUNNEL

A short round hardwood rod which is inserted into corresponding holes in two pieces of timber so as to connect them.

Also, a short round steel rod which is inserted into corresponding holes in a concrete floor slab and the foot of a door jamb.

Also, a pin made of slate, stone, or non-ferrous metal which is inserted into corresponding holes in adjoining stones to connect them.

GANG-NAIL CONNECTOR PLATE

A galvanized steel plate with a large number of nails punched out at right angles. The plate is used to connect pieces of timber, the nails being hydraulically pressed into the timber. The plates are made in a range of sizes and with three sizes of nail.

GUSSET

A metal plate which is used to connect structural members by means of bolts, screws or rivets.

LEAD PLUG

Lead which is cast in a groove cut in two adjoining stones in a course so as to connect them. Also, a small cylindrical rod of lead which is driven into a pre-drilled hole in a wall so as to provide a fixing for a screw.

LONGSCREW

A short length of mild steel tube with a parallel thread externally at both ends, one thread being long enough to take a back-nut and coupler. It is used to join tubes which cannot be rotated.

OAKLEY CLIP

A small bar bent to form a hook with a threaded hole which is screwed on to a bolt and used to hold cladding sheets to a structural member.

SHEAR PLATE CONNECTOR

A timber connector made of mild steel or malleable cast iron which consists of circular plate with a central hole and a circumferential flange. The flange is fitted into a corresponding groove in the timber and spreads the load of a bolted connection.

SPLICE BAR

A steel reinforcing bar which overlaps another.

SPLIT-RING CONNECTOR

A timber connector made from steel strip which consists of a ring with double bevelled sides and round milled edges. The connector is inserted into a pre-cut circular groove made in both timber members which are connected by a bolt, nut and washers.

TIE BAR
A steel bar positioned to take tensile stress and to connect two components.

TIMBER CONNECTOR also CONNECTOR
Split-ring, shear-plate and toothed-plate discs made of steel or cast iron used with bolts to connect timber members.

TOOTHED PLATE CONNECTOR also BULLDOG PLATE
A circular or square plate with a central hole and a ring of triangular teeth projecting alternately from opposite faces at right angles to the plate. The plate is positioned between adjoining timber members and connected by means of a bolt, nut and washers.

TURNBUCKLE
A coupling with a screw thread at both ends which is used to connect two bars and adjust the tension.

WALL TIE also TIE IRON
A piece of twisted wire or strip made of galvanized steel or non-ferrous metal that is laid across a cavity wall to connect the two leaves. A *butterfly wall tie* and a *twisted-wire tie* are particular forms.

Fastenings

BUTTON
A small piece of wood or metal which is screwed to a door frame and able to be turned so as to keep the door shut.

FLOOR CLIP also ACOUSTIC CLIP or BULLDOG CLIP
A specially shaped sherardized steel strip which is cast into a concrete floor slab or screed and nailed to flooring battens. The clip may incorporate a pad of rubber or similar material to reduce sound transmission.

GRAVITY TOGGLE
A toggle that is pivoted on a fixing screw so that it can be passed through a hole in the fixture and the board or panel and allowed to drop down and rest against the back face. The screw is then tightened to complete the fastening.

HANGER also STIRRUP STRAP
A steel strip which is fastened to adjoining timber members or is fastened to a timber member and built into a wall.

HOLDERBAT
A cast iron or steel bar with a semi-circular hook at one end and a corresponding semi-circular bar which is screwed to it so as to clamp a pipe. The plain end of the bar is built into the wall or support structure. Another type is fixed to the structure with nails or screws.

HOLDFAST
A cast iron or steel spike having a flattened end with a hole in it. The spike is driven into a wall joint and a screw is inserted in the hole to fasten a timber member or other fixture.

JOIST HANGER also WALL HANGER
A specially shaped hanger which is used to support the end of a timber joist. It is nailed or screwed to the joist and built into the supporting wall or fastened to another joist.

LATCH
A metal bar used to fasten a door. The bar is pivoted on the door so that it engages a hook fixed to the door frame. Alternatively, a latch is the bevelled bar controlled by a spring and moved by a door handle in a door lock.

LUG
A metal bar which is fastened to a window or door frame and built into the jamb of the wall construction.

RIVET
A headed shank that is used to fasten two parts by inserting the shank through a hole in both pieces and forming a head with the projecting part of the shank.

SPRING TOGGLE
A toggle with two wings and a spring attached to a fixing screw so that it can be passed through a hole in the fixture and the board or panel. The toggle wings then spring apart and rest against the back face. The screw is then tightened to complete the fastening.

STRAP
A shaped steel strip which is fitted around a pipe and fastened by means of bolts or screws to a supporting structure.

THREE-WAY STRAP
A steel plate shaped with three arms used to fasten three timber members which are in the same plane and meet at a node. The strap is usually fastened with coach screws or bolts.

TOGGLE also TOGGLE BOLT
A special fastening which is used to make a fixing to a thin board or panel. See *spring toggle* and *gravity toggle.*

Fittings also pipe fittings

CAPILLARY FITTING
A short copper tube which is used to join the ends of two copper tubes. The inside diameter of the fitting is slightly larger than the outside diameter of the tubes and contains two rings of solder which are melted so as to fill the space between the tubes and the fitting.

COMPRESSION FITTING
A brass fitting which is used to join the ends of two copper tubes by means of nuts which compress glands round the tubes.

COLLAR
A metal tube which is fitted into the end of a pipe or into which a pipe is fitted.

COUPLING also COUPLER or SOCKET
A short collar which is used to join the screwed end of two pipes. It is screwed internally at each end.

GLAND also OLIVE
A brass or soft copper ring which is used in a compression fitting to seal the gap between the tube and the fitting.

JOINTING RING also JOINT RING or
COMPRESSION RING
A ring of rubber or similar material which is used to
seal the joint between two drainpipes.

NIPPLE
A short pipe with an external taper thread at both ends
which is used to join two internally threaded pipes.

SLEEVE PIECE also, THIMBLE or FERRULE or
LINER
A short brass or copper tube which is used to join
pipes of different materials.

SOCKET
The enlarged end of a pipe into which the end of
another pipe of the same diameter is fitted.

SPIGOT
The end of a pipe which is inserted into a socket of a
pipe of the same diameter.

TUBULAR
A pipe fitting made of mild steel in the form of a collar,
bend, T or other junction.

UNION also PLUMBER'S UNION or CAP AND
LINING
A pipe fitting screwed at one end to fit a steel pipe and
having a brass sleeve at the other end for soldering to a
lead pipe.

Hinges

BACK-FLAP HINGE
A hinge similar in design to a butt hinge, but with wider
flaps that are screwed to the face of the door and door
frame.

BUTT HINGE also BUTT
A hinge which consists of a central pin and two flaps,
one being fixed to the joint face of the door frame and
one to the edge of the door.

COUNTER-FLAP HINGE
A hinge used for the flap of a shop counter which
allows the flap to rotate through two right-angles and
lie flat on the counter.

H-HINGE also PARLIAMENT HINGE or SHUTTER
HINGE
A hinge with projecting flaps, commonly used for an
outside shutter or to permit a door to clear an architrave
and open through two right angles.

LIFT-OFF BUTT also LOOSE BUTT HINGE
A hinge formed so that one flap can be lifted off the
central pin.

LOOSE-PIN BUTT also PIN HINGE
A hinge formed with a hinge pin which can be removed.
It allows a door to be removed without unscrewing the
flaps.

RISING BUTT HINGE also RISING BUTT
A hinge formed with a helical surface between the two
flaps. It causes the door to be raised about 12 mm as it
opens and to clear a carpet.

STRAP HINGE also BAND-AND-HOOK HINGE or
CROSS-GARNET HINGE or T-HINGE or HOOK-
AND-RIDE HINGE or BAND-AND-GUDGEON
HINGE
A hinge with one flap in the form of a wrought iron
strip which is screwed to the ledge of a door or gate.

Hooks

BITCH
A bar made of steel with a spike at each end, one being
at right angles to the other, and both at right angles to
the bar.

CABIN HOOK
A bar with a hooked end which slots into an eye so as to
form a lock for a door or casement.

CRAMP also CRAMP-IRON
A U-shaped bar made of non-ferrous metal which is
used to lock together adjoining stones in a masonry
wall.

DOG
A U-shaped bar made of steel with a spike at each end
which is used to lock together two heavy timbers.

GATE HOOK also GUDGEON
A bar with a pin at right angles to it at one end and a
spike at the other end which is driven into a timber post
or built into a pier to support a gate hinge.

GLAZING CLEAT
A small non-ferrous clip which is inserted in a hole in a
metal window frame to hold the pane of glass in
position.

PIPE CLAMP
A U-shaped strip of steel which is placed over a pipe to
hold it in position.

PIPE HOOK
A bar with a curved hook at one end and a spike at the
other end which is driven into timber or a joint in a wall
so as to support and grip a pipe of similar diameter.

SCREW HOOK
A small bar with a curved or square hook at one end and
a wood screw at the other end which is screwed into
timber to form a bracket.

SHOULDERED SCREW HOOK
A screw hook with a shoulder between the screw and
the hook.

WALL HOOK
A bar with a square hook at one end and a spike at the
other end which is driven into the joint of a wall so as
to support a pipe or a timber joist.

Nails

ANNULAR NAIL
A nail with a ringed shank that increases the resistance to withdrawal. Non-ferrous material is used for external joinery.

CEDAR SHAKE NAIL
A nail of copper or aluminium that is used for fixing cedar cladding to walling.

CLOUT NAIL also SLATE NAIL or FELT NAIL
A galvanized nail with a large round flat head that is used to fix roofing felt, sash cords and fencing rails.

CONVEX HEAD ROOFING NAIL also SPRING-HEAD ROOFING NAIL or NIPPLE HEAD NAIL
Normally made of galvanized steel or aluminium and used for fixing corrugated roof sheeting to timber purlins.

CUT CLASP NAIL also CUT NAIL or CLASP NAIL
Cut by shearing from steel sheet and used to fix heavy carpentry, especially to masonry.

CUT FLOOR BRAD also FLOOR BRAD or BRAD
Cut from steel sheet and used to fix floor boards to timber joists.

CUT LATH NAIL
A cut nail that is used to fix laths.

CUT SHARP POINT CANADA CLASP NAIL
A heavy cut nail of rectangular section with a shank which tapers towards a rectangular head and also towards a rectangular point.

DOWEL also DOWEL PIN
A short round wire nail that is pointed at both ends.

DUPLEX HEAD NAIL also DOUBLE HEAD SHUTTER NAIL
A nail with two separate heads that is used to make temporary fixings and that can be easily withdrawn.

EXTRA LARGE HEAD CLOUT NAIL also, FELT NAIL
Normally made in galvanized steel or aluminium and used to fix felt.

GIMP NAIL also GIMP PIN
A small pin with a relatively large head.

GLAZING SPRIG also GLAZIER'S POINT
A small headless nail that is used to hold a glass pane in position while putty is applied around the frame.

HARDBOARD PANEL PIN also HARDBOARD PIN
Made with a round or square section shank and a diamond profile head that is hidden below the face of the hardboard when driven home.

LATH NAIL
A wire nail with a small head that is used to fix plaster and other laths to softwood.

LOST HEAD NAIL
A wire nail with a shank of round or oval cross-section. When used for fixing flooring the head of the nail can be punched below the surface and the hole filled.

MASONRY NAIL also DRIVE PIN
A hardened steel pin that can be driven into ordinary bricks with a hammer or into pre-drilled holes in harder bricks or concrete.

OVAL BRAD HEAD NAIL also OVAL-WIRE BRAD
A nail made from oval steel wire. It must be distinguished from a cut floor brad.

PANEL PIN or PIN
A small round wire nail used to fix plywood and in joinery. It is easily driven home and the head may be punched below the surface.

PIPE NAIL also CHISEL POINT NAIL
A large round wire nail used to fix some types of rainwater brackets to brickwork and masonry.

PLASTERBOARD NAIL (JAGGED SHANK)
A galvanized or sherardized wire nail, with a countersunk head and serrated shank used to fix plasterboard to softwood.

ROUND PLAIN HEAD NAIL also ROUND WIRE NAIL or FRENCH NAIL
A steel nail used in carpentry. Brass wire is used for escutcheon pins and aluminium wire for slate nails.

SLEEVED NAIL
A nail with an outer sleeve which is expanded as the nail is driven home.

SQUARE TWISTED SHANK FLAT HEAD NAIL also DRIVE SCREW or SCREW NAIL or HELICALLY THREADED NAIL
A galvanized helically threaded nail used to fix corrugated or similar sheeting to softwood.

STAPLE
A U-shaped galvanized steel wire with equal legs.

TACK also CLIP
A short sharply pointed nail used to fix fabric to wood or carpet to flooring.

TENTERHOOK
A staple that has one leg longer than the other.

TILE PEG
A steel or aluminium nail with a clout head and a dumped or, alternatively, a sharp point, used for fixing roofing tiles.

TRAM NAIL
A large wire nail with a flat or raised head and a chisel point.

WASHER HEAD SLAB NAIL also PURLIN NAIL
A long small diameter steel, copper or aluminium alloy nail used to fix slabs to softwood.

WIGGLE NAIL also CORRUGATED FASTENER or JOINT FASTENER or MITRE BRAD
A small piece of corrugated steel which is used to connect the edges of two boards.

Screws

SCREW
A fastening made of steel, brass, stainless steel, aluminium, silicon bronze or nickel-copper alloy, with a spiral or helical thread and a slotted head which may be of several different kinds.

COACH SCREW
A large wood screw with a gimlet point and a square head for making fastenings to timber or joining timber members. A pilot hole is drilled and the square head is turned with a spanner.

DOWEL SCREW also HAND-RAIL SCREW
A small diameter rod threaded at each end which is used in conjunction with two nuts to connect adjacent lengths of handrail. It should be distinguished from a handrail bolt.

GRUB SCREW also SET SCREW
A small short screw with a slotted head which is used to lock a collar on a shaft or a door handle on a spindle or to provide a similar form of fastening.

MACHINE SCREW
A screw with a helical thread and a blunt end which is used for screwing into metal or for threading with a nut.

ROOFING SCREW
A short screw with a gimlet point which is used for fastening roofing sheets to a supporting member, usually in conjunction with a plastic washer.

SELF-TAPPING SCREW
A screw with a hardened thread which makes a thread in the material into which it is screwed. It is screwed into a pre-drilled hole of the required diameter. There are several different points, threads and heads.

WOOD SCREW formerly called a SCREW NAIL
A screw with a spiral thread and a pointed end which is used for fixing into wood. Alternative heads include countersunk head, raised countersunk head, round head and dome head.

Chapter 5
Jointing

5.1 THE PROCESS OF JOINTING

The nature of jointing

The construction of a building consists in the putting together of its component parts to form a structure. The parts are put together or assembled sequentially and additively. Each part is added to or placed next to a preceding part. Each part adjoins another. The addition of parts is the adjoining of parts and the adjoining of parts produces joints. Consequently joints are the inevitable concomitant of construction. From this viewpoint the process of building is the jointing of building components or the making of joints between them.

The development of new materials and different forms of construction has not altered this basic building process which is one of simple addition. The change is in the material and form of the components and the method of making the new forms of joint.

5.2 JOINTING OPERATIONS

Jointing, or the making of a joint, is also itself a sequential process. It can be analysed as a set of sequential operations. There is often only one possible sequence for a given joint and the joint is the outcome of the sequence.

Each of the operations required to form the joint can be related directly to one of the building components or one of the jointing products used to form part of the given joint. The three principal jointing operations are positioning the building components, fixing them by means of jointing products and protecting the joint with other jointing products. These operations in whatever form are dependent upon the method used to assemble the building: the method of assembly.

Methods of assembly

There are, in principle, two methods of assembly that may be used in the construction of a building. They may be used separately or in combination. The two methods have already been referred to in Chapter 3.2 in relation to the widths of gaps between adjoining building components.

The two methods may be distinguished by the gap widths or by the degree of accuracy obtained in the positioning of the components or by the procedures used in the setting out and positioning of the building components.

We shall term the first method of assembly *close fit*, and the second method of assembly, *loose fit*.

5.3 CLOSE AND LOOSE FIT

Close fit

The first method of assembly is characterized by building components which are designed to be fitted together on site easily and accurately. The fitting is achieved by manufacturing the components to relatively close tolerances, using jigs, and designing connections that are self-positioning. The method has been developed over the past two hundred years, especially in mechanical engineering. The theory of tolerances embodies standard tolerances, limits and tolerances for commonly used shafts and holes for general engineering purposes, and recommendations on selected fits.

This method of assembly is the one used in the erection of most steel frameworks for building. The erection procedure, as in mechanical engineering assembly is essentially sequential in the sense that each component of the structure is fastened to one that has already been placed in position. The final structure behaves as a single object.

Loose fit

The second method of assembly is characterized by building components which are intended to be positioned on site independently of one another. The tolerance on the gap width is relatively large being designed to allow for induced and inherent deviations. Induced deviations are dimensional variations due to the manufacturing, setting out and positioning of the building components. Inherent deviations are dimensional variations due to the nature of the material used and its behaviour under stress as, for example, when it is loaded or subject to changes in temperature or moisture content. With this method of assembly jointing products must be designed to suit the relatively large gap between adjoining building components and the probable variations in gap width.

This method of assembly is the one used in the construction of walling in blockwork or brickwork. The procedure of laying blocks is based on the concept that each block occupies a specified space designed to take it and that there is a standard gap between blocks with a clearance of 10 mm. The blocks are positioned independently of each other and although the procedure is essentially additive it need not be sequential. Work can start at both ends of a wall and the intermediate blocks are then positioned in between so that each block occupies its own allocated space and so that the standard clearance between adjacent blocks is maintained. The blocks are not self-positioning and therefore the exercise of skill is required in the setting out, location, and positioning of the blocks and in the application of the jointing material.

Close fit or loose fit

Although both methods of assembly are in use independently and can be recognised in theory as distinct ways of positioning and fixing building components, there are certain situations in a building where either method can be used. When a timber window is to be used in an opening within a brick wall in accordance with the first method of assembly, the window is first placed in position on the window sill. The bricks are then laid tightly against the window frame so that there is virtually no gap between the jamb of the frame and the brickwork. Alternatively, when the second method of assembly is used, the brickwork is constructed first so as to form an opening to take the window. The window is then inserted at a later stage in the construction. In this case the brickwork opening must be large enough to permit the subsequent insertion of the window. Also, the gap widths must be wide enough for the gaps to be satisfactorily filled and sealed.

It follows that these two methods of assembly require two quite different kinds of joints and that the jointing products needed will also differ.

5.4 FIXING OF JOINTING PRODUCTS

After two building components have been positioned to form a joint, the first operation related to the jointing products is to clean the surfaces of the joint profiles that will be in contact with the products. The surfaces may be unclean due to corrosion on metal, oil and resin on timber, powder and loose material on concrete and masonry, or dust and contamination generally because of lack of protection. The jointing products themselves may also be unclean before application as a result of insufficient protection.

Jointing products intended to provide fixing by adhesion are particularly dependent upon the existence of absolutely clean surfaces just prior to application. Adhesives, joint sealing compounds and gaskets or flashings with adhesive coatings, may also require the application of a specially selected primer to the surfaces in order to ensure adhesion. The primer is intended to modify the porosity of the surfaces so as to meet the requirements of the particular adhesive being used and so secure a satisfactory bond.

Jointing products which depend upon compression and surface contact such as baffles, cover strips, flashings and gaskets also require clean surfaces. In addition, however, the surfaces must be free from defects, such as pin-holes or air bubbles, which might spoil the surface continuity and which would produce an uneven interface between the component and the jointing product.

The installation and fixing of jointing products is closely related to the particular joint in a particular situation. For this reason, each joint illustrated in Part II has, in addition to a list of its jointing products, a description of the sequence of assembly including the operations involved and special points to be noted.

5.5 JOINTING IN THE FACTORY

Building joints are primarily made on the building site. However, the use of larger or more complex building components enables some of the jointing operations to be carried out under factory conditions. Quality control can then be better than under site conditions. It is also possible to carry out operations quite different from those able to be done on site.

Factory operations may be divided into those of fabrication and assembly. It is possible in the factory to increase the complexity of and the work involved in the fabrication and, by so doing, simplify the assembly operations, both in the factory and subsequently on the site.

Factory operations also permit the use of jigs, tools, and methods of measurement which can lead to close tolerances and a high degree of control of the dimensions of the products.

The manufacture of a door set is an example of the transfer of certain jointing operations from the site to the factory. The door is made and fitted to the door frame in the factory. The component parts are made accurately so as to enable them to be assembled with ease and without the need for fitting and adjustment as is normally required on site to hang a door on a door frame. The component sent to the site is larger, replaces a large number of parts and reduces the work otherwise required on site.

New materials, new forms of fabrication, and new approaches to design are changing the component parts and the sub-assemblies. The number of joints and the methods of jointing are correspondingly being affected. These changes which are taking place in the factory, in the first place, will subsequently lead to new jointing methods on the building site.

In general, there is a long-term tendency for fabrication operations to take place primarily under factory conditions and for assembly operations to become the principal operations on the building site. Under such conditions, jointing operations carried out in the factory will differ considerably from those carried out on the building site.

Part II
Examples from practice

Introduction

As far as is known, this book is a first attempt to bring together the principal joints that are used and needed in the present day construction of buildings. The joints illustrated and described in this part are actual examples carefully selected from the recommendations of specialist firms throughout the industry and from authoritative technical sources of reference.

The drawings of joints included in this part are specific cases and every effort has been made to ensure their accuracy. The joints illustrated are not diagrammatic or representative or typical or standardized. They form a collection of actual examples of good recognised practice in their respective areas. They are believed to be workable and reliable when used in the positions indicated and within the limitations stated or implied.

Each joint shown has been designed to meet a particular set of conditions that is likely to occur at the place in the building where the joint is intended to be located. Although the examples selected are regarded as workable, it is in the nature of our current open-ended technology that improvements can and will be made in the near or more distant future.

Extreme conditions will require special and unusual designs. Such designs are not the subject of this part and are not included. But the joints shown should serve as a reminder of the principal requirements of a particular situation and provide a basis for modification to meet other, perhaps more severe, conditions. They can serve as starting points for the design of other, perhaps improved, details that make use of newer materials, forms or processes. They may also serve as a basis for establishing a set of standards for a single element, a particular building, or a set of buildings.

There is probably no such thing as a standard joint or a typical or type joint. Every joint in a building is in a unique place in a particular building on a particular site in its own micro-climate. Each joint is part of a building considered as a whole. Each joint is in a unique place not only in a particular building but also in its place on earth. In this sense, no joint is ever exactly the same as another because it is subject to its own set of forces.

Every joint must necessarily be designed on assumptions about its immediate surroundings and the generally prevailing conditions. When the conditions change, and that may well happen during the life of its building, a joint will no longer perform as predicted or as expected.

Nevertheless, it is still possible to select joints that are generally suitable for a given situation in the building, since a given situation tends to have its own particular set of performance requirements. It is for this reason that the selected joints or sets of joints have been grouped in this chapter under their respective element, which is according to their place in the building. The place where a joint is found generates a set of conditions that apply to joints in the vicinity, in spite of changes of material, form and method of assembly.

The method of assembly of each joint illustrated has been broken down into a sequence of operations based upon the components to be joined and the jointing products used. The sequence of assembly is indicated on the drawings and in the description by a sequence of numbers. Where alternative sequences are possible, only one has been chosen and shown.

FOUNDATIONS: Steel stanchions

A The normal method of fixing a steel stanchion to a concrete foundation base is by means of foundation bolts that are set in position before the concrete is poured. The foot of the column has a baseplate welded to it and sometimes flange stiffeners. The baseplate is levelled with shims and the washers and nuts are fitted. Grout is then packed under the baseplate and allowed to set. The sleeves for the holding down bolts are not shown in the drawing.

1 Foundation bolts
2 Concrete foundation base
3 Steel stanchion
4 Nut and washer
5 Grout filling

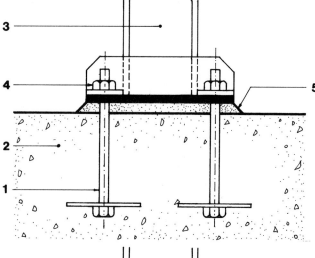

B An alternative method of fixing a steel stanchion is to cast a socket in the concrete foundation slightly larger than the overall size of the stanchion and with a level base at a predetermined level. The stanchion has a based plate welded to it that transmits the load directly to the foundation. The stanchion is lowered into the socket, plumbed, and temporarily held in position while grout is poured into the socket and allowed to set.

1 Concrete foundation pad
2 Concrete socket
3 Steel stanchion
4 Grout

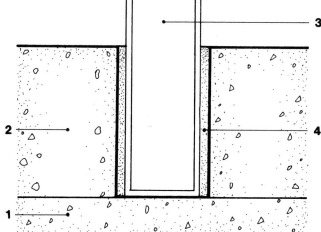

C Another method of fixing a steel stanchion to a foundation slab is to cast a concrete socket above the top of the slab. The base of the stanchion is then at slab level and the socket is filled with grout after erection and positioning of the stanchion.

1 Concrete foundation slab
2 Concrete socket
3 Steel stanchion
4 Grout

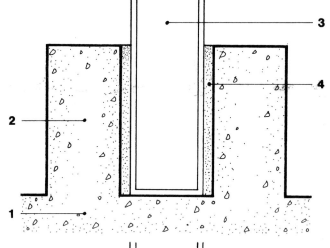

D When a steel stanchion requires to have a pinned base instead of a fixed base, it is normal to use only two foundation bolts that are fixed to the stanchion baseplate with nuts and washers. The baseplate is placed on shims, the stanchion is plumbed and grout is packed under the baseplate to set. The sleeves for the holding down bolt are not shown in the drawing.

1 Foundation bolt
2 Concrete foundation base
3 Steel stanchion
4 Nut and washer
5 Grout

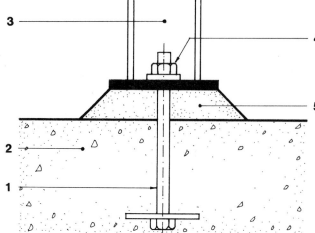

FOUNDATIONS: Concrete columns

A The lower end of the concrete column has reinforcement that is welded to a steel base plate. The fixing of the base plate to the foundation is similar to that normally used for steel stanchions. Vertical adjustment is by means of the aligning screws. The column can be positioned for height and plumb and is then sometimes temporarily braced. The gap between the base plate and the foundation can be filled fairly easily and the presence of the filling can be checked.

1 Holding-down bolts
2 Concrete base
3 Concrete column
4 Aligning screws
5 Packing shims
6 Filling grout

B The bottom of the socket is cast below the required position of the column base so as to provide a gap for a mortar bed or packing shims. The lower faces of the column and the sides of the pocket are sometimes roughened so as to transfer some of the load to the foundation from that taken solely by end bearing. The column is normally plumbed by the use of wedges.

1 Concrete foundation
2 Packing shims or mortar bed
3 Concrete column
4 In situ mortar or concrete filling

C The socket for the column is constructed above the level of the surrounding foundation and is reinforced as necessary. Packing shims are placed at the bottom of the socket to give the required level of the actual column that is to be positioned. The base of the column is shaped to permit improved flow of the in situ concrete or mortar that fills the gap between the column and the socket. The column is normally held plumb by the use of wedges.

1 Concrete socket
2 Packing shims
3 Concrete column
4 In situ mortar or concrete

D Reinforcement starter bars are placed in the foundation to project from it. Packing shims are positioned in the normal manner to give the required level for the base of the column. The column is located over the starter bars and the pocket is then filled with grout. It is possible for the grout to be of a different mix from that of the column which may lead to a reduction in the strength and stiffness of the joint when compared with other joints shown.

1 Starter reinforcing bars
2 Concrete base
3 Packing shims
4 Column
5 Grout in pocket of column

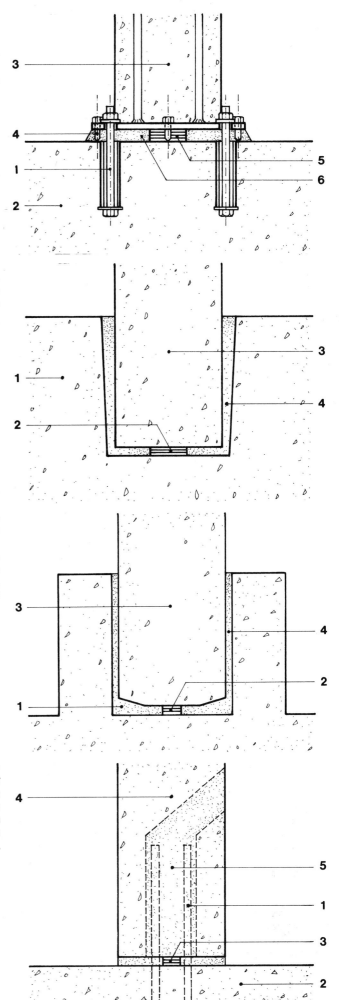

FOUNDATIONS: In situ concrete basements

SCALE 1:5

A A kicker joint consists of a horizontal construction joint between an in situ concrete wall and a continuous upstand section of that wall cast integrally with the base slab. The joint is sealed against water by means of a waterstop in the form of a plain web section and end bulbs extruded from a high grade natural rubber. The width of section depends upon the thickness of concrete, the size of aggregate and the position of the reinforcement. It should not be used where shear movement is possible.

1 Concrete upstand cast in situ with base slab
2 Rubber plain web waterstop
3 Concrete wall cast in situ

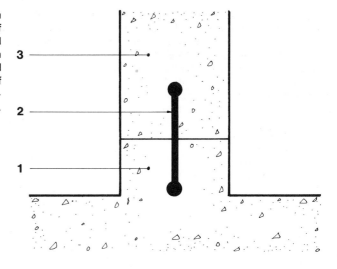

B An expansion joint for a concrete slab that is intended to take movements of up to 40 mm and to prevent the passage of water is formed with a centre bulb waterstop placed centrally across the joint. The waterstop is a section extruded from a high grade natural rubber with a centre bulb. The width of section depends upon the thickness of concrete, the size of aggregate and the position of the reinforcement.

1 Concrete slab
2 Rubber centre bulb waterstop
3 Concrete slab

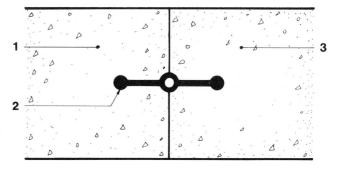

C An alternative form of expansion joint for a concrete basement slab is formed with a baseplate profile waterstop. The waterstop is placed on the sub-base and does not interrupt the stop end shuttering. The end bulbs of the profile provide a firm key in the concrete. The stop end shuttering is positioned centrally and parallel to the waterstop. The concrete slab is then cast in two stages.

1 Extruded PVC baseplate profile waterstop
2 Concrete base slab
3 Butt joint
4 Concrete base slab

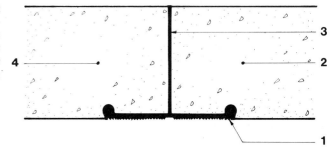

D When a joint is provided in a concrete basement slab for contraction or expansion and is required to take both horizontal and vertical movement, a centre bulb profile waterstop is used. The waterstop is fixed into split shuttering and the concrete is cast on one side. When the concrete is set, the shuttering is removed and a compressible filler placed in position below and above the centre bulb. A temporary batten is used to form a slot for the joint sealing compound. The second concrete slab is then cast.

1 Rubber centre bulb waterstop
2 Concrete base slab
3 Compressible filler
4 Concrete base slab
5 Two-part polysulphide sealing compound

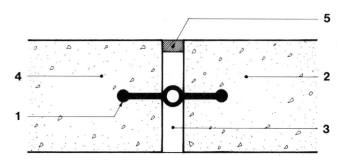

FOUNDATIONS: Concrete slabs

A A sealed expansion joint in a concrete ground slab used as a hardstanding or a paved area such as a garage or factory floor. The joint faces must be dry, clean and free from loose stones, dust and grit. An expansion strip is used to take up expansion and to provide support for the sealant that, in this case, is a hot poured, rubberized pitch fuel-resistant sealing compound. It contains no bitumen and is not therefore attacked by greases and certain fats.

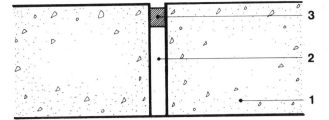

1 Concrete slab
2 Expansion strip
3 Sealant (recessed 3 mm to 9 mm below surface of slab)

B When the concrete slab is covered with a granolithic screed the expansion joint is made with an expansion strip and sealant. The sealant, however, must connect the concrete slabs below the screed. It is recessed below the surface of the slab 3 mm to 9 mm to allow for upward movement of the sealant when the slabs expand and compress the strip.

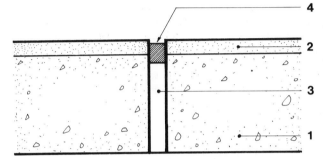

1 Concrete slab
2 Granolithic screed
3 Expansion strip
4 Sealant

C When a concrete slab is of a sufficiently large area and subject to contraction during the course of drying out, cracks are avoided by deliberately providing contraction joints. The separate slabs are cast independently and a groove is provided at the top of the joint to take a sealant. Initially there is no gap between the two slabs that are kept separated by a strip of polythene.

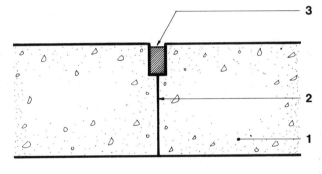

1 Concrete slab
2 Polythene separating strip
3 Sealant

D An alternative method of allowing for contraction in a concrete slab is to form an induced contraction joint that consists of a combination of a groove cast in the top of the slab and a fillet cast along the underside, both being intended to induce a crack at a predetermined position. The groove is filled with a sealant.

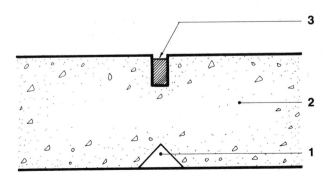

1 Fillet
2 Concrete slab
3 Sealant

FOUNDATIONS: External walls

A Timber framed external wall on solid ground floor

The foundation for the external wall of a light timber framework is normally constructed as a concrete edge beam cast with the ground floor site slab. The outside edge of the beam must be accurately set out to the outer face of the timber studwork. The slab is covered with a damp-proof membrane which is joined to the damp-proof course under the wall plate. The wall plate is then bolted down to the edge beam.

1 Concrete edge beam and ground slab
2 Damp-proof membrane
3 Timber wall plate 100 mm x 50 mm
4 Anchor bolt 12 mm diameter at 2400 mm centres
5 Plywood sheathing 8 mm thick
6 Breather membrane
7 Timber cladding

B Cavity brickwork external wall on brick base

The base for an external walling in cavity brickwork is built on a concrete footing or on trench fill and is taken to a height of not less than 150 mm above ground floor level. The concrete floor slab is cast to the same level and covered with a damp-proof membrane which connects with the damp-proof course laid on the inner leaf of the brickwork.

1 Brickwork base
2 Concrete slab 100 mm thick
3 Damp-proof course
4 Damp-proof membrane
5 Brickwork outer leaf
6 Brickwork inner leaf

C Brick clad timber framed external wall on solid ground floor

When a light timber framework is clad with a brickwork outer leaf, the concrete edge beam is rebated to provide a separate support for the outer leaf at a height of not less than 150 mm above ground floor level and 75 mm below the top of the ground slab. The damp-proof membrane on the slab connects with the damp-proof course under the wall plate and at the base of the outer leaf. The wall plate is bolted to the concrete with anchor bolts.

1 Concrete edge beam and ground slab
2 Damp-proof course
3 Damp-proof membrane
4 Timber wall plate 100 mm x 50 mm
5 Anchor bolt 12 mm diam. at 2400 mm centres
6 Plywood sheathing 8 mm thick
7 Breather membrane
8 Brickwork outer leaf

D Brick clad timber framed external wall on brick base

The brick base outer leaf is built to a height of not less than 150 mm above ground floor level and 75 mm below the top of the ground slab. The brick base inner leaf is built up to the level of the ground slab. The damp-proof membrane under the ground slab is laid to connect with the damp-proof course under the wall plate which is bolted to the brickwork base with anchor bolts.

1 Brickwork base
2 Damp-proof course
3 Damp-proof membrane
4 Concrete ground slab
5 Timber wall plate 100 mm x 50 mm
6 Anchor bolt 12 mm diam, at 2400 mm centres
7 Plywood sheathing 8 mm thick
8 Breather membrane
9 Brickwork outer leaf

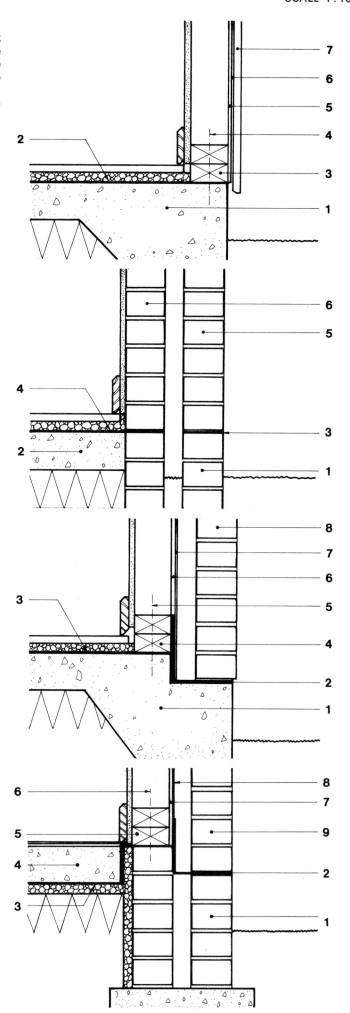

FOUNDATIONS: Dense concrete and rubble walls

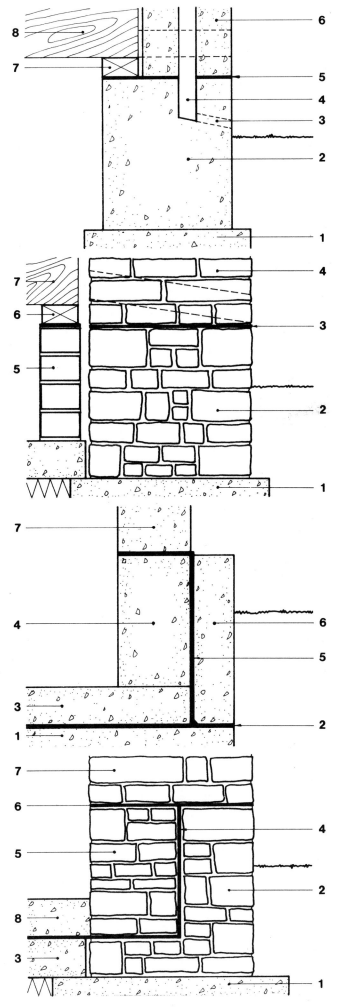

A The concrete foundation wall for a dense concrete cavity wall rests on a concrete footing and is normally taken up to the level of the damp-proof course at a minimum height of 150 mm above finished ground level. The wall cavity, however, may be extended downwards into the foundation and be connected to weepholes for drainage just above ground level.

1 Concrete footing
2 Concrete foundation
3 Weephole
4 50 mm cavity
5 Damp-proof course
6 Dense concrete wall
7 Timber plate
8 Floor joist

B The rubble foundation wall for a solid rubble wall may rest on dense impervious stone footings or on a concrete pad. The foundation wall should be taken up to a minimum height of 150 mm above finished ground level. The ground floor is kept independent of the wall and is supported on a separate sleeper wall built on the oversite concrete slab.

1 Concrete pad
2 Rubble foundation wall
3 Damp-proof course
4 Solid rubble wall
5 Sleeper wall
6 Timber plate
7 Floor joist

C Where the finished floor level is below the outside ground level, a vertical damp-proof course is applied to the outside face of the foundation wall to connect with the horizontal damp-proof course at a minimum height of 150 mm above ground level. The vertical damp-proof course is protected from damage and deterioration by a separate external wall.

1 Concrete foundation slab
2 Asphalt damp-proof course
3 Concrete floor slab
4 Foundation wall
5 Asphalt vertical damp-proof course
6 Concrete external wall
7 Dense concrete wall

D Where the finished floor level is below the outside ground level and is separated by a rubble wall, a vertical damp-proof course connects the damp-proof course over the site slab with the horizontal damp-proof course at a minimum height of 150 mm above ground level. The external foundation wall is built first, followed by the vertical damp-proof course and the internal foundation wall.

1 Concrete foundation pad
2 External rubble foundation wall
3 Concrete site slab
4 Asphalt damp-proof course
5 Internal rubble foundation wall
6 Asphalt damp-proof course
7 Rubble wall
8 Concrete site slab

A Timber framed external wall

When a suspended timber floor is used in conjunction with light timber framed construction the floor joists are supported on a continuous wall plate which is anchored to the external brickwork base. The header joist is placed over the wall plate to provide additional support for the external wall.

1 Brickwork base
2 Anchor bolt 12 mm diameter
3 Damp-proof course
4 Timber wall plate
5 Timber floor joist
6 Timber header joist

B Brick clad timber framed external wall

When a suspended timber floor is used in conjunction with light timber framed construction which is clad in brickwork, the floor joists are supported on a separate internal sleeper wall. The wall plate rests on a damp-proof course and is anchored to the sleeper wall.

1 Brickwork sleeper wall
2 Anchor bolt 12 mm diameter
3 Damp-proof course
4 Timber wall plate
5 Timber floor joist
6 Timber header joist

C Brick partition

When a suspended timber floor is used in conjunction with a load-bearing partition, the partition is supported on its own foundation. The floor joists rest on a wall plate which is carried on a separate sleeper wall. A damp-proof course is provided along the top of the sleeper wall and under the wall plate.

1 Brickwork sleeper wall
2 Damp-proof course
3 Timber wall plate
4 Timber floor joist

D Cavity brickwork external wall

When a suspended timber floor is used in conjunction with an external wall of cavity brickwork, the floor joists are fixed to a wall plate on a separate sleeper wall that is carried on the concrete ground slab.

1 Brickwork sleeper wall
2 Damp-proof course
3 Timber wall plate
4 Timber floor joist

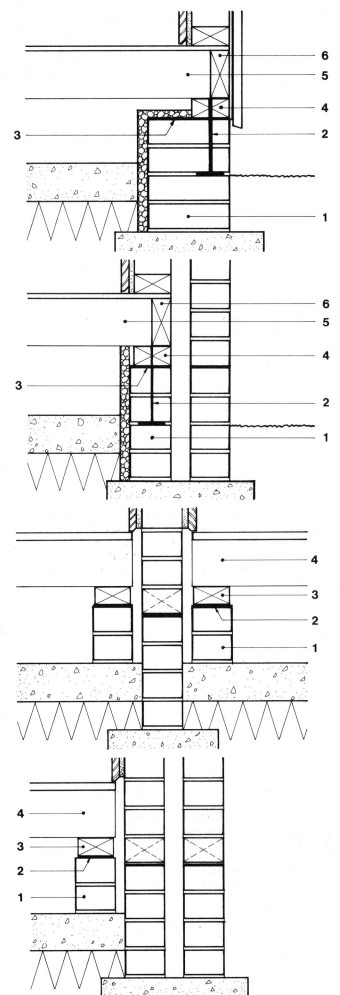

FOUNDATIONS : Balustrade posts

A There are a number of alternative methods that are used to fix the posts of balustrades to a concrete foundation base. A simple method with low initial cost is to temporarily support the post plumb in both directions and at the required level prior to pouring the concrete base around the post. The depth of the foot of the post below ground level should be not less than 300 mm.

1 Square tubular steel post
2 Concrete foundation base

B Another method is to cast the concrete foundation base with pockets at the positions required for the posts before the delivery and erection of the posts. The post is fitted with a base place and foundation bolts which are lowered into the hole and grouted in after the posts have been levelled and balustrade lined up.

1 Concrete foundation base
2 Square tubular steel post with base plate
3 Foundation bolt
4 Grout

C An alternative method of fixing the posts is to cast the concrete foundation base and make use of anchors that permit of vertical adjustment. The post with a base plate attached is fitted over the anchor bolts. The base plate is then levelled and grouted, and the anchor nuts tightened.

1 Concrete foundation base
2 Square tubular steel post with base plate
3 Anchor bolt

D A fourth method of fixing the post is to cast into the concrete foundation base a steel socket slightly larger than the post and with its base at the required level. The post is then lowered into the socket and a sealing compound applied around the gap at the top of the socket. In the event of damage it is possible to withdraw the post and replace it with a new post and new sealing compound.

1 Steel socket with base plate
2 Concrete foundation base
3 Square tubular steel post
4 Sealing compound

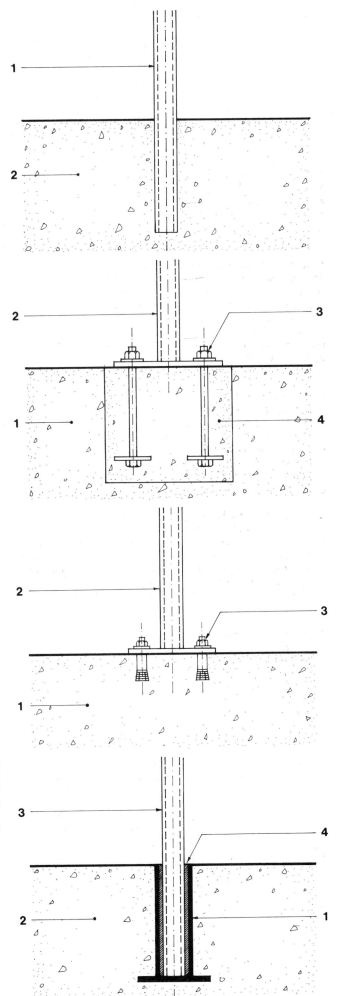

A Asphalt tanking applied internally
When foundations below ground level are to be tanked internally, the concrete base is laid and the external walls built to 150 mm above ground level. The asphalt membrane is then applied in three coats to the internal face of the base slab and the external walls. Angle fillets are formed at the internal junctions of the horizontal and vertical membranes. A sand:cement screed is laid horizontally to provide a protective layer for the asphalt. A concrete inner wall is then cast to serve as a loading coat to prevent the asphalt being forced off by water pressure.

1 Concrete base slab
2 External brick wall
3 Asphalt 28 mm thick horizontally, 18 mm thick vertically
4 Asphalt angle fillet
5 Sand:cement screed 50 mm thick
6 Concrete inner wall

B Asphalt tanking applied externally
When foundations below ground level are to be tanked externally, the horizontal asphalt membrane is laid first on the concrete base and is covered with a protective screed and a concrete loading coat. The vertical external walls are then built. The asphalt membrane is applied in three coats to the external face and jointed with an angle fillet to the horizontal membrane, which must be kept clean. A brick protective panel is then built externally to prevent the asphalt being subsequently damaged.

1 Concrete base slab
2 Asphalt 28 mm thick
3 Sand:cement screed 50 mm thick
4 Reinforced concrete loading coat
5 External brick wall
6 Asphalt 18 mm thick
7 Asphalt angle fillet
8 Brick wall protective panel

C Bitumen sheet tanking applied internally
When foundations below ground level are to be tanked internally with bitumen sheeting, a bituminous strip is first applied at the angle between the base slab and the external wall. The two layers of bitumen sheet are then applied, the horizontal layers being protected by a screed. A concrete loading coat is applied over the screed and against the vertical layers of sheeting.

1 Concrete base slab
2 External brick wall
3 Angle strip
4 Bitumen sheet
5 Sand:cement screed 50 mm thick
6 Reinforced concrete loading coat

D Bitumen sheet tanking applied externally
When foundations below ground level are to be tanked externally with bitumen sheeting, the base concrete is formed with an upstand to take a bituminous angle strip. The two horizontal layers of bituminous sheet are then laid and turned up and over the upstand. A protective screed is laid and the reinforced concrete loading slab and wall are constructed. The sheet is turned up against the outside of the concrete wall, the vertical bitumen sheet is applied in two layers and a protective brick panel is then built externally.

1 Concrete base slab
2 Angle strip
3 Bitumen sheet
4 Sand:cement screed 50 mm thick
5 Reinforced concrete loading coat
6 Bitumen sheet
7 Brick wall protective panel

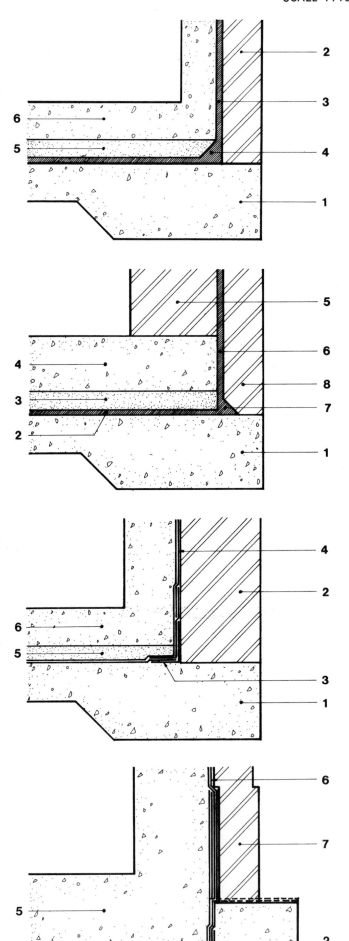

FOUNDATIONS : Tanking to column bases

A Asphalt tanking to column base

When the foundation for a concrete column stands below ground level and asphalt tanking is provided, and where the slab is required to be thickened under the column, the asphalt is taken over the sinking and angle fillets are applied at the junction between the slopes and the horizontal. The asphalt is laid in three coats and covered with a protective screed. The in situ concrete slab and column base are then added.

1 Concrete base slab
2 Asphalt 28 mm thick
3 Angle fillet
4 Sand : cement screed 50 mm thick
5 Concrete slab and column

B Bitumen sheet tanking to column base

When the foundation for a concrete column stands below ground level and tanking is by means of bitumen sheet, the surface of the base is primed with a coat of bitumen solution or bitumen emulsion. The first layer of bitumen sheet is then bonded with hot bitumen. Subsequent layers are bonded similarly, the joints between layers being lapped at least 100 mm. The sheet is covered with a protective screed. The in situ concrete slab and column are then added.

1 Concrete base slab
2 Bitumen sheet in three layers
3 Sand : cement screed 50 mm thick
4 Concrete slab and column

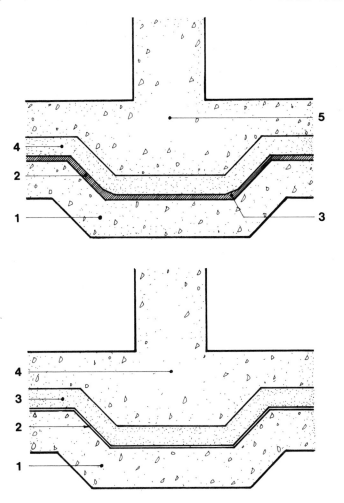

A   The **mortise-and-tenon joint**, also called a **mortise joint**, was used in traditional timber frame construction normally between members at right angles to one another. A rectangular slot, the mortise, is cut in one member, and a corresponding projection, the tenon, cut on the other member. A hole is drilled through both members which are then connected with an oak peg of uniform cross-section.

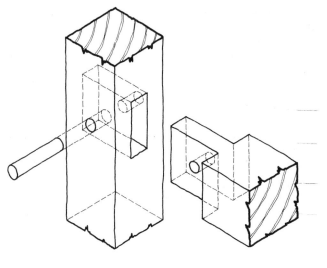

B   The **halved joint** is normally an **angle joint** but may be used to form a **lengthening joint**. It is usually made between two members of the same thickness. One half of the thickness is cut away from the face of one member and a corresponding half from the back of the other. The cut surfaces are placed together and fixed with a dowel or, more often today, with glue and screws. The joint is commonly used in carpentry.

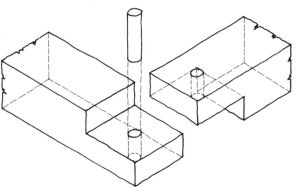

C   **Cocking**, also called **cogging**, or **corking** is the name given to a joint between a beam and a wall plate. A square notch is cut out of the wall plate and a corresponding notch is cut near the end and on the underside of the beam. When a notch is cut on both sides of the wall plate the joint is known as double-notched cogging. The solid tooth left projecting upwards from the wall plate is called a cog.

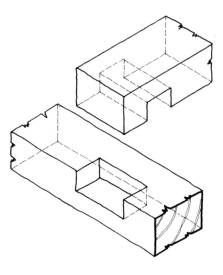

D   The **skew notch joint** is used to connect timber members at an angle with one another as, for example, a roof joist on to a wall plate, sill or purlin. A notch is cut at the required angle in the plate and the end of the joist is cut to match the notch. A hole is drilled through both members which are then connected with an oak peg.

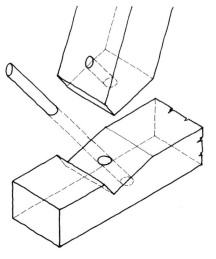

FRAMES : Timber post-and-beam construction

A The earliest form of post-and-beam construction has a solid timber section for both the post and the beam. For a rigid connection, the joint between the post and beam, formerly made with a mortise-and-tenon, is now made with a strap iron and an angle strap secured with bolts.

1 Timber post 100 mm x 100 mm
2 Timber beam 250 mm x 100 mm
3 Strap iron
4 Angle strap
5 12 mm diameter bolt

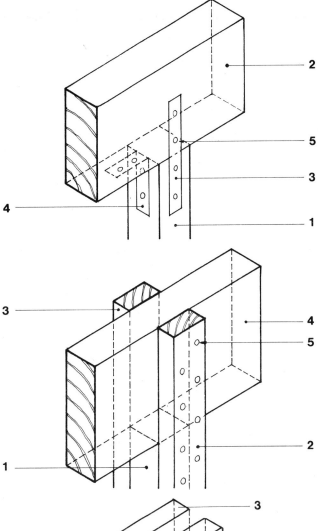

B An alternative form of construction is to make the post of three sections with the beam supported on the central section and held on both sides by the two outer sections that act as gussets. The fixing is by means of nails.

1 Timber post 100 mm x 100 mm
2 Timber side post 100 mm x 50 mm
3 Timber side post 100 mm x 50 mm
4 Timber beam 300 mm x 100 mm
5 Nail

C A third form of construction is to assemble two beams on both sides of a single post and to fix them with a single 12 mm diameter bolt combined with 2 toothed plate connectors.

1 Timber post 200 mm x 50 mm
2 Timber beam 300 mm x 50 mm
3 Timber beam 300 mm x 50 mm
4 12 mm diameter bolt with 2 toothed plate connectors 65 mm diameter

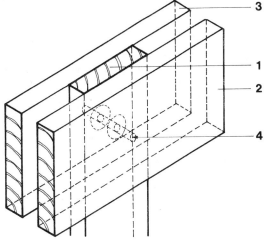

D An alternative form of construction is to form a beam of three pieces and a post of three pieces. The central section of the post has a beam section on both sides. The side sections of the post support the side sections of the beam. Fixing is made with nails.

1 Timber post section 100 mm x 50 mm
2 Timber post section 150 mm x 75 mm
3 Nail
4 Timber beam section 200 mm x 50 mm
5 Timber beam section 250 mm x 75 mm

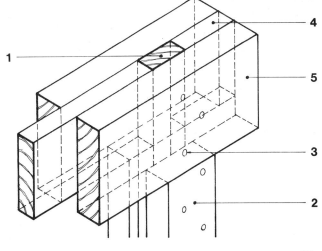

FRAMES: Floor joist hangers

A Heavy duty joist hanger on brickwork or blockwork
The connection of a heavy timber joist to a wall of brickwork or blockwork may be made by means of a heavy duty joist hanger manufactured for standard joist widths from 38 mm to 150 mm and depths from 125 mm to 250 mm. The end of the joist is placed against the face of the wall and both sides are nailed with square twisted nails 32 mm long through the pre-punched holes of the hanger.

1 Brick wall
2 Galvanized mild steel joist hanger 2.7 mm thick
3 Timber joist
4 Sherardized square twisted nail 32 mm

B Medium duty joist hanger on brickwork or blockwork
For connection to a gable wall a joist hanger is used with a hooked upper flange which straddles the wall and a horizontal seating that projects 90 mm to support the joist. The underside of the end of the joist is nailed to the hanger through the pre-punched holes.

1 Brick wall
2 Galvanized mild steel joist hanger 2.7 mm thick
3 Timber joist
4 Sherardized square twisted nail 32 mm

C Light duty joist hanger on timber joist
For connections between timber joists which are positioned at right angles to one another, as between a joist and a trimmer, a light duty joist hanger is used. The hanger is pressed from light-gauge galvanized steel and has pre-punched holes. No notching of the joists is required and the plasterboard is nailed directly to the underside of the joists. The hanger is nailed firmly to both joists with square twisted nails.

1 Timber joist
2 Galvanized mild steel joist hanger 1 mm thick
3 Timber joist
4 Sherardized square twisted nail 32 mm

D Medium duty joist hanger on timber joist
Where additional bearing capacity is required, a joist hanger with two legs is used, the legs being bent across the top of the support joist and securely nailed to it. Hangers are manufactured to suit joist widths from 38 mm to 50 mm and depths from 125 mm to 250 mm.

1 Timber joist
2 Galvanized mild steel joist hanger 1 mm thick
3 Timber joist
4 Sherardized square twisted nail 32 mm

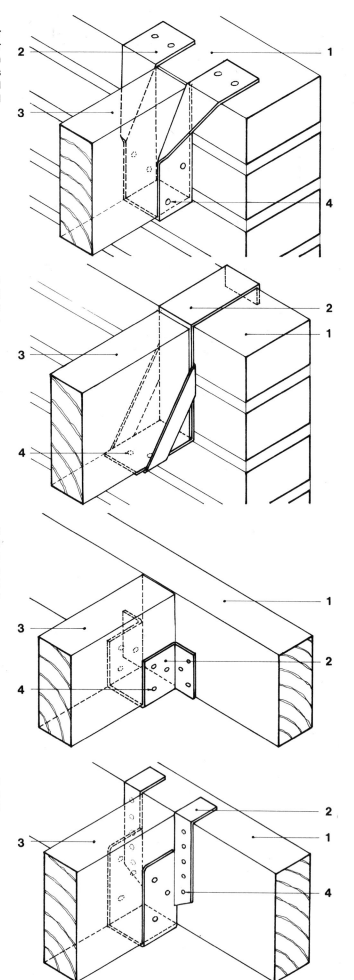

FRAMES: Jointing of timber sections

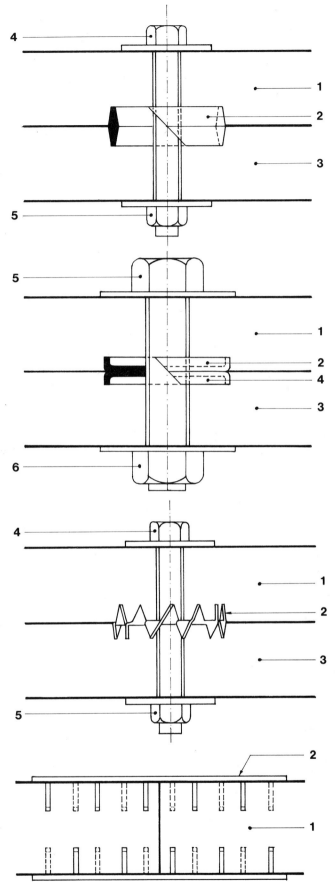

A A bolt hole is bored in the two timbers to be joined 1.5mm larger than the bolt size. Circular grooves half the depth of the ring are cut in opposite faces of timbers using a special grooving tool which centres in the hole already drilled. The split-ring connector is then placed in the groove in one timber and the other timber is fitted over it. The two timbers are drawn tightly together with the bolt that remains in position.

1 Timber section
2 Double-bevelled split-ring timber connector 64 mm internal diameter
3 Timber section
4 Bolt and washer M12 diameter
5 Nut and washer (special large diameter round)

B A bolt hole is drilled through both timbers. Circular grooves are cut in opposite faces of the timber sections to be joined by means of a special tool. A shear plate connector is placed in each groove so that its back is flush with the surface of the timber. The two timbers are then bolted firmly together.

1 Timber section
2 Shear plate timber connector
3 Timber section
4 Shear plate timber connector
5 Bolt and washer M20 diameter
6 Nut and washer (special large diameter round)

C A hole is drilled through both timbers 1.5 mm diameter larger than the bolt. The toothed plate connector is centred over the holes, the bolt placed in position and firmly tightened, forcing the teeth of the connector into both timbers. There can be a gap between the timbers with a clearance equal to the thickness of the central connector plate.

1 Timber section
2 Round toothed plate connector
3 Timber section
4 Bolt and washer M12 diameter
5 Nut and washer (special large diameter round)

D The gang-nail connector plate is a steel plate with integral teeth punched out at right angles to the plane of the plate. The plate overlaps adjoining timber members and the teeth are pressed into the timber by means of a special hydraulic press.

1 Timber section
2 Gang-nail connector plate

FRAMES: Steel beam connections

SCALE 1 : 10

A A common method of connecting a steel beam to a steel stanchion is by means of an end plate shop-welded to the beam before assembly and bolted to the stanchion on site.

1 Steel stanchion
2 Steel beam
3 Steel end plate welded to beam
4 Bolt

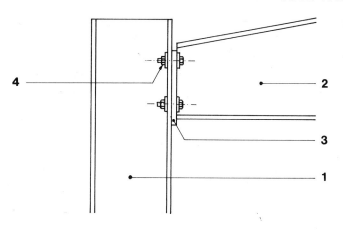

B A method of fixing a steel beam to a concrete column is by means of a steel support plate welded to the lower flange near the end of the beam. The plate contains two slotted holes: one on each side of the beam. Two anchor studs are inserted into the top of the column and the plate is bolted to the studs.

1 Concrete column
2 Steel beam
3 Steel plate
4 Anchor stud

C One method of fixing a steel beam to the top of a brick wall is by means of a support plate combined with tie bars. The support plate is shop-welded to the lower flange of the beam before assembly and is fixed to the concrete padstone with two stud anchors: one on each side of the beam. Another plate welded to the top flange of the beam is connected to two tie bars held down by the upper part of the brick wall.

1 Brick wall
2 Concrete padstone
3 Steel support plate
4 Steel beam
5 Anchor stud
6 Steel plate
7 Tie bar

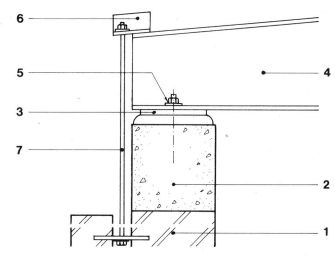

D A common method used to connect steel purlins to a main support beam is by means of steel plates welded on to the top flange of the beam. The purlins are independently bolted to the plate, a gap being allowed for between the ends of purlins to provide for ease of assembly.

1 Steel beam
2 Steel plate
3 Steel purlin
4 Bolt

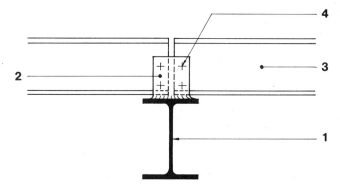

FRAMES: Fire protection of structural steel

A Structural steel sections need fire-resistant casings to give fire protection for a required period. Fire resistance of 30 mins is provided by a casing of 9 mm asbestos composition sheet with 25 mm x 25 mm corner battens and 6 mm fillets fixed inside the horizontal joints.

1 Structural steel column not less than 45 kg/m
2 6 mm cover fillet
3 9 mm casing
4 25 mm x 25 mm corner battens
5 Self-tapping screw 32 mm at 230 mm centres

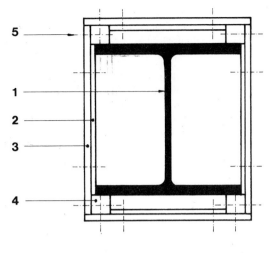

B Fire protection for a period of not less than 2 hours is given by providing thick fire-resistant casings screwed to one another and fillets placed inside the casings to cover the horizontal joints.

1 Structural steel column not less than 45 kg/m
2 6 mm fillet
3 25 mm panels
4 Wood screw 64 mm at 230 mm centres

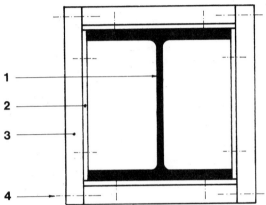

C Fire protection for a period of not less than 4 hours is given by providing two layers of fire resistant casings with screw fixings. The inner set of casings are first screwed together and the outer casings are then fixed so that horizontal joints are staggered.

1 Structural steel column not less than 45 kg/m
2 25 mm inner panel
3 50 mm wood screw at 600 mm centres
4 25 mm outer panel
5 50 mm wood screw at 230 mm centres

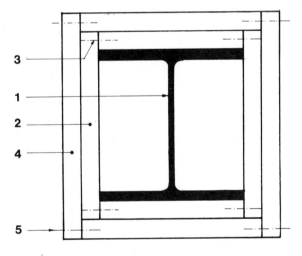

D An alternative method of column casing is the use of a pre-fabricated steel casing with a lining of asbestos composition sheet bonded to the inside. The thickness of the lining is made to suit the period of fire protection required.

1 Structural steel column not less than 45 kg/m
2 Galvanized sheet steel casing 0.71 mm thick, U-shape
3 Snap-on lid with locking device

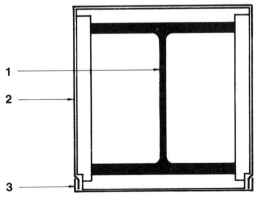

FRAMES : Structural steel

A Floor beam—Column Elevation
The connection between a steel floor beam and column is by
means of high strength friction grip bolts inserted through
pre-drilled holes in the flanges of the stanchion and the end
plate of the beam. The column is a standard rolled steel column
section and the beam is fabricated from a castellated rolled
steel joist with flat plates 12 mm thick welded at both ends. A
cleat is fixed to the stanchion to provide bearing for the floor
beam during assembly and ensure alignment of the holes in the
beam with those in the stanchion.

1 Rolled steel column
2 Steel floor beam
3 Steel high strength friction grip bolt
4 Steel angle cleat

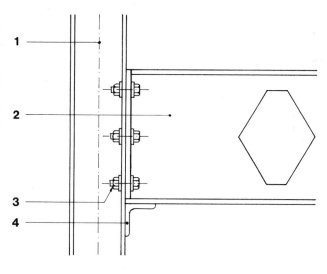

B Floor beam—Column Plan
The beam is positioned on the temporary cleat. The bolts are
inserted and tightened up. The cleat may be removed if required
after the assembly of the frame is completed

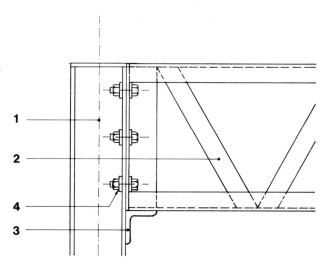

C Roof beam—Column Elevation
The joint between the roof beam and stanchion of the structural
steel frame is in the form of a bolted connection. The stanchion
is a standard rolled steel column section with both flanges pre-
drilled. The beam is of welded construction consisting of upper
and lower flanges formed of channel sections joined by angles.
The end of the beam has a welded T drilled with holes to match
those in the stanchion. An angle cleat is welded to the stanchion
to facilitate assembly.

1 Structural steel column
2 Steel fabricated roof beam
3 Steel angle cleat
4 High strength friction grip steel bolt 18 mm diameter

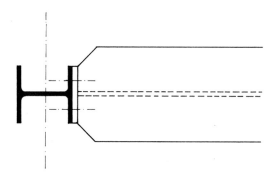

D Roof beam—Column Plan
The roof beam is positioned on the angle cleat and bolted to the
stanchion with six 18 mm diameter high strength friction grip steel
bolts. If required, the cleat may be removed after the assembly of
the frame is complete.

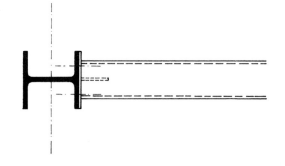

FRAMES : Structural steel

A The joint between the perimeter tie beam and the perimeter structural column of a structural frame is in the form of a bolted connection. The stanchion that consists of a rolled steel column section may be positioned with its web parallel to the span of the beam or at right angles to it. In the former case the connection is by means of an angle and in the latter case by means of a flat plate. Both the angle and flat plate are fitted on site, thereby utilising a single length of beam for both conditions. The perimeter beam consists of a castellated rolled steel channel of constant length. The tolerance on the length of the beam is taken up in the clearance between the end of the beam and the joint face of the flange of the stanchion. The clearance can also include an allowance for different flange thicknesses of the alternative stanchion sections that are manufactured.

1 Structural steel stanchion
2 Castellated rolled steel channel
3 Steel angle
4 High strength friction grip steel bolt 18 mm diameter

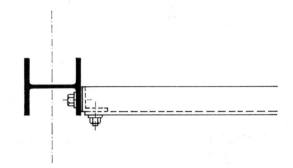

B One leg of the angle is bolted to the end of the web of the perimeter beam with three high strength friction grip 18 mm diameter steel bolts. The beam is then lifted into position and the other leg of the angle is bolted to a flange of the stanchion.

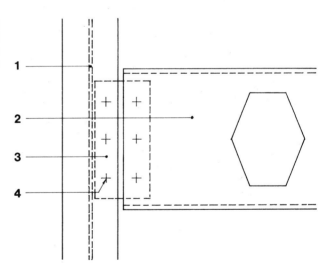

C When the stanchion is orientated with the web at right angles to the span of the perimeter beam, the connection is made by means of a flat plate drilled with holes that are positioned so as to correspond with those in the web of the beam. The same bolts are used as in A above.

1 Structural steel stanchion
2 Castellated rolled steel channel
3 Steel flat plate
4 HSFG steel bolt 18 mm diameter

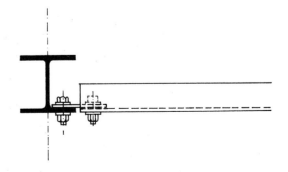

A There are a number of alternative ways of jointing a concrete beam to a concrete column by means of steel connectors. A mild steel box section filled with concrete is cast into the column and projects beyond it so as to form a channel bracket. A similar section is cast into the end of the beam. The beam bracket is positioned and connected to that of the column with a friction grip bolt. Another bolt connects the top of the beam to the column. The gap is then filled with in situ concrete.

1 Concrete column
2 Concrete beam
3 High strength friction grip bolt
4 Mild steel bolt
5 In situ concrete

B A second method of making the joint consists in casting into the column a mild steel T section that projects to form a shelf bracket and a mild steel angle that projects for welding to a tie bar at the top of the beam. Two mild steel plates are cast in the end of the beam and project so as to rest on the T section. The beam plates are positioned and supported on the column bracket and then welded to it. A tie bar is welded to the angle. The gap is then filled with in situ concrete.

1 Concrete column with mild steel T and angle cast in
2 Concrete beam
3 Mild steel plate
4 Tie bar welded to angle
5 In situ concrete

C A third method of making the joint consists in casting into the concrete column a mild steel box section that projects to provide a bracket, and casting into the end of the concrete beam a mild steel T section with a recess below it at the end. The beam is supported on the bracket that is then welded on site to the T section. Continuity steel is fixed through the column and along the top of the beam. The recess is then filled with in situ grout.

1 Concrete column
2 Mild steel box section
3 Concrete beam
4 Continuity steel
5 Mild steel T section
6 Slot inside of beam to permit welding of connection

D A fourth method of making the joint is to cast a section of RSJ in the column so that it projects to provide a support bracket. Two mild steel plates are cast into the end of the beam and project from it. A mild steel bearing plate is welded to the underside of the beam plates and to the top flange of the RSJ when the beam is in position on site. The gap between the end of the beam and the column is filled with in situ concrete.

1 Concrete column
2 Section of rolled steel joist
3 Concrete beam
4 Mild steel plate
5 Welded connection
6 In situ concrete

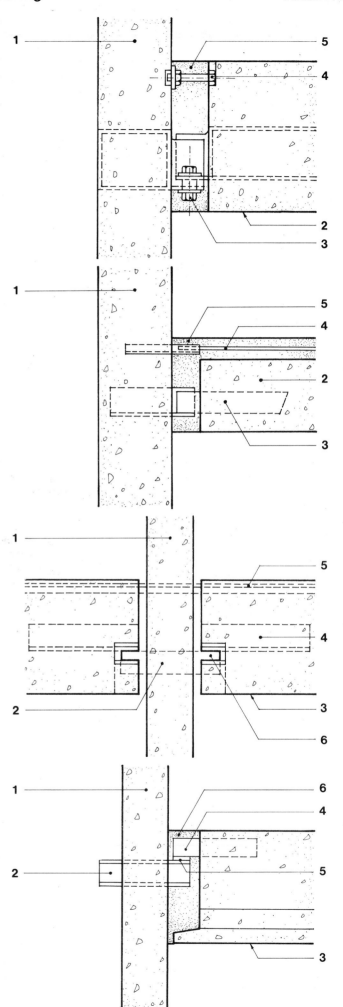

FRAMES: Beam to column joints: Concrete bearing

A There are a number of alternative methods used to join a concrete beam to a concrete column in those cases where the beam bears directly on to the column or on to a corbel that is part of the column. One method is to connect a flange of a short length of steel angle to the lower end of the beam by means of an anchor socket. The lower flange of the angle rests on the top of the column and is bolted to a threaded bar cast into it. Continuity bars are provided at the top of the beam. The gap is filled with in situ concrete.

1 Concrete column
2 Threaded bar cast in column
3 Concrete beam
4 Anchor socket
5 Steel angle
6 Continuity steel

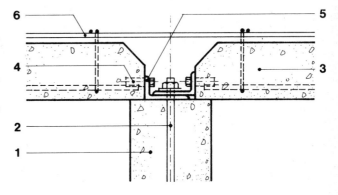

B A second method is to cast a column with a corbel to support the end of the beam. A flexible bearing pad is provided to reduce possible stress concentration and a dowel to position the underside of the end of the beam. When the beam is in position continuity steel is passed through the column and along the top of the beam. The gap between the beam and column is fitted with in situ grout.

1 Concrete column
2 Flexible bearing pad
3 Concrete beam
4 Steel dowel
5 Continuity steel
6 In situ grout
7 Screed

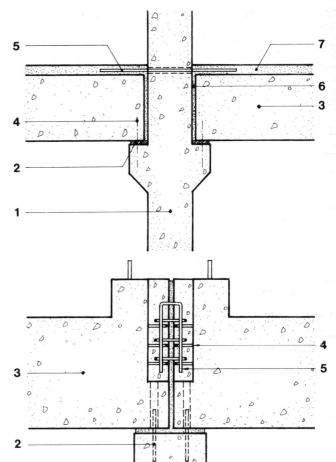

C A third method is to provide holes for a dowel in the top of the column and the underside of the end of the beam. The beam is positioned on the top of the column by means of the dowel and fixed on a mortar bed. Hoop bars that project from the end of adjacent beams are linked with connecting bars and the gap between the beams is filled with in situ concrete.

1 Concrete column
2 Steel dowel
3 Concrete beam
4 Hoop bars
5 Connecting bars

D A fourth method is to cast a corbel at the top of the column with a profile that corresponds with a flange on the end of the beam. The end of the beam is positioned and supported on the corbel, the two being connected by means of two bolts fitted in holes passing vertically through the beam flange and the corbel. The gap between the joint face of the beam and the corbel is filled with in situ grout.

1 Concrete column
2 Concrete beam
3 Bolts
4 Hole for grout
5 In situ grout

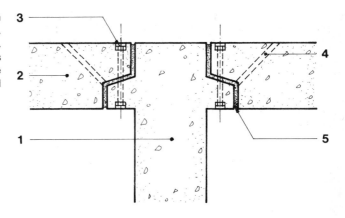

A A number of alternative methods are used to make the joint between columns of reinforced concrete. The use of turnbuckles to connect the splice bars of the upper and lower columns permits adjustment to be made to plumb and level without the need for additional support or temporary bracing before the gap between the ends of the columns is filled with in situ concrete. It is important to ensure that the gap is completely filled. The in situ concrete filling has been omitted from the drawing for clarity.

1 Lower splice bar with right hand thread
2 Upper splice bar with left hand thread
3 Turnbuckle

B A second method of connecting two concrete columns is to weld a connecting plate to the underside of the four upper column bars. The connecting plate is drilled with four holes at the corners to take the four lower column bars that are bolted to it. This method, like the one above, enables adjustment to be made to plumb and level before the gap between the columns is filled with in situ concrete.

1 Lower column bar
2 Upper column bar
3 Connecting plate
4 Connecting nut

C A third method of connection is by means of mild steel plates. Two plates are cast in each column and one pair forms a lap joint with the other pair. High strength friction grip bolts are used to connect the two plates of one column to the two plates of the other. Adjustment is not possible with this method and the holes in the plates have to be accurately positioned.

1 Lower column mild steel plate
2 Upper column mild steel plate
3 High strength friction grip bolt

D A fourth method has two bars with threaded ends that project from the lower column up into a pocket cast in the upper column. Nuts are fastened on to the bars. The upper column is temporarily supported while the gap between the columns is filled and the pocket in the upper column is filled with grout.

1 Lower column bar
2 Pocket in upper column
3 Nut

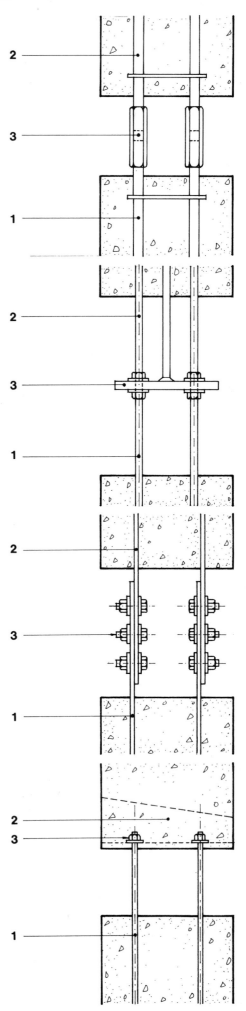

FRAMES: Structural aluminium

A The joint between the beam and column of the aluminium portal frame made of box members is formed with two gussets. The holes through the end of the beam and the head of the column are pre-drilled before assembly. The two gussets are positioned on opposite sides of the column and connected to it with through bolts. The beam is placed between the gussets and connected on site with through bolts.

1 Aluminium alloy box column made up of 2 channels
2 Aluminium alloy gusset 10 mm thick
3 Mild steel bolt 16 mm diameter
4 Aluminium alloy box beam
5 Mild steel bolt 16 mm diameter cadmium plated

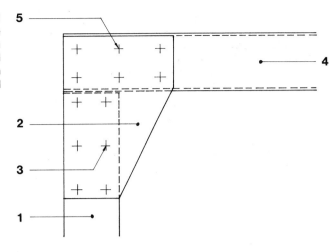

B The box column is shop fabricated from 2 channels that are connected by batten plates on the inside, rivetted to the channels with countersunk solid rivets or bolted with countersunk bolts. The beam is fabricated in the same way. The holes to take the gussets are pre-drilled and reamed to ensure a tight fit on site.

1 Aluminium alloy box column made up of 2 channels
2 Aluminium alloy gusset 10 mm thick
3 Mild steel bolt 16 mm diameter
4 Aluminium alloy box beam
5 Mild steel bolt 16 mm diameter cadmium plated

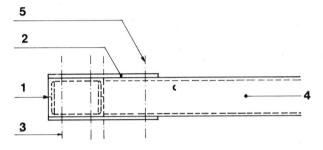

C An intermediate column supports the beam of the portal frame. It is connected to the beam by means of two gusset plates that are shaped to take the connecting bolts in positions required to resist the applied loads. The through bolts are of the same type as used to make the connection in A above.

1 Aluminium alloy box column
2 Aluminium alloy gusset 10 mm thick
3 Mild steel bolt 16 mm diameter
4 Aluminium alloy box beam
5 Mild steel bolt 16 mm diameter cadmium plated

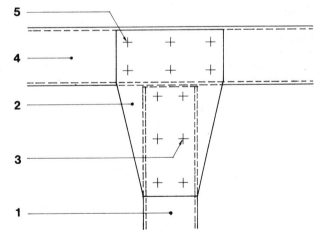

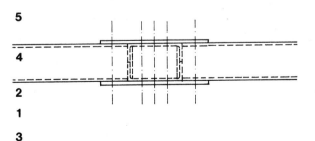

A Bearing on brickwork wall

The fully precast reinforced concrete slabs have projecting concrete nibs which rest on the top of the brickwork wall thereby providing a gap 200 mm wide to take the hoop reinforcing bars projecting from the edge of the slabs. A steel tie bar is passed through the hoops and the gap is filled with concrete. The floor slabs as laid are covered with a screed not less than 35 mm thick.

1 Load-bearing brickwork support wall 215 mm thick
2 Precast reinforced concrete slab 200 mm wide, 150 mm thick
3 Steel tie bar
4 Concrete in situ filling
5 Screed 35 mm thick

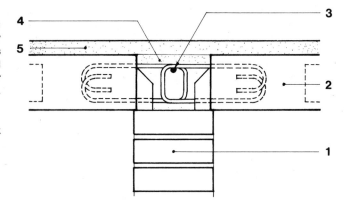

B Joint between floor slabs

The fully precast reinforced concrete slabs are 1200 mm wide and have urea formaldehyde cores to reduce the dead weight of the slab. The flanges along the lower edge of each slab are butted together and the gap between the joint faces of adjacent slabs is filled with concrete.

1 Precast reinforced concrete slab 150 mm thick
2 Concrete in situ filling
3 Screed 35 mm thick

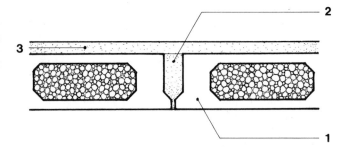

C Bearing on rolled steel joist

When the reinforced concrete floor slabs are designed as composite construction with a rolled steel joist, the joist is designed to take the tension and steel studs are welded to the top flange to transmit shear forces to the slabs. The concrete nibs projecting from the end of each slab bear on the top flange of the rolled steel joist and leave a gap for the projecting steel hoops, the steel tie bar and the concrete in situ filling. The spacing of the studs is arranged to suit the spacing of the reinforcement projecting from the slabs.

1 Rolled steel joist
2 Precast reinforced concrete slab 150 mm thick
3 Steel tie bar
4 Concrete in situ filling

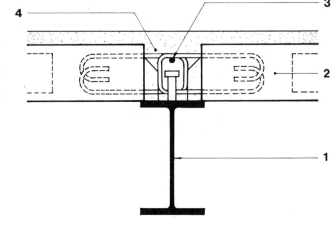

D Junction of longitudinal and transverse joint

The 4-way joint at the junction of the longitudinal joint between the ends of slabs and the transverse joint between the sides of slabs is filled with concrete in situ filling.

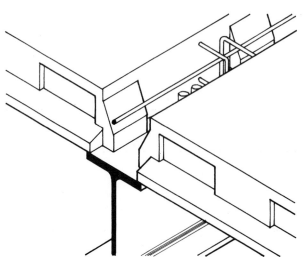

A Floor Slab—Steel Beam

The end of the floor slab is centred on the rolled steel joist with a nominal gap width of 13 mm between opposite slabs. A special stainless steel clip is then slotted over the top flange of the rolled steel joist and hammered into the side face of the slab. A clip with projections of the opposite hand is fixed on the opposite side of the slab. Reinforcing bar is placed in rebates in the top edges of the slab to provide continuity.

1 Rolled steel joist
2 Lightweight concrete floor slab
3 Stainless steel clip (Sheffield clip)
4 Steel reinforcing bar for continuity

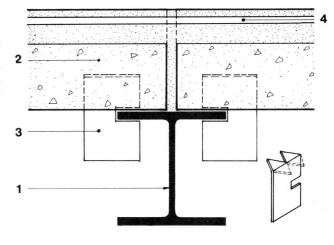

B Floor Slab—Steel Beam

An alternative method of fixing is by means of a Derby cleat that consists of a mild steel plate with a slot that is welded on the centre line of the top flange of the rolled steel joist. The end of the floor slab is butted against the cleat with a nominal gap width of 13 mm between opposite slabs. The bar for continuity is passed through the slot in the cleat.

1 Rolled steel joist
2 Mild steel plate with slotted hole (Derby cleat)
3 Lightweight concrete floor slab
4 Steel reinforcing bar for continuity.

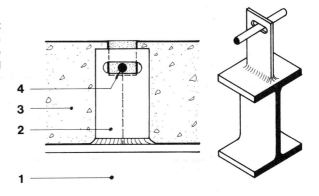

C Floor Slab—Concrete Beam

When the top surface of the concrete beam is not true and plane a bed of mortar is provided to give a level bearing for the floor slabs. Mild steel stirrups are cast in the beam on the centre line at right angles to its length to project bar below the top of the slabs. The slabs are positioned on the beam, bars for continuity are placed in the rebates along the edges of the slabs and other bars are passed through the stirrups and over the continuity bars.

1 Reinforced concrete beam
2 Mortar bed
3 Mild steel stirrup 6 mm diameter rod
4 Mild steel bar 6 mm diameter
5 Lightweight concrete floor slab
6 Steel reinforcing bar for continuity

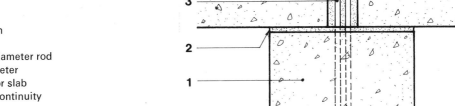

D Floor Slab—Concrete Beam

An alternative method of fixing is by means of mild steel stirrups cast in the beam on the centre line parallel to its length to project 12 mm below the top of the slabs. The ends of the slabs are butted against the stirrups with a nominal gap width of 13 mm between opposite slabs. Bars to provide continuity are passed through the stirrups and rest in rebates along the edges of the slabs.

1 Reinforced concrete beam
2 Mortar bed
3 Mild steel stirrup 6 mm diameter rod at 600 mm centres
4 Lightweight concrete floor slab
5 Steel reinforcing bar for continuity

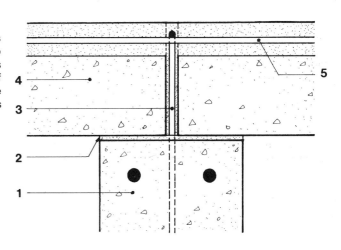

FRAMES: Joint with high strength friction grip bolts

A Hexagon head bolt with load indicator washer
Joints in structural steelwork made with high strength friction grip bolts (HSFG) provide a simple method of transmitting loads by means of the friction on the contact faces developed through the high clamping force resulting from correctly tightened high strength bolts. The bolt is fitted in a clearance hole so that it is not subject to bearing or shear forces. The special load indicator washer is placed under the head of the bolt.

1 Steel plates
2 Load indicator washer *before* tightening
3 HSFG bolt
4 Hardened steel washer
5 Steel nut
6 Load indicator washer *after* tightening

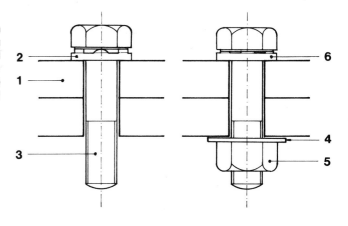

B Hexagon head bolt with load indicator washer and taper washer
When the steelwork has taper flanges, taper washers are fitted either under the nut or under the load indicator washer.

1 Steel plates
2 Load indicator washer
3 Taper washer
4 HSFG bolt
5 Flat round washer
6 Steel nut

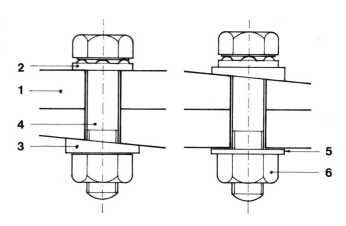

C Countersunk head bolt with load indicator washer under nut
When a countersunk head HSFG bolt is used, the load indicator washer is placed under the nut with a special nut faced washer in addition. The holes should be sufficiently well aligned to permit bolts to be placed freely in position. A flat round washer is positioned under the nut or bolt head, whichever is to be rotated during tightening. Tightening is by means of special tools.

1 Steel plates
2 Countersunk head HSFG bolt
3 Load indicator washer *before* tightening
4 Special nut faced washer
5 Steel nut
6 Load indicator washer *after* tightening

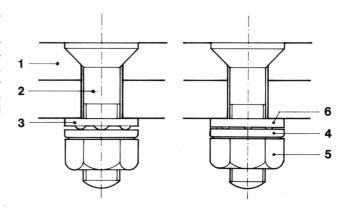

D Load indicator washer
The load indicator washer is a specially hardened washer with protrusions on one face (as shown opposite). The protrusions bear against the underside of the bolt head, or the nut-faced washer, leaving a gap. As the nut is tightened, the protrusions are flattened and the gap reduced. A specified average gap, measured by feeler gauge corresponds to the induced shank tension. Once tightened the bolt will remain tight and maintain the tension between the specified maximum and minimum limits during its working life. When the load indicator washer is used under a bolt head the specified average gap is 0.40 mm.

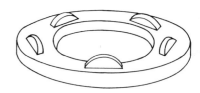

STAIRS: Safety treads and aluminium nosings

A Single strip insert straight edged tread

Plugs are cast into the concrete and prepared timber battens of the same size as the insert are placed in the required position and at the correct depth. After the concrete has set, the battens are removed. The insert is positioned with rough side upwards, the top surface being 1 to 2 mm proud of the topping, and is fixed with adhesive and countersunk wood screws. Matching plugs are then tapped into place to cover the screw heads.

1 Timber plug in concrete step
2 Polychloroprene type adhesive
3 Single strip vinyl plastic insert straight edged tread
4 Galvanized countersunk wood screw at 100 mm centres
5 Plug to match tread

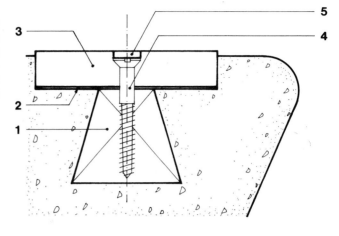

B Round edged (bull-nosed) tread

The concrete is placed to within about 6 mm of the required height and the tread with special lugs welded to the underside is pressed into position with the rough side on top. Instead of casting in during construction, an alternative method is to use adhesive and screws as described in A above.

1 Concrete step
2 Special lug welded to tread
3 Round edged (bull nosed) vinyl plastic tread with non-slip grain

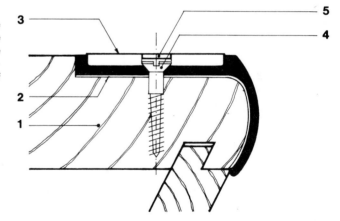

C Aluminium nosing to timber tread

The edge of the timber tread is rebated and shaped to fit the aluminium nosing section. A coat of adhesive is applied to the surface of the tread and the underside of the nosing and the nosing is then fixed with countersunk wood screws in counter-bored holes. Matching plugs are inserted to cover the heads of the screws.

1 Timber tread
2 Adhesive
3 Aluminium nosing with non-slip insert
4 Countersunk wood screw at 250 mm centres
5 Plug to match insert material in nosing

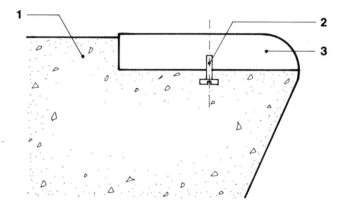

D Aluminium nosing to concrete tread

The concrete steps must be true and accurate. The top of the concrete and the underside of the nosing are coated with adhesive. The nosing is then positioned and fixed with counter-sunk wood screws into fixing plugs in the concrete. Matching plugs are inserted to cover the heads of the screws.

1 Concrete tread
2 Fixing plug
3 Adhesive
4 Aluminium nosing with non-slip insert
5 Countersunk wood screw at 250 mm centres
6 Plug to match insert material in nosing

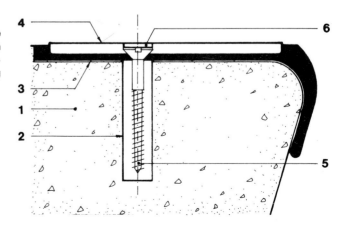

ROOFS : Concrete roof tile

A Ridge

A layer of untearable roofing felt is laid over the rafters and fixed with clout nails. Softwood battens are nailed to the rafters with round plain head nails. The roof tiles are laid on the battens and a dentil course is laid in the troughs of each tile on both sides of the ridge. The ridge tiles are bedded in continuous mortar bed and their butt joints are filled with mortar.

1 Roofing felt fixed with clout nails
2 Timber batten 38 mm x 19 mm fixed with round plain head nails 50 mm long
3 Concrete roof tile
4 Continuous edge mortar bed 1 : 3 cement : sand
5 Special tile slips
6 Concrete half round ridge tile

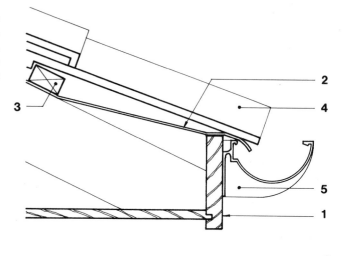

B Eaves

The fascia board is fixed to the end of the rafters and a layer of untearable roofing felt is nailed to the rafters and extends over the tilting fillet and well into the gutter. Softwood battens are nailed to the rafters with round plain head nails. The roof tiles are laid on the battens starting with the tile at the eaves that projects to overlap the gutter.

1 Timber fascia board
2 Roofing felt
3 Timber batten 38 mm x 19 mm
4 Concrete roof tile
5 Plastic gutter bracket

C Verge

A plain undercloak course is bedded on the outer leaf of the brick wall so as to project 38 mm to 50 mm over the face of the wall. It must not tilt inwards. The roof tiles are bedded on the undercloak. The bedding of a suitable colour is struck off and given a wood float finish.

1 Brick wall
2 Plain tile face down
3 Roofing felt
4 Timber batten 38 mm x 19 mm
5 Mortar bedding 1 : 3 cement : sand
6 Concrete verge tile 38 mm to 50 mm overhang

D Abutment

The roofing felt is laid and turned up against the outside wall. Softwood battens are nailed to the rafters with round wire nails. The roof tiles are laid and fitted closely against the wall. Lead cover flashing, stepped to suit the tile courses, is dressed down over the nearest roll of the adjacent tiles.

1 Brick wall
2 Roofing felt
3 Timber batten 38 mm x 19 mm
4 Concrete roof tile
5 Stepped lead cover flashing 19 kg per sq m
6 Damp-proof course

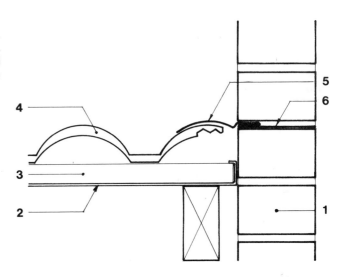

ROOFS : Chimney stack flashings

A Back gutter flashing

The back gutter or upper flashing of a chimney stack is made with a minimum gutter width of 150 mm. The flashing extends up under the roof slating or tiling for at least 200 mm and the top edge is folded back 25 mm to serve as a water check. The flashing is folded up the back of the stack for a height of not less than 100 mm. At each corner the flashing is returned 50 mm round the side faces of the stack and positioned to cover the gutter flashing upstand.

1 Tiles or slates
2 Zinc back gutter flashing
3 Zinc cover flashing

B Side flashing with single-lap tiling or sheet material

When the roof covering is single-lap tiling or sheet material, no soakers are used and the side flashing is extended at its lower edge to meet the roof covering and folded across for a distance of not less than 100 mm. The free edge is held with zinc clips 40 mm wide which are nailed to the roof battens at 300 mm centres.

1 Tiles or sheet roof covering
2 Zinc side flashing
3 Zinc clip

C Side flashing with plain tiles or slates

Soakers are cut and folded to extend at least 100 mm under the tiles or slates and 75 mm up the side of the stack. The soakers are fitted between the courses of tiles and are covered by the side flashing. The side flashing is cut with steps to fit the joints in the stack and with the lower edge stiffened by a 25 mm fold. The distance between the edge of the fold and the internal angle of a step is not less than 50 mm. The upper edges of the side flashing are turned into the joints of the stack, wedged and pointed.

1 Zinc soaker
2 Tiles or slates
3 Zinc side flashing

D Front apron flashing

The front apron or lower apron flashing of a chimney stack is made with its lower edge folded under for a distance of 12 mm to stiffen it. The apron extends down the roof slope from the chimney face for at least 125 mm. The apron is turned up against the stack for a height of not less than 75 mm. The apron is cut at each corner and returned round each side of the stack. A gusset is cut to fit the triangular gap in the apron, lapped 25 mm, and is soldered into position.

1 Zinc apron flashing
2 Zinc gusset
3 Solder

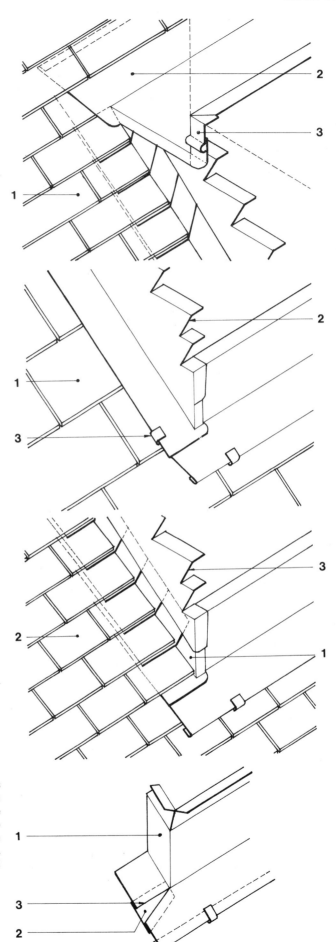

ROOFS : Lead sheet roofing

A The joint between lead sheets that runs with the fall of the roof is made with a wood-cored or a hollow roll. The wood roll is formed by dressing the edges of the lead sheet over a shaped wooden core. The underlap is nailed to the core with flat-headed cut copper nails at 150 mm centres. The overlap extends 35 mm onto the surface of the adjoining bay.

1 Timber decking
2 Felt underlay
3 Wood roll
4 Lead sheet
5 Flat-headed cut copper nail
6 Lead sheet

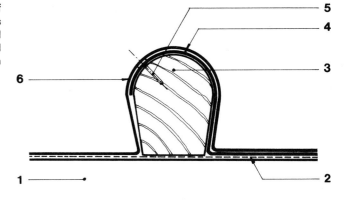

B The hollow roll is made by first forming a standing welt with the copper clips, then turning over the overlapping sheet and turning this welt into a roll. The clips are fixed at about 700 mm centres.

1 Timber decking
2 Felt underlay
3 Copper clip 50 mm wide
4 Brass countersunk screw
5 Lead sheet underlapping
6 Lead sheet overlapping

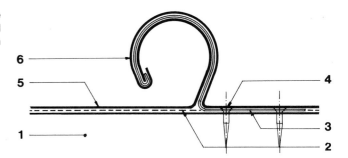

C For pitched roof coverings over 30 degrees slope, the wood roll is shaped to take copper clips fixed at about 600 mm centres to support the lead sheet. The underlapping and overlapping edges of the two sheets are welted together at the side of the roll with the clips incorporated within the welt.

1 Timber decking
2 Felt underlay
3 Lead sheet
4 Wood roll
5 Copper clip
6 Flat-headed cut copper nail
7 Lead sheet

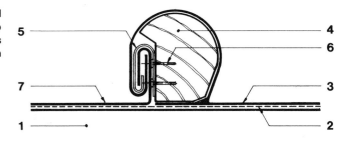

D The single welt may be used as an alternative to rolls for a joint that runs with the fall of the roof provided that the depth of flow of rainwater is not above about 6 mm. Copper clips 50 mm wide are screwed with two screws each to the decking at 600 mm centres. The edges of the adjoining lead sheets are folded at 90 degrees. A welt is formed including the clips and is lightly dressed down to roof level.

1 Timber decking
2 Felt underlay
3 Copper clip 50 mm wide
4 Brass countersunk screw
5 Lead sheet underlapping
6 Lead sheet overlapping

ROOFS : Lead drips and laps

A   Normal drip for roof slope up to 15 degrees

The joint across the fall of a flat roof or a low pitched roof up to
15 degrees is formed with a drip. The step is normally not less
than 50 mm deep. The lower sheet is turned up and over the
edge and is fixed with flat headed copper nails to the top edge of
the step which is rebated for a width of 25 mm to take the sheet.
The overlapping sheet is taken down the drip and across the
underlay for a width of 40 mm.

1 Decking
2 Felt underlay
3 Lead underlapping sheet
4 Copper nail
5 Lead overlapping sheet

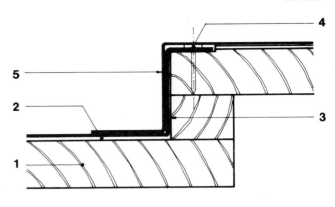

B   Minimum drip for roof slope up to 15 degrees

When the roof slope is sufficient and the flow of water is not
excessive, the step may be reduced to 40 mm deep provided
than an anti-capillary groove is formed in the upstand of the
step. Otherwise, the sheets are laid and fixed as in A above.

1 Decking
2 Felt underlay
3 Lead underlapping sheet
4 Copper nail
5 Lead overlapping sheet

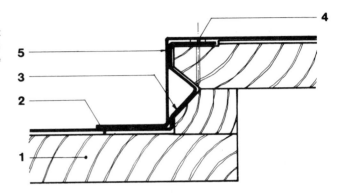

C   Splayed drip roof slope up to 15 degrees

An alternative form of drip across the fall of a flat or low pitched
roof up to 15 degrees is formed with a splayed step 75 mm
deep. The underlapping sheet is fixed as in A above. The overlapping sheet is taken down the face of the step for the full depth.

1 Decking
2 Felt underlay
3 Lead underlapping sheet
4 Copper nail
5 Lead overlapping sheet

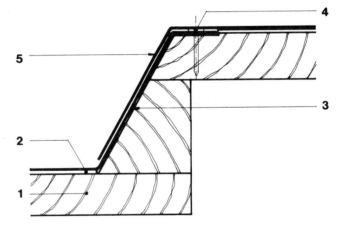

D   Lap for roof slope steeper than 15 degrees

For roof slopes greater than 15 degrees, the joint across the fall
of the roof is formed with a lap. The underlapping sheet is laid
on underlay and fixed with two rows of large headed copper
nails at 75 mm centres. Copper clips 50 mm wide are then
nailed to the decking to hold down the free edge of the overlapping sheet. The overlapping sheet is laid to give an overlap
equivalent to a vertical height of 75 mm.

1 Decking
2 Felt underlay
3 Lead underlapping sheet
4 Copper nail
5 Copper clip
6 Copper nail
7 Lead overlapping sheet

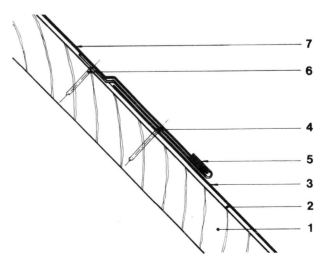

ROOFS : Traditional copper sheet roofing

A One of the two main systems of traditional copper roofing is the batten roll system named after the method used to join adjacent roofing sheets in the direction of the roof slope. It may be used on all pitches.

1 Decking
2 Brown inodorous roofing felt
3 Copper clip 38 mm wide at 450 mm centres maximum
4 Timber square roll 40 mm wide x 40 mm high
5 Copper roofing sheet
6 Copper roofing sheet
7 Copper capping strip

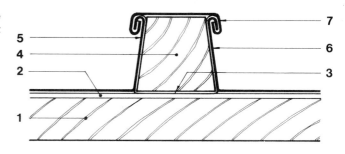

B Where a roof has a pitch of between 1 degree and 5 degrees, drips 65 mm deep and spaced not more than 3 m centres, depending on the thickness of the copper, must be used. Felt is fixed to the decking with copper nails. Copper clips 50 mm wide are nailed to the drip edge. The lower roofing sheet is turned up. The upper roofing sheet is positioned and the lower edge turned over to make the welt.

1 Decking
2 Drip edge
3 Brown inodorous roof felt
4 Copper clip
5 Copper nail
6 Copper roofing sheet
7 Copper roofing sheet

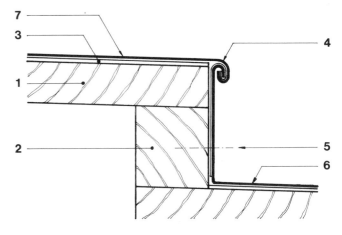

C Copper clips of the same thickness as the roofing sheet are fastened to the decking by two copper nails or two brass screws close to the turn-up. The clips are 38 mm wide spaced at not more than 460 mm centres. The roll is positioned over the clips and they are turned up on each side to retain the copper roof sheeting in position.

1 Deck
2 Roofing felt
3 Copper clip
4 Copper nails
5 Roll
6 Roofing sheet
7 Copper capping strip

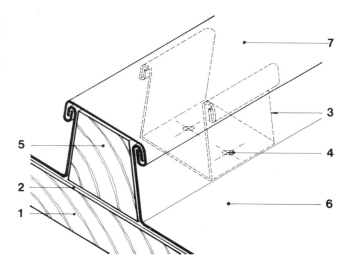

D The drawing shows the forming of the joint between the square roll and the longitudinal drip. A capping piece is fitted over the sloped off lower end of the roll and the roofing sheets are welted to it. The lower edge of the capping piece is turned over the drip.

1 Capping piece
2 Roofing sheet
3 Drip
4 Capping strip

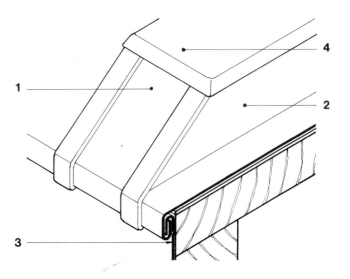

ROOFS : Traditional copper sheet roofing

A Ridge

The ridge of a traditional copper roof is formed with a wood roll cut to suit the slopes of the roof. Clips, 50 mm wide, are nailed with two copper nails or screwed with two brass screws and placed two per bay of the roofing sheet. They pass under the roll of the ridge and turn up each side. The roof sheets are turned up the sides of the roll and a capping strip is held by the two seams.

1 Decking
2 Roofing felt
3 Copper clip
4 Wood roll
5 Roofing sheet
6 Capping strip

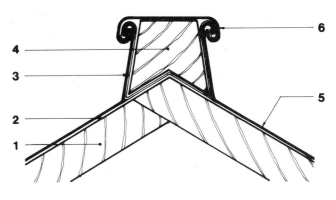

B Eaves

The eaves of a traditional copper roof is formed with a drip apron. A continuous fixing strip is nailed to the back of a wood roofing batten that is then securely screwed to the fascia board. The roof sheeting is laid with the lower edge projecting beyond the batten. A drip apron is then joined by continuous seams to the continuous fixing strip and the roofing sheet.

1 Fascia board
2 Batten
3 Copper nail
4 Copper continuous fixing strip
5 Copper drip apron
6 Roofing felt
7 Copper roofing sheet

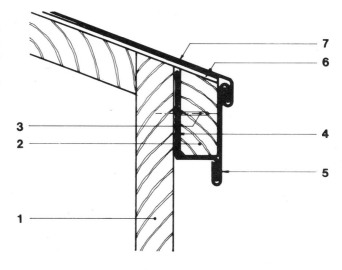

C Verge

The verge of a traditional copper roof is normally formed by covering the barge board with a copper drip apron. A continuous fixing strip is nailed to the barge board with copper nails. Clips for the verge seam are fixed at 300 mm centres. The drip apron is placed in position and seams are formed with the continuous fixing strip and with the roofing sheet.

1 Barge board
2 Continuous fixing strip
3 Copper nail
4 Drip apron
5 Roofing felt
6 Roofing sheet

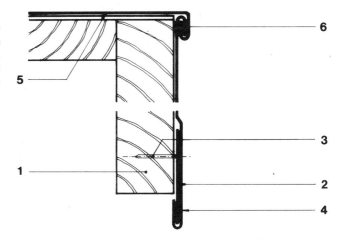

D Abutment

At the abutment of a traditional copper roof with the use of a standing seam the end of the seam is flattened to assist in folding the sheet to form the upstand. At a square abutment a timber angle fillet is firmly fixed to the decking.

1 Decking
2 Timber angle fillet
3 Roofing felt
4 Roofing sheet
5 Roofing sheet

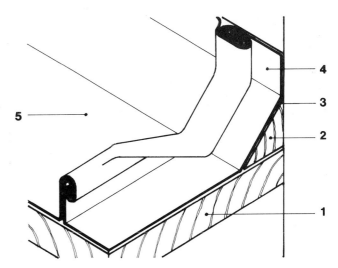

ROOFS : Traditional copper sheet roofing

A The second main system of traditional copper roofing is named the standing seam system after the method used to join adjacent copper sheets in the direction of the slope. Roofing felt is nailed with copper nails to the decking. Copper clips are fixed to the decking. The roofing sheets are turned up on both sides of the clips and a seam is formed at a height of not less than 25 mm. Standing seams may be used on roofs where the pitch is 6 degrees or greater.

1 Decking
2 Roofing felt
3 Copper clip
4 Copper nail
5 Roofing sheets

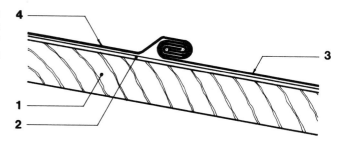

B The transverse joints used with standing seams are double lock welts for pitches from 6 degrees to 40 degrees and single lock welts for pitches above 40 degrees. The seams are formed by turning the ends of the sheets and incorporate clips as shown in the following drawing.

1 Decking
2 Roofing felt
3 Lower roofing sheet
4 Upper roofing sheet

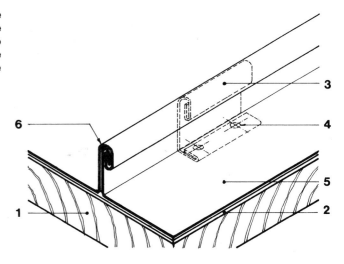

C The standing seams are held in position by copper clips of the same thickness as the roof sheeting that is used, fixed to the decking with two copper nails (or two brass screws) close to the turn-up. The clips should not be less than 38 mm wide spaced at a maximum of 380 mm centres along the length of the roof slope.

1 Decking
2 Roofing felt
3 Copper clip
4 Copper nails
5 Roofing sheet
6 Roofing sheet

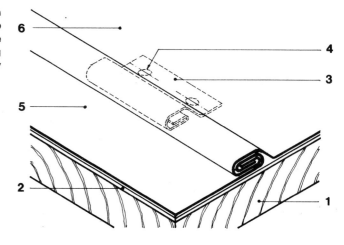

D The cross seams or welts, as they are also called, are held in position by copper clips that are nailed to the decking with two copper nails or two brass screws close to the turn-up. The clips are 50 mm wide and are spaced apart, one per roofing sheet bay for double lock welts and two per roofing sheet bay for single lock welts.

1 Decking
2 Roofing felt
3 Copper clip
4 Copper nail
5 Lower roofing sheet
6 Upper roofing sheet

ROOFS: Long strip copper roofing

A Timber roll joint

The normal joint on a copper roof that runs from ridge to eaves is a standing seam. However, on a long roof allowance has to be made for thermal movement and a timber roll joint is positioned about every twelve bays. Felt is nailed to the decking. Clips are placed under the roll and screwed to the decking. Roofing sheets are placed in position and the ends folded into the capping strip welt.

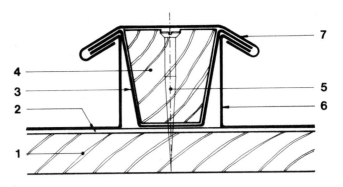

1 Decking
2 Brown inodorous roofing felt laid with butt joints
3 Copper clips 38 mm wide at about 450 mm centres
4 Square timber roll
5 Brass screw
6 Roofing panel of 0.6 mm thick hard temper copper strip
7 Copper capping strip

B Longitudinal drip

The length of long strip copper roofing sheet is limited to 8.5 m. For longer roof slopes a longitudinal horizontal joint is made in the form of a drip. The height of the drip must be not less than 65 mm. The felt is nailed with copper nails to the decking. The top end of the lower panels is turned up and folded into the lining plate welt. The lining plate is fixed with copper nails or brass screws. The upper layer of roofing felt covers the lining plate and the upper roofing panels are positioned so that the lower edges can be folded to form the welt and drop.

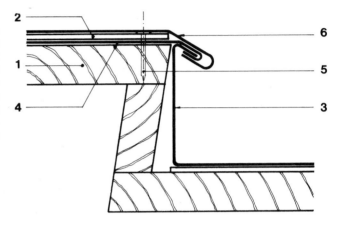

1 Decking
2 Brown inodorous roofing felt laid with butt joints
3 Copper roofing panel
4 Copper lining plate
5 Copper nails or brass screws
6 Copper roofing panel

C Verge

The joint at the verge is formed around a timber batten on the edge of the decking. The decking is covered with a felt underlay and roofing panel which is folded to form an upstand. A continuous copper lining plate is nailed to the top of the batten at 80 mm centres. A copper capping is then placed in position and welts formed with the roofing panel on the inside and the drop apron on the outside.

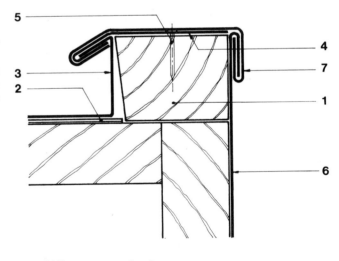

1 Timber batten
2 Felt underlay laid with butt joints
3 Copper roofing panel
4 Copper lining plate
5 Copper nail 25 mm long
6 Copper drop apron
7 Copper capping

D Eaves

The joint at the eaves is formed over a batten fixed to the top of the fascia board. A continuous copper fixing strip is nailed to the batten and welted to the drop apron. A continuous copper lining plate is fixed with two rows of copper nails, each row at 80 mm centres along the edge of the decking. The copper roofing panel is laid on felt underlay and a welt formed at the edge with the lining plate and the drop apron. The fold of the roofing panel projects an additional 10 mm to accommodate thermal movement along its length.

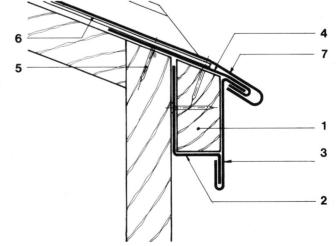

1 Timber batten
2 Continuous copper fixing strip
3 Copper drop apron
4 Copper lining plate
5 Copper nail
6 Felt underlay
7 Copper roofing panel

ROOFS : Traditional zinc sheet roofing

A One system of traditional zinc roofing named the cap roll system makes use of shaped wood rolls running with the fall of the roof to join the sides of the zinc sheets. The roof panels are pre-formed before being placed in position. Sides are turned up 35 mm to fit against the rolls leaving a gap of 5 mm at the angle to allow for thermal movement. The zinc roll capping is a standard pre-formed component.

1 Decking
2 Roofing felt
3 Zinc sheet fixing clip
4 Wood roll
5 Zinc roofing sheet panel
6 Zinc roofing sheet panel
7 Zinc roll capping

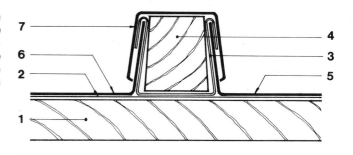

B The horizontal joint or cross welt between the roofing sheets is made with a single welt for roof slopes of 15 degrees or more, and with a drip at least 50 mm deep for roof slopes of less than 15 degrees. Zinc clips, two per bay, are fixed to the decking with galvanized clout nails. The lower end of a roof panel is pre-formed with a single welt 30 mm wide so as to engage with a similar welt 25 mm wide on top edge of the lower panel.

1 Decking
2 Roofing felt
3 Zinc sheet fixing clip
4 Galvanized clout nail
5 Upper roofing sheet
6 Lower roofing sheet

C The edges of the roofing panel and the wooden roll are held in position by zinc sheet fixing clips spaced along the rolls at not more than 1 m centres. The clips are nailed to the decking with two galvanized clout nails and turned over the turned-up edges of the roofing sheets.

D The joint between the roll and the horizontal drip is formed with a stop end that consists of a separate zinc sheet capping piece that is shaped to fit the capping and turned over at the lower end to fit the bead of the drip (or the welt where it is used).

1 Decking
2 Roofing felt
3 Roof sheet panel
4 Zinc sheet stop end capping

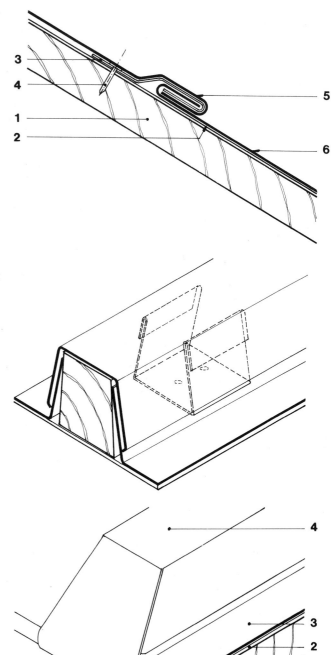

ROOFS : Zinc sheet roofing

A Ridge

The ridge of roll cap zinc roofing is formed with a wood roll 75 mm high and tapered slightly from 35 mm wide at the base to 30 mm wide at the top. The top edges of roofing panels are turned up the sides of the roll and a standard machine-formed zinc capping, as used for the roof rolls, is fixed in lengths not exceeding 1.1 m with holding-down clips.

1 Decking
2 Roofing felt
3 Zinc sheet fixing clip
4 Wood roll
5 Roofing sheet
6 Roofing sheet
7 Zinc capping

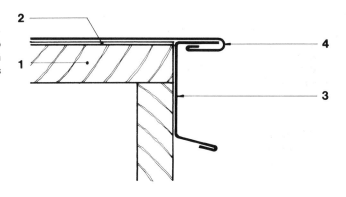

B Eaves

The eaves of roll cap zinc roofing is formed by means of a pre-formed apron that is folded outwards with a flange of 25 mm to engage with the welted ends of the roof panel. An apron deeper than 100 mm has the lower edge secured with clips spaced at about 450 mm centres.

1 Decking
2 Roofing felt
3 Zinc pre-formed apron
4 Zinc roof sheeting panel

C Verge

The verge of a roll cap zinc roofing may be formed in the same way as the eaves as in B above or alternatively with an apron and a wood roll and capping. The apron is secured by means of fixing clips.

1 Decking
2 Roofing felt
3 Zinc sheet fixing clip
4 Wood roll
5 Zinc sheet apron
6 Roof sheeting
7 Zinc capping

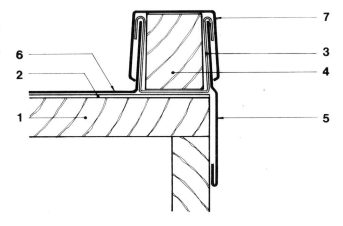

D Abutment

At an abutment with a wall the roof sheeting is turned up for a height of not less than 100 mm and the upstand covered by a preformed zinc apron flashing so as to give at least 50 mm cover. The top edge of the flashing is folded into a groove in the wall a minimum distance of 10 mm and wedged at 600 mm centres. The bottom edge is stiffened with a half round bead or a fold.

1 Decking
2 Roofing felt
3 Roof sheeting
4 Zinc apron flashing
5 Zinc wedge

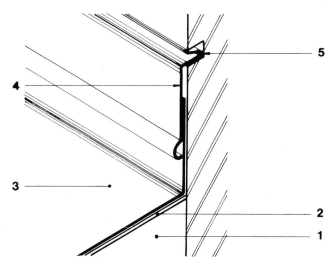

ROOFS : Zinc standing seam sheet roofing

A The joint between zinc roofing sheets that runs in the direction of the fall of the roof is made in the form of a standing seam. The adjacent panels are pre-formed with turned up edges, one of 40 mm and the other of 30 mm, a space of 5 mm being left between the bays to allow for thermal movement. Zinc sheet fixing clips are incorporated. The seam is then formed by folding twice to make a double welt standing about 25 mm above the roof surface.

1 Decking
2 Roofing felt
3 Zinc roofing clip
4 Zinc roofing panel
5 Zinc roofing panel

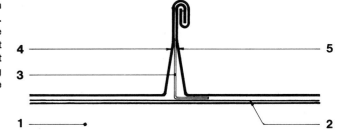

B The horizontal joint between zinc roofing sheets is made with a single cross welt for roof slopes of 40 to 90 degrees, a double cross welt for slopes of 20 to 40 degrees and a drip for slopes between 4 and 20 degrees. The welted edges are secured with two zinc clips per bay nailed to the decking with galvanized clout nails.

1 Decking
2 Zinc sheet fixing clip
3 Galvanized clout nail
4 Upper roofing panel
5 Lower roofing panel

C Zinc sheet fixing clips, 40 mm wide x 75 mm long are fixed along the line of the seam at 450 mm centres. For roof coverings with panels not exceeding 3 m long the fixing clips are nailed to the decking with galvanized clout nails. For longer lengths, a proportion of the clips are a sliding type which retains the sheets, but allows for thermal movement.

D At the intersection of a standing seam and a horizontal drip, the standing seam is folded over with the open face downward to enable the seam to be folded over the top edge of the drip.

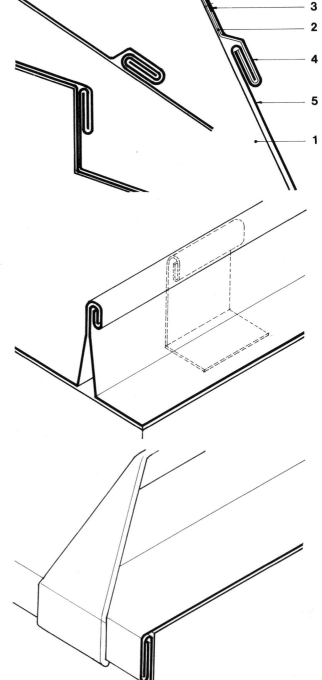

ROOFS : Flat aluminium sheet roofing

A Roofing that consists of interlocking profiled aluminium sheet may be fitted to different supporting structures with the appropriate screws. Timber decking is covered with an underlay of no 1 inodorous felt to BS747 type 4 'A' (ii) Brown suitable for use with aluminium. The first pre-formed sheet is then fixed with wood screws including a nylon washer. The second sheet is hinged at 90 degrees over the first and locked down into position.

1 Timber decking
2 Underlay of no 1 inodorous felt
3 Profiled aluminium interlocking sheet
4 Wood screw with nylon washer
5 Profiled aluminium interlocking sheet

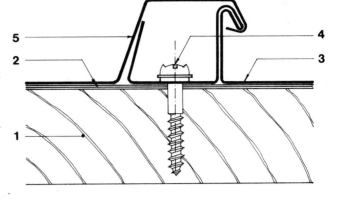

B When the sheet is used on steel purlins, self-adhesive tape is first applied to the bearing surfaces of the steelwork. The channel of the first sheet is screwed to the purlin with self-drilling self-tapping screws. The second sheet is hinged at 90 degrees over the first and locked down into position. The procendure is repeated for subsequent sheets.

1 Steel purlin
2 Self-adhesive tape
3 Profiled aluminium interlocking sheet
4 Self-drilling self-tapping screw
5 Profiled aluminium interlocking sheet

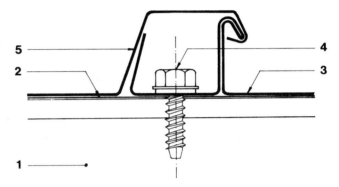

C When insulation is required over a boarded roof or over a concrete slab, wood battens are first fixed to the supporting structure and the insulation is placed between them. An underlay of no 1 inodorous felt is applied and the first profiled sheet is fixed to the battens with screws located in the channel of the sheet. The second sheet is then hinged at 90 degrees over the first and locked down into position.

1 Supporting structure (boarded roof or concrete slab)
2 Wood batten
3 Insulation
4 Underlay of no 1 inodorous felt
5 Profiled aluminium interlocking sheet
6 Screw
7 Profiled aluminium interlocking sheet

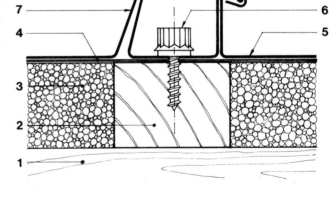

D When insulation is required over a steel supporting structure, wood battens are fixed to the steel purlins with self-tapping screws, the holes in the batten being counterbored to take the head of the screws. Insulation is placed between the battens. The aluminium profiled sheeting is then fixed as in C above.

1 Steel purlin
2 Wood batten
3 Self-tapping screw
4 Underlay of no 1 inodorous felt
5 Profiled aluminium interlocking sheet

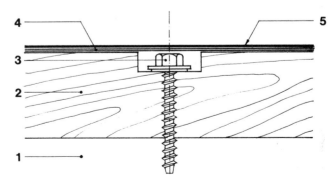

ROOFS: Parapet upstands

A At the junction of a roof with a parapet wall and when the roof covering is roofing felt, the layers of felt are taken up the wall for a height of at least 150 mm. The bend is supported by an angle fillet of cement mortar or wood. The upstand is covered with a metal apron flashing to give a cover of at least 75 mm.

1 Brick wall
2 Roof structure
3 Cement mortar angle fillet
4 Bitumen compound
5 Bituminous roofing felt
6 Zinc apron flashing
7 Damp-proof course

B At the junction of a roof with a parapet wall and when the roof covering is lead sheet, the sheet is turned up the face of the wall not less than 150 mm. The top of the upstand is covered with a lead apron flashing to give a cover of not less than 75 mm and the top edge is turned into a brick joint or groove 25 mm deep. Lead wedges are inserted at 600 mm intervals. The flashing should be in lengths not exceeding 7 m with laps not less than 100 mm.

1 Brick wall
2 Roof structure
3 Felt underlay
4 Lead sheet
5 Lead apron flashing
6 Lead wedge

C At the junction of a roof with a parapet wall and when the roof covering is copper sheet, the roofing sheet is turned up against the wall for a minimum height of 150 mm and held in position with upstand clips at 450 mm centres fixed to the wall with two brass screws per clip. A copper cover flashing not longer than 1800 mm and 150 mm deep is welted to the roofing sheet and the top of the clips. The upper edge of the cover flashing is folded at least 25 mm into a mortar joint and wedged with copper wedges.

1 Roof deck
2 Copper clip 38 mm wide on 460 mm centres
3 Brass round head wood screw
4 Copper roofing sheet
5 Copper cover flashing
6 Copper wedge

D At the junction of a roof with a parapet wall and when the roof covering is copper sheet, another form of flashing is by means of a hanging flashing. The roofing sheet is turned up against the wall for a height of 150 mm and is held in position by copper clips, each fixed with two brass screws to the wall. The clips are turned down over the top of the sheet and welted to the hanging flashing. The lower end of the flashing is folded to give increased stiffness and the upper end is turned into a mortar joint 25 mm deep and wedged with copper wedges.

1 Roof deck
2 Copper clip 38 mm wide on 460 mm centres
3 Brass round head wood screw
4 Copper roofing sheet
5 Copper hanging flashing
6 Copper wedge

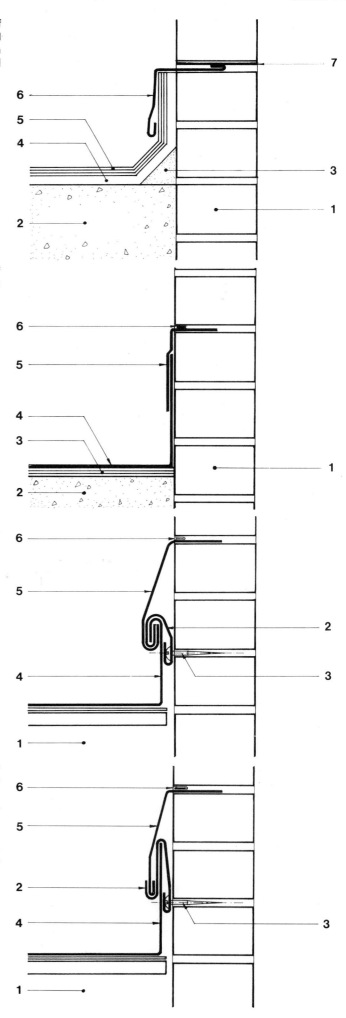

ROOFS: Asphalt parapet upstands

A The junction of mastic asphalt roofing laid on a structural concrete slab parapet wall is characterized by the asphalt upstand which is bonded firmly to the brickwork, requires solid support from below, and a full angle fillet between the horizontal and vertical asphalt. The top of the apron requires protection to ensure that no water gets between the asphalt and brickwork.

1 Structural concrete slab
2 Screed
3 Vapour barrier bedded in hot bitumen
4 Sand:cement rigid infill
5 Pre-felted expanded polystyrene board bedded in hot bitumen
6 Fibre insulating board bedded in hot bitumen
7 Sheathing felt underlay
8 Two coats of mastic asphalt
9 Solar reflective treatment to surface
10 Metal apron flashing
11 Damp-proof course

B The junction of mastic asphalt roofing laid on a structural timber roof deck with a brick parapet wall is characterized by an asphalt upstand that is kept clear of the brickwork, is fully supported by the decking and its timber edge fillet, and has a full angle fillet between the horizontal and sloping asphalt. The top of the apron is protected by interlocking metal flashings that allow for movement of the timber roof structure. A reflective treatment should be applied to the asphalt surface.

1 Plasterboard ceiling
2 Insulation
3 Timber joist
4 Timber decking
5 Timber fillet nailed to boarding along the edge
6 Sheathing felt underlay
7 Two coats of mastic asphalt
8 Metal cover flashing
9 Metal apron flashing
10 Damp-proof course

C The junction of mastic asphalt roofing with a brick parapet wall on a balcony is formed with an integral asphalt angle fillet and upstand skirting. A layer of sheathing felt is placed over the insulation board which is laid on a vapour barrier over the structural concrete slab. The mastic asphalt is laid in two coats comprising a base coat, 10 mm thick, and a hardened top coat 15 mm thick, laid breaking joint. The upstand and fillet are formed in two coats, the upstand being 13 mm thick. Protection of the roof from solar radiation must be considered.

1 Structural concrete slab
2 Bitumen felt vapour barrier
3 Cork board insulation
4 Sheathing felt underlay
5 Roofing grade asphalt 25 mm thick in two layers
6 Sand and cement pointing

D The junction of mastic asphalt roofing with a brick parapet wall of a car park is formed with an integral asphalt and upstand skirting. A layer of sheathing felt is placed over the concrete slab to provide a separating membrane. The asphalt is laid in three coats: a base coat 10 mm thick, a second coat 10 mm thick breaking joint and a top finishing coat grade 30 mm thick. The skirting is formed of two coats 13 mm thick laid upon cleaned brickwork with joints raked out.

1 Structural concrete slab
2 Sheathing felt underlay
3 Roofing grade asphalt 20 mm thick in two layers
4 Roofing grade finishing coat 30 mm thick
5 Sand and cement pointing

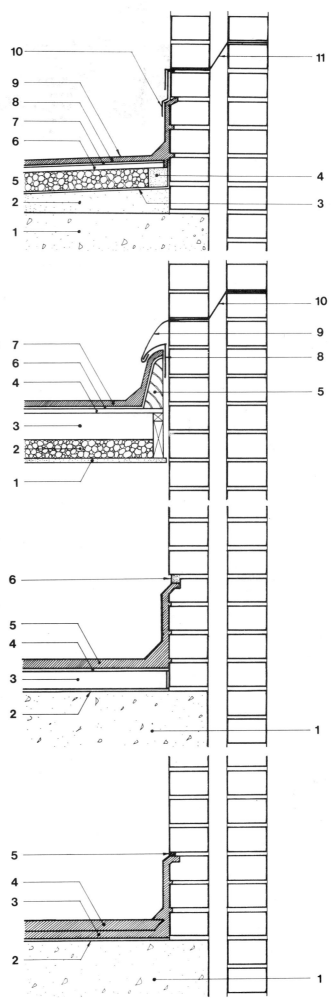

ROOFS: Flat paved concrete slab

A Paved roof
The concrete roof slab is swept clean and covered with a felt underlay laid loose and two coats of roof asphalt. Insulation slabs are then laid loose with tight butt joints and with all joints staggered. Paving slabs of hydraulically pressed precast concrete are laid dry with butt joints on inorganic felt levelling pads placed at the corners of each slab.

1 Concrete roof slab
2 Two-coat roof asphalt on felt underlay
3 Foam polystyrene insulation slab 50 mm thick
4 Inorganic felt levelling pad 100 mm x 100 mm
5 Precast concrete slab 50 mm thick laid dry

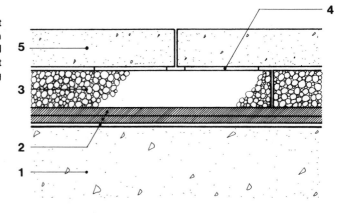

B Paved roof with upstand
The concrete roof slab is covered with a felt underlay laid loose and two coats of asphalt that are taken up the abutment for a minimum height of 150 mm, tucked into a groove 25 mm x 25 mm and pointed with mortar. The insulation layer is laid dry with joints closely butted and staggered. The paving slabs are laid on small felt levelling pads and stopped short of the wall a distance of 100 mm, the space being filled with gravel to allow for movement of the paving slabs.

1 Concrete roof slab
2 Two-coat roof asphalt on felt underlay
3 Foam polystyrene insulation slab 50 mm thick
4 Inorganic felt levelling pad 100 mm x 100 mm
5 Precast concrete paving slab 50 mm thick laid dry
6 Gravel 100 mm wide

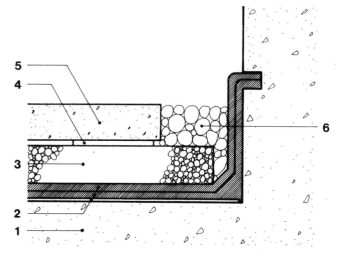

C Verge
The concrete roof slab is covered with a felt underlay laid loose and a two-coat layer of asphalt that is taken up the slope of the verge upstand and tucked into a groove 25 mm x 25 mm. The insulation slab is laid dry with joints closely butted and staggered. The precast concrete paving slabs are laid only on felt levelling pads and stop short of the verge to leave a channel that is filled with gravel.

1 Concrete roof slab and upstand
2 Two-coat roof asphalt on felt underlay
3 Foam polystyrene insulation slab 50 mm thick
4 Inorganic felt levelling pad 100 mm x 100 mm
5 Precast concrete paving slab 50 mm thick laid dry
6 Gravel strip: minimum gravel size 15 mm

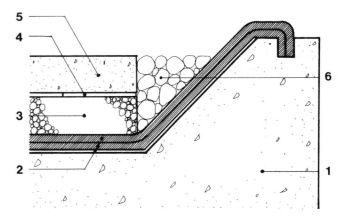

D Rainwater outlet
The concrete roof is laid flat and outlets for rain water are provided at about 6 m centres. A collar is fitted into the top of the rainwater pipe and the asphalt is finished around the outlet. Water is able to seep through the joints of the paving slabs and the insulation to the waterproof membrane. The insulation and paving slabs are laid over the top of the rainwater outlet.

1 Concrete roof slab
2 Internal rainwater pipe
3 Metal collar
4 Two-coat roof asphalt on felt underlay
5 Foam polystyrene insulation slab 50 mm thick
6 Inorganic felt levelling pad 100 mm x 100 mm
7 Precast concrete paving slab 50 mm thick laid dry

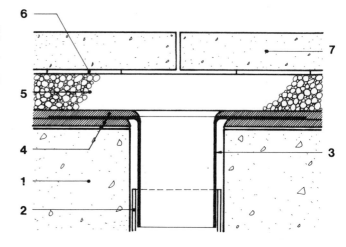

ROOFS: Flat roof with gravel layer

A Gravel layer roof

The concrete roof slab is swept clean and covered with a two-layer waterproof membrane. Insulation slabs of foam polystyrene are laid loose with tight butt joints and with all joints staggered. The slabs are covered with gravel having a minimum gravel size of 15 mm in a layer not less than 50 mm thick. The gravel is laid loose, and to an even thickness over the roof area.

1 Concrete roof slab
2 Two-layer bitumen-polymer waterproof membrane
3 Foam polystyrene insulation slab 50 mm thick
4 Gravel layer minimum 50 mm thick: minimum gravel size 15 mm

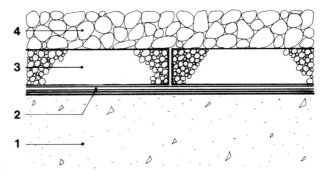

B Abutment

At an abutment the waterproof membrane is taken up the wall for a minimum height of 150 mm and tucked into a chase 25 mm x 25 mm formed along the wall that is then pointed with mortar. The polystyrene slabs are laid with joints closely butted and staggered. Gravel is laid loosely in a layer of even thickness not less than 50 mm thick so as to completely cover the insulation right up to the wall.

1 Concrete roof slab
2 Two-layer bitumen-polymer waterproof membrane
3 Foam polystyrene insulation slab 50 mm thick
4 Gravel layer minimum 50 mm thick: minimum gravel size 15 mm

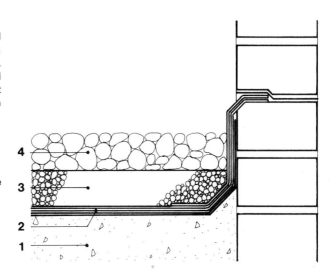

C Verge

The concrete roof slab is covered with a two-layer waterproof membrane that is taken up the slope of the verge upstand and over the top to form a welted apron that is nailed to a continuous nailing strip. The insulation layer is laid dry with joints closely butted and staggered. Gravel with a minimum size of 15 mm is then laid loosely in a layer not less than 50 mm thick to an even thickness over the whole of the roof area and around the edges of the slabs at the verge upstand.

1 Concrete roof slab
2 Two-layer bitumen-polymer waterproof membrane
3 Foam polystyrene insulation slab 50 mm thick
4 Gravel layer minimum 50 mm thick: minimum gravel size 15 mm

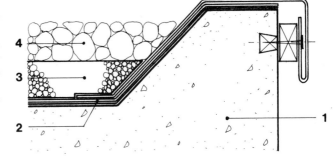

D Rainwater outlet

Rainwater pipes are placed internally at about 6 m centres. A collar fits into the top of the pipe and the roofing membrane is turned down over the rim of the collar. A gravel guard is fitted into the top of the collar. The insulation slab is cut to fit round the guard.

1 Concrete roof slab
2 Internal rainwater pipe
3 Metal collar
4 Two-layer bitumen-polymer waterproof membrane
5 Gravel guard
6 Foam polystyrene insulation slab 50 mm thick
7 Gravel layer minimum 50 mm thick: minimum gravel size 15 mm

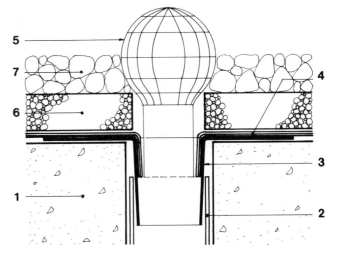

A Ridge

The joint at the ridge between the two roof slopes covered with protected steel corrugated sheeting is made with a cover flashing with a lap of 200 mm on both sides that is fixed together with the top edge of each sheeting to the timber purlin with steel roofing drive screws. For roofs of 15 degree pitch and over, the end lap of the roofing sheet is 150 mm minimum. The gap between the trough of a corrugation and the flashing is filled with a foamed polyurethane closer piece.

1 Timber purlin
2 Protected steel corrugated roof sheeting
3 Foamed polyurethane closer piece
4 Ridge flashing
5 Steel roofing drive screw 6 mm diameter

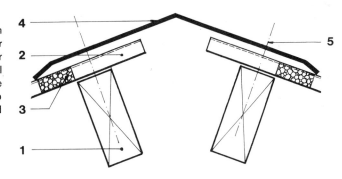

B Eaves

The joint at the eaves between the roof sheeting and the vertical cladding is made with an eaves flashing that is positioned over the cladding for a height of 125 mm and under the roof sheeting for a length of 225 mm. It is fastened, together with the sheeting, to the timber purlin by means of steel roofing drive screws 6 mm diameter. A closer piece is fitted in the corrugation between the flashing and the roof sheeting.

1 Timber purlin
2 Vertical cladding
3 Eaves flashing
4 Foamed polyurethane closer piece
5 Protected steel corrugated roof sheeting
6 Steel roofing drive screw 6 mm diameter

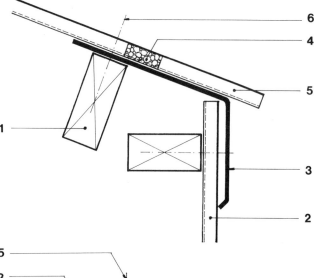

C Verge

The joint at the verge between the roof sheeting and the vertical cladding is made with a corner flashing that covers the ends of both sheets and has a lap vertically and horizontally of 125 mm. The flashing is fastened, together with the sheeting, to the timber purlin by means of drive screws through the crown of the corrugations.

1 Timber purlin
2 Vertical cladding
3 Protected steel corrugated roof sheeting
4 Corner flashing
5 Steel roofing drive screw 6 mm diameter

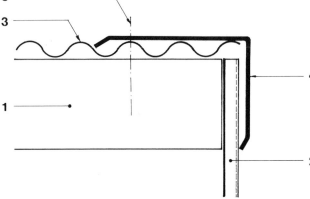

D Abutment

The joint between the roof sheeting and the vertical cladding at an abutment is made with an apron flashing that extends behind the cladding vertically for a height of 220 mm and down over the roof slope for a length of 225 mm. The apron flashing is fastened, together with the sheeting, to the timber purlin by means of drive screws through the crown of the corrugations.

1 Timber purlin
2 Protected steel corrugated roof sheeting
3 Apron flashing
4 Vertical cladding
5 Steel roofing drive screw

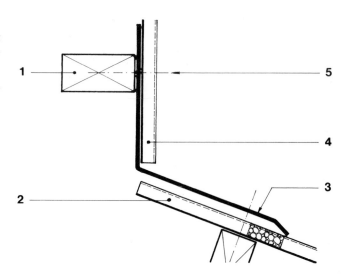

ROOFS : Asbestos corrugated roofing sheet

A Ridge

When a sloping roof is covered with asbestos corrugated roofing sheet the ridge is constructed of two asbestos ridge pieces that are formed to fit over the corrugations of the roofing sheet and to make a curved lap joint along the ridge. The ridge pieces are adjustable for position and are fastened with hook bolts to the roof purlins.

1 Steel purlin
2 Asbestos lining sheet
3 Insulation
4 Roofing sheet
5 Asbestos close fitting ridge piece
6 Galvanized steel hook bolt

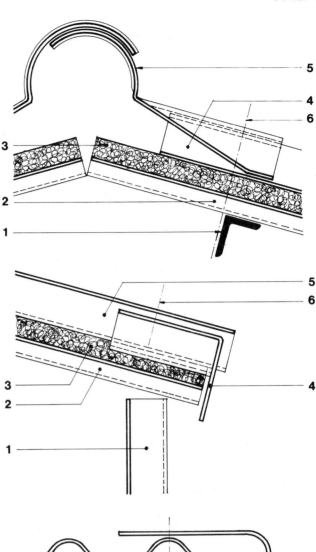

B Eaves

The joint at the eaves between the wall cladding sheet and the roofing sheet is made by means of a special asbestos eaves closer piece formed with corrugations along one side to match the roofing sheet and a flange along the other side to serve as a flashing. The eaves closer piece is fastened to the roofing sheet with roofing bolts positioned at the ridge of the corrugations.

1 Asbestos wall cladding sheet
2 Asbestos lining sheet
3 Insulation
4 Asbestos eaves closer piece
5 Asbestos roofing sheet
6 Galvanized steel roofing bolt

C Verge

The joint at the verge between the wall cladding sheet and the roofing sheet is made by means of a specially formed asbestos barge board which is fastened to the roofing sheet with roofing bolts and to the end wall purlin with hook bolts.

1 Asbestos wall cladding sheet
2 Steel purlin
3 Asbestos lining sheet
4 Insulation
5 Asbestos roofing sheet
6 Asbestos barge board
7 Galvanized hook bolt

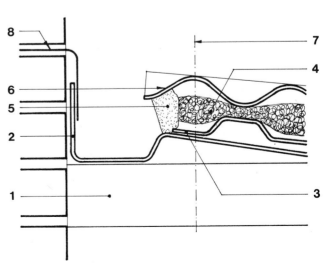

D Abutment

The joint at the abutment of roofing sheets and a gable wall is made with an asbestos secret gutter that is formed with an upstand along one side and a sloped ridge along the other side. The edge of the roofing sheet is bedded on a mortar bed laid on wire mesh. The upstand of the gutter is positioned against the inner face of the wall and a metal flashing makes a lap joint. The gutter is fastened to the roof purlins by hook bolts which also fix the roofing sheet.

1 Steel purlin
2 Asbestos secret gutter
3 Asbestos lining sheet
4 Insulation
5 Mortar bed on wire mesh
6 Asbestos roofing sheet
7 Galvanized hook bolt
8 Metal flashing

ROOFS : Wood wool slabs

A The fixing of wood wool slabs to timber joists may be made by means of a thick plate washer and a galvanized nail that has a round shank and a large diameter head. Two washers are required across the width of a slab and the nails must be not less than 100 mm long.

1 Timber roof joist
2 Wood wool slab 50 mm thick
3 Washer 1.6 mm thick plate 76 mm square
4 Galvanized steel nail 3 mm diameter 100 mm long

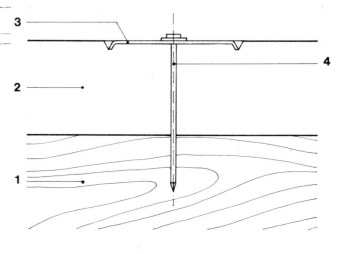

B An alternative method of fixing a wood wool slab suitable for use with fully interlocking edge channel reinforcement is by means of galvanized nails driven through both flanges of one channel. Five nails are used across the width of slab. When the channels do not interlock, each channel is nailed separately.

1 Timber roof joist
2 Wood wool slab 50 mm thick with fully interlocking reinforcing channels
3 As 2
4 Galvanized steel nail 3 mm diameter 100 mm long

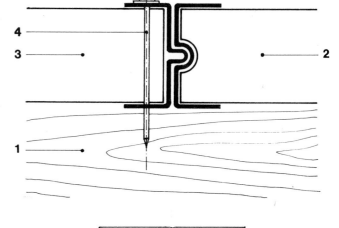

C The fixing of wood wool slabs to a steel supporting structure of channel beams or angle purlins may be made by means of a specially shaped clip with a long and short leg. The long leg is bent round the flange of the steelwork and the short leg has a split end that is bent in opposite directions over the top edges of adjacent slabs so as to lie on the surface.

1 Rolled steel joist
2 Galvanized steel clip 1.6 mm thick, 40 mm wide
3 Wood wool slab 50 mm thick
4 Wood wool slab 50 mm thick

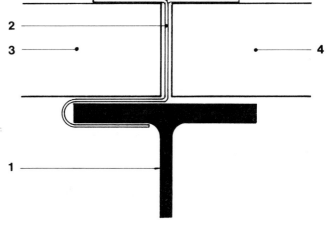

D An alternative method of fixing wood wool slabs to a steel supporting structure is by means of short lengths of bar welded to the structural member. The bars that also serve to locate the slabs are bent over the top edge of the slab and covered by the screed.

1 Rolled steel joist
2 Galvanized steel bars 6 mm diameter, 100 mm long
3 Wood wool slab 50 mm thick
4 Wood wool slab 50 mm thick

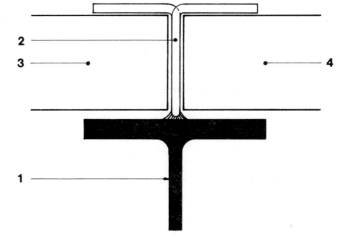

A　A standard and traditional method of fixing cladding sheets to steel purlins is by means of a steel hook bolt. A more recent design makes provision for a plastic covered square steel nut that is screwed to the threaded top of the hook bolt. A plastic covered cap completes the assembly.

　1　Steel angle purlin
　2　Metal cladding sheet
　3　Hook bolt
　4　Coloured plastic covered square steel nut
　5　Coloured plastic covered cap

B　An alternative method of fixing metal cladding sheets to steel purlins is to use a roofing bolt and a U-clip. The clip is held in position by a washer and nut on the lower end of the roofing bolt. The head of the roofing bolt is fitted with a plastic washer and a plastic cover.

　1　Steel angle purlin
　2　Metal cladding sheet
　3　Steel roofing bolt
　4　Galvanized steel U-clip
　5　Round steel washer
　6　Square nut
　7　Coloured plastic washer
　8　Coloured plastic cover

C　The fixing of metal cladding sheets to pre-stressed concrete rails or purlins shown is by means of a purpose-made hook bolt that is fitted through a pre-drilled hole in the sheet and held up against the flange of the rail (or purlin) by a square plastic coated nut. A plastic coated cap is fitted last to completely protect the bolt end from corrosion or unsightly rust marks.

　1　Pre-stressed concrete purlin flange
　2　Metal cladding sheet
　3　Steel purpose-made hook bolt
　4　Plastic coated square nut
　5　Plastic coated cap

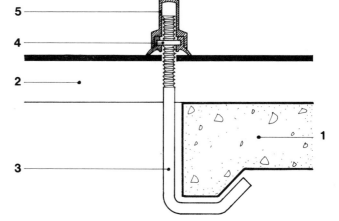

D　An alternative method of fixing cladding sheets to concrete purlins is to use an Oakley clip that is either tapped or has a clearance hole. The roofing bolt is passed through a pre-drilled hole in the cladding sheet and screwed until the clip is fastened firmly against the flange of the purlin. The bolt head is then covered with a plastic cover.

　1　Pre-stressed concrete purlin (or rail) flange
　2　Metal cladding sheet
　3　Coloured plastic washer
　4　Steel mushroom head roofing bolt
　5　Steel Oakley clip
　6　Coloured plastic bolt head cover

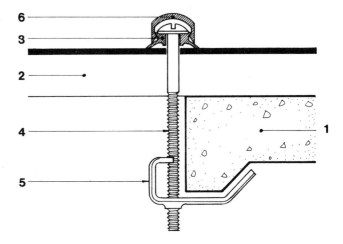

A Fixing of the asbestos cement cladding sheet to the timber purlin is by means of a steel wood screw with a coloured plastic head and plastic ring washer. A special socket to fit over the plastic head can be used with a carpenter's brace or similar hand tool or with an electric power drill having a controlled low speed drive.

1 Timber support purlin
2 Asbestos cement sheet
3 Plastic ring washer
4 Bright zinc plated and passivated steel wood screw with coloured plastic head.

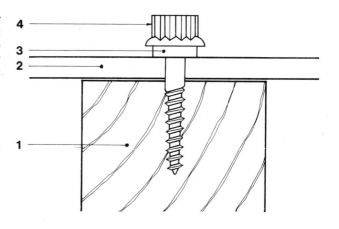

B Fixing of metal cladding sheet that is thin or of relatively low strength to a timber purlin or beam is also by means of a steel wood screw, but with a special large diameter washer designed to spread the load. The wood screw shown has a coloured plastic cap and large diameter plastic washer head.

1 Timber support purlin
2 Steel or aluminium cladding sheet
3 Large diameter plastic ring washer
4 Bright zinc plated and passivated steel wood screw with bi-hexagon coloured plastic head and plastic washer head

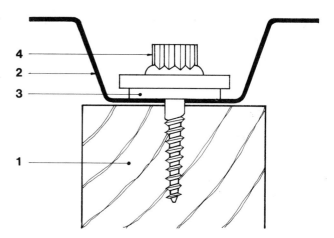

C Another method of fixing cladding sheets directly to timber purlins or beams is by means of a square twisted shank flat head nail. The nail shown is driven home with a hammer and is used together with a special washer and a cover that clips over the head of the nail.

1 Timber support purlin
2 Aluminium or steel cladding sheet
3 Square twisted shank flat head nail
4 Coloured plastic washer with integral skirt
5 Coloured plastic cover

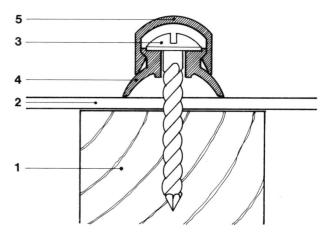

D An alternative method of fixing cladding sheets to timber purlins is to use an annular nail. The nail is driven home with a hammer and used in conjunction with a round flat plastic washer.

1 Timber support purlin
2 Aluminium or steel cladding sheet
3 Round flat plastic washer
4 Steel annular nail

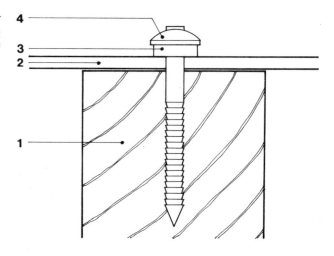

ROOFS : Cladding sheets

A The aluminium, steel, or plastic sheet is secured to the purlins or the framework made of steel or other metal by means of cadmium plated and passivated hardened steel self-tapping screws that are fitted with plastic ring washers and coloured plastic heads. The sheet and purlin is pre-drilled with a hole slightly smaller than the diameter of the screw. The screws are used either in the ridge of the corrugation as shown or in the valley.

1 Steel purlin
2 Hole pre-drilled
3 Cladding sheet of steel, aluminium or plastic
4 Self-tapping steel screw with plastic ring washer and plastic head

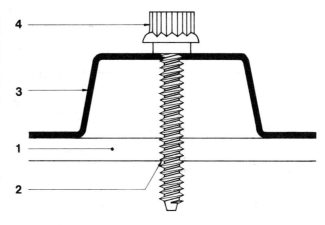

B When the cladding sheets are thin or weak and high wind pressures are likely, the load at the fixing position can be spread over the sheet by means of a large diameter washer. The washer is made of steel encased in plastic and the underside is slightly dished to provide a good water seal on flat surfaces.

1 Steel purlin
2 Hole pre-drilled
3 Cladding sheet of aluminium, steel or plastic
4 Steel washer encased in plastic
5 Self-tapping steel screw with plastic head

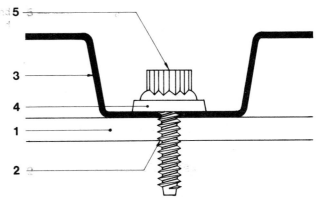

C The cladding sheets are secured to one another at a seam or overlap by means of a self-tapping screw and a plastic ring washer. The sheets are pre-drilled with a 3 mm diameter hole for a 4.9 mm diameter screw. The normal length of screw is 19 mm. The whole of the work is carried out from the outside of the roof.

1 Aluminium, steel or plastic corrugated sheet
2 Second corrugated sheet
3 Plastic ring washer
4 Self-tapping steel screw with plastic head

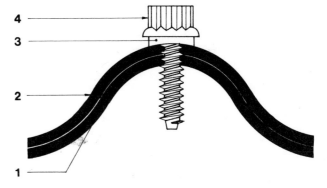

D An alternative method of fixing cladding sheets where they overlap is by means of nut and bolt. The bolt shown is used with a plastic ring washer and a square nut.

1 Aluminium, steel or plastic troughed sheet
2 Second troughed sheet
3 Plastic ring washer standard diameter
4 Bright zinc plated and passivated carbon steel bolt (or aluminium bolt) with bi-hexagon coloured plastic head
5 Square (or hexagon) nut

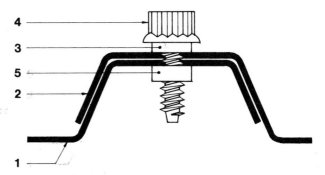

ROOFS : Roofing felt and asphalt eaves

A The edge of a flat concrete roof covered with 3 layer bituminous felt may be protected and finished with an extruded aluminium alloy section roof edge trim. After the first layer of felt has been laid, the edge trim is fixed with galvanized or cadmium plated countersunk screws or aluminium screws at least 25 mm long at 300 mm centres. A gap of 3 mm is left between adjacent 3 m lengths of section and an internal jointing sleeve is inserted and locked on one side only to permit movement.

1 Concrete curb
2 First layer of roofing felt
3 Roof edge trim of extruded aluminium alloy section
4 Countersunk screw galvanized, cadmium plated or aluminium
5 Internal jointing sleeve
6 Second layer of roofing felt
7 Third layer of roofing felt

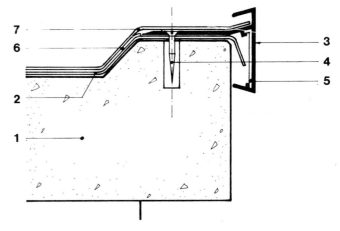

B The edge of a flat roof covered with asphalt may be finished with a roof edge trim designed to take asphalt. Sheathing felt is first laid on the roof structure. The lower surfaces of the roof edge trim are coated with bituminous primer and the edge trim is fixed to the concrete curb. The two layers of asphalt are then laid so as to fill both channels of the edge trim.

1 Concrete curb
2 Sheathing felt underlay
3 Roof edge trim of extruded aluminium alloy section
4 Countersunk screw galvanized, cadmium plated or aluminium
5 First layer of asphalt
6 Second layer of asphalt

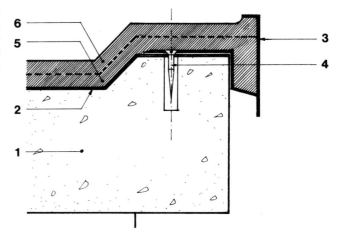

C An alternative method to form the eaves of a flat concrete roof covered with roofing felt is by means of a mineral surfaced felt flashing. The concrete slab is covered with bituminous roofing felt laid in hot bitumen. The felt flashing is then nailed to the plug in the edge of the slab and turned up and over the top edge of the slab. A second layer is applied followed by a third layer. The flat roof is covered with stone chippings to reflect solar heat.

1 Concrete slab
2 Bituminous roofing felt laid in hot bitumen : first layer
3 Mineral surfaced felt flashing
4 Clout nail
5 Bituminous roofing felt : second layer
6 Bituminous roofing felt : third layer
7 Stone chippings laid in bituminous adhesive

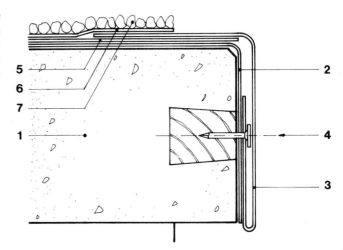

D When the flat roof consists of trough section aluminium or steel roof decking, an aluminium angle is rivetted to the edge of the decking to form a soffit and an eaves closer. Insulation is bonded to the decking with hot bitumen and a first layer of bituminous roofing felt laid in hot bitumen. The felt flashing is then nailed to the eaves and turned up and over the top edge of the roof decking. A second layer of felt is applied to the roof followed by a third layer, both layers being laid in hot bitumen.

1 Trough section aluminium or steel roof decking
2 Aluminium angle section
3 Pop rivet
4 Fibre board insulation
5 Bituminous roofing felt : first layer
6 Mineral surfaced felt flashing
7 Bituminous roofing felt : second layer
8 Bituminous roofing felt : third layer

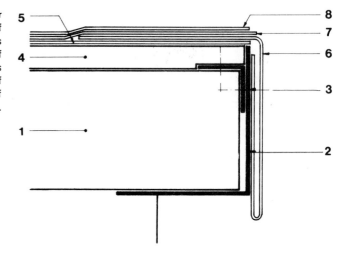

ROOFS: Roof patent glazing

A Abutment

When patent glazing bars are used to form roof glazing the bars are supported at their top end on a wall plate. The lower flanges of the glazing bar are slotted into a special fixing plate that is screwed to the wall plate. The glass is held in position by the extruded aluminium capping. The top end of the bar and glass is covered with a lead flashing.

1 Timber wall plate
2 Aluminium fixing plate
3 Round head wood screw 38 mm long
4 Extruded aluminium alloy glazing bar at 622 mm centres
5 Glass 6 mm thick
6 Sheet lead flashing

B Eaves

The joint between the glazing bar and the wall plate at the eaves is formed by means of a special fixing plate. The plate is slid on to the lower flanges of the glazing bar and is screwed through the weather strip to the wall plate. The glass is supported at the lower end by an aluminium glass stop which is bolted to the end of the glazing bar.

1 Timber wall plate at eaves
2 Aluminium weather strip
3 Aluminium fixing plate
4 Round head wood screw 38 mm long
5 Extruded aluminium alloy glazing bar
6 Aluminium glass stop
7 Fixing bolt
8 Glass 6 mm thick

C Verge

The glazing bar at the end of a run of bars has a special end capping formed of an extruded aluminium section which is screwed to the top flange of the glazing bar with stainless steel pan head self-tapping screws. The centre-line of the end bar is positioned 18 mm from the face of the end wall and the gap is covered with a lead flashing.

1 Extruded aluminium alloy glazing bar
2 Greased asbestos cord
3 Glass 6 mm thick
4 Extruded aluminium end capping
5 Stainless steel pan head self-tapping screw
6 Sheet lead flashing

D Glazing

The glazing bars are spaced apart at 622 mm centres for glass 610 mm wide. The fixing plates at top and bottom are adjustable and are accurately set out to ensure that the bars are parallel. The glass is bedded on greased asbestos cord fitted into a groove in the glazing bar, and is held down by an extruded aluminium capping that is screwed to the top flange of the bar by stainless steel pan head self-tapping screws. The minimum recommended pitch for the glazing bars is 15 degrees to the horizontal.

1 Aluminium fixing plate
2 Extruded aluminium alloy glazing bar
3 Greased asbestos cord
4 Glass 6 mm thick
5 Extruded aluminium capping
6 Stainless steel pan head self-tapping screw 13 mm

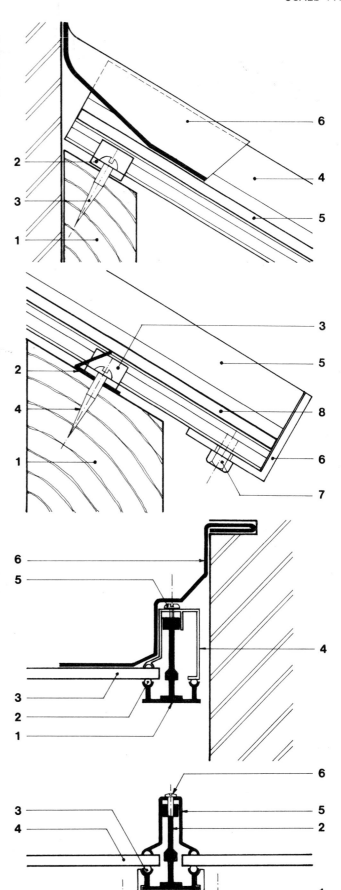

ROOFS : Glass channel units

A Abutment

The aluminium channel section is carried on a timber wall plate and screwed to the wall. A pitch polymer strip on the lower flange of the section supports the glass channel unit. An expanded polystyrene filler is inserted to form a backing for the aluminium clip with its neoprene wedging strip. An aluminium flashing is fixed to the wall and over the section, the clip and the capping of the glass units.

1 Timber wall plate
2 Aluminium channel section
3 Zinc or cadmium coated steel screw 50 mm long
4 Pitch polymer strip
5 Glass channel unit up to 2500 mm long without purlin support
6 Expanded polystyrene filling
7 Aluminium clip with neoprene wedging strip.
8 Aluminium flashing
9 Aluminium capping section

B Eaves

An aluminium clip is screwed to the top of the wall and carries a continuous aluminium support angle. A pitch polymer strip is used to bed the glass unit. Adjacent flanges are capped as shown in detail D below. The ends of the cappings are firmly held in place by the pitch polymer pads on the inside faces of the aluminium angle.

1 Concrete support wall
2 Aluminium clip
3 Zinc or cadmium coated steel screw
4 Pitch polymer strip
5 Glass channel
6 Pitch polymer pad
7 Continuous angle in aluminium
8 Aluminium capping section

C Verge

A recommended method of jointing at the verge is to overhang the glass unit. The edge support is covered with a continuous strip of pitch polymer to form a bed for the glass unit. The flange of the unit is covered with a pitch polymer pad held down by an aluminium strip which is screwed to the edge beam.

1 Timber end support beam
2 Pitch polymer strip
3 Glass channel unit
4 Pitch polymer pad
5 Aluminium clip 50 mm wide at 600 mm centres
6 Zinc or cadmium plated wood screw

D Seam

The clearance between two adjacent glass units is maintained at 3 mm by PVC spacers approximately 3 mm thick. The flanges of the units are placed upwards in this case and are covered by a special aluminium capping section which contains gun grade sealing compound. The capping is gently tapped into position and covered at the upper end by flashing and at the lower end by an aluminium angle.

1 Glass channel unit
2 PVC spacers 3 mm thick
3 Glass channel unit
4 Aluminium capping section
5 Gun grade sealing compound

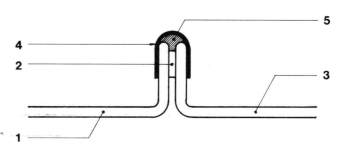

ROOFS: Aluminium rooflights

SCALE 1:2

A Single glazed fixed domed rooflight
The rooflight frame has welded corners and rests on the top of the curb which is part of the roof construction. It is held down by clips that are hooked over a corresponding hook around the frame and screwed to the side of the curb. The acrylic formed dome is held down on all four sides by continuous glazing beads.

1 Timber curb
2 Aluminium rooflight frame
3 Aluminium adjustable fixing clip
4 Stainless steel wood screw
5 Clear acrylic single glazed formed dome
6 Continuous aluminium glazing bead

B Double glazed fixed domed rooflight with permanent ventilation
The same rooflight frame as in A above is supported on special aluminium fixing clips that provide a clearance of 13 mm around the rooflight frame between the frame and the top of the curb. The clip is screwed to a timber plug in the top of the curb. Two separate acrylic domes are clipped to the rooflight frame.

1 Concrete curb
2 Special aluminium adjustable fixing clip
3 Stainless steel wood screw
4 Aluminium rooflight frame
5 Clear acrylic single glazed formed outer dome
6 Continuous aluminium glazing bead
7 Clear acrylic single glazed formed inner dome
8 Aluminium glazing clip.

C Double glazed opening domed rooflight
The opening rooflight has an aluminium frame formed of a section incorporating a skirt and a hinge. The hinge slides over a hinge pin that is part of a clip screwed to the top of the rooflight curb. The rooflight frame is double glazed with acrylic formed domes held in position by a continuous clip-on aluminium glazing bead on the outer dome and glazing clips on the inner dome.

1 Timber curb
2 Aluminium clip with hinge pin
3 Stainless steel wood screw
4 Aluminium rooflight frame
5 Clear acrylic single glazed formed inner dome
6 Aluminium glazing clip
7 Clear acrylic single glazed formed outer dome
8 Continuous aluminium glazing bead

D Double glazed fixed flat rooflight
The rooflight frame is the same as in A above and is supported on the top of a concrete curb to which it is fixed by hook clips that are screwed to wood plugs set in the curb. The frame is double glazed with two sheets of wired cast glass. The outer sheet is retained on all four sides by a continuous aluminium glazing bead and the inner sheet by glazing clips.

1 Concrete curb
2 Aluminium rooflight frame
3 Aluminium fixing clip
4 Stainless steel wood screw
5 Georgian wired cast glass 6 mm
6 Aluminium glazing clip
7 Georgian wired cast glass 6 mm
8 Continuous aluminium glazing bead

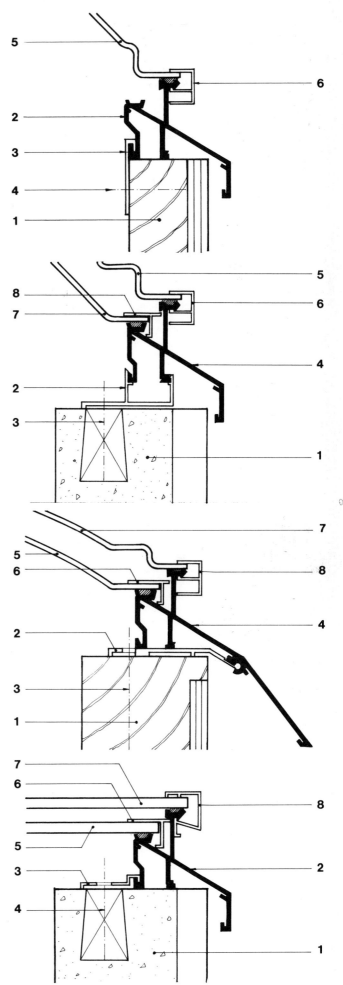

ROOFS : Timber double glazed roof window

A Head frame to roof

The rafters are trimmed at the head to clear the lining. An apron flashing is positioned against the top of the frame and its sides overlap the side flashings. It is pinned along its top to the frame. A cover flashing is then screwed to the frame of the opening sash and overlaps the apron flashing.

1 Roof rafter
2 Roof window frame
3 Aluminium upper apron flashing
4 Pin
5 Cover flashing

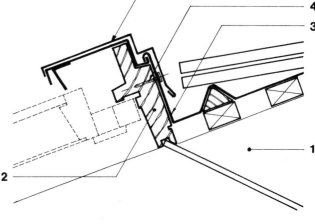

B Sill frame to roof

The rafters are trimmed at the sill to clear the vertical lining. The roof window is positioned and the lower apron flashing that is dressed over the tiles is placed against the frame with its return ends on the sides of the frame. It is pinned along its top to the frame. The cover flashing that is screwed to the frame of the opening sash then overlaps the top of the apron flashing.

1 Roof rafter
2 Roof window frame
3 Roof tile
4 Lower apron flashing
5 Pin
6 Cover flashing

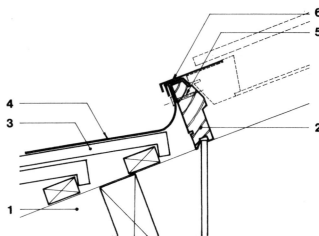

C Side frame to roof

The rafters are trimmed to the head and sill trimmers so as to provide an opening 60 mm wider than the width of the window. The roof window is positioned and supported on the rafters on both sides with two brass angle brackets placed about 120 mm from the top and the bottom that are screwed to the window frame and the rafters. An apron flashing is placed against the side of the frame and pinned to it along its top edge. The cover flashing on the window sash overlaps the apron flashing.

1 Roof rafter
2 Roof window side frame
3 Brass angle bracket screwed to frame and rafter
4 Apron flashing
5 Pin
6 Cover flashing

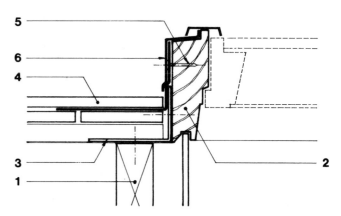

WALLS : Concrete lintels and facing brickwork

A   With flat arch and window in back position
The outer leaf of the cavity wall is in facing brickwork and the window opening is spanned with a brick flat arch. The inner leaf is supported by means of a reinforcement precast concrete lintel. A stepped damp-proof course is positioned to cross the cavity and project beyond the top of the window head to form a waterbar. Weepholes are formed in the vertical joints of the flat arch to drain the cavity.

1   Cast concrete reinforced lintel
2   Damp-proof course
3   Brick flat arch
4   Plaster 13 mm thick

B   With flat arch and window in forward position
The outer leaf of the cavity wall is in facing brickwork and the window opening is spanned with a brick flat arch. The inner leaf is supported by means of a reinforced precast concrete lintel. A stepped damp-proof course is positioned to cross the cavity and go between the underside of the brick arch and the head of the window.

1   Cast concrete reinforced lintel
2   Damp-proof course
3   Brick flat arch
4   Plaster 13 mm thick

C   With boot lintel and window in back position
When the facing brickwork is required to run across the opening without the construction of a brick arch, both leaves of the cavity wall are supported on a reinforced concrete boot lintel cast in situ. The stepped damp-proof course is carried across the cavity and projects beyond the top of the lintel. Weepholes are formed in the vertical brick joints above the lintel at about 800 mm centres

1   Reinforced cast concrete boot lintel
2   Damp-proof course
3   Brick horizontal course
4   Plaster 13 mm thick

D   With support angle and window in forward position
An alternative method used to support the facing brickwork across the opening without the construction of a brick arch is by means of a hot-dip galvanized steel angle. The inner leaf of the wall is supported by a precast concrete lintel. The stepped damp-proof course is carried across the cavity and over the top of the steel angle to project beyond the head of the window.

1   Hot-dip galvanized steel angle
2   Precast reinforced concrete lintel
3   Damp-proof course
4   Brick horizontal course
5   Plaster 13 mm thick

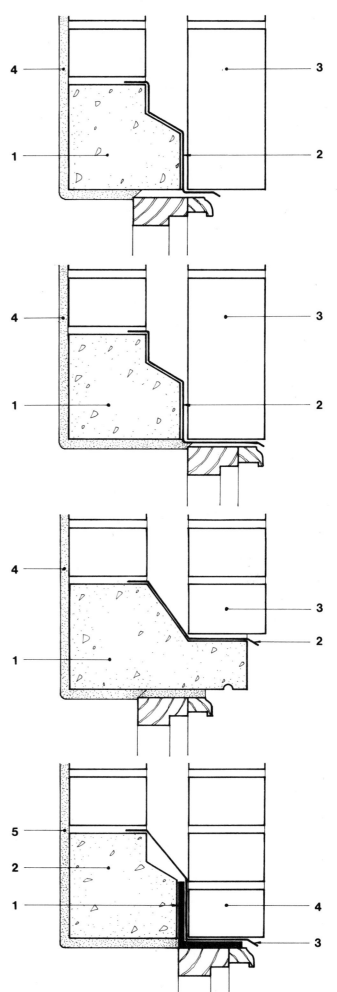

WALLS: Steel lintels

A Opening in brick faced cavity wall
For a clear span up to 1350 mm and for normal loading a galvanized steel lintel 150 mm deep is used as a support for the outer brick leaf. The inner leaf is carried on a precast reinforced concrete lintel. The steel lintel serves as a damp-proof course across the cavity and has a minimum bearing of 150 mm on both sides of the opening.

1 Precast reinforced concrete lintel
2 Hot-dip galvanized steel lintel
3 Brickwork facing
4 Plaster 13 mm thick

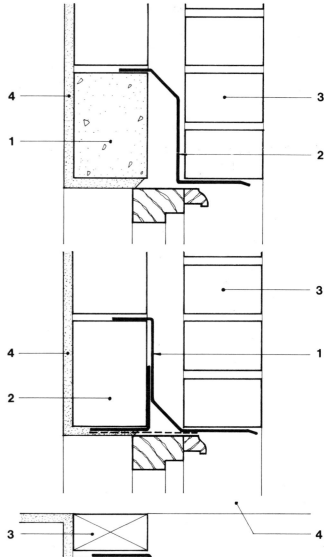

B Opening in brick faced cavity wall
For a clear span up to 1800 mm and for normal loading a galvanized steel lintel 150 mm deep with two lower flanges is used to support both leaves of the wall. Expanded steel mesh is welded to the underside of the flanges to provide a key for plaster.

1 Hot-dip galvanized steel lintel
2 Concrete block
3 Brickwork facing
4 Plaster 13 mm thick

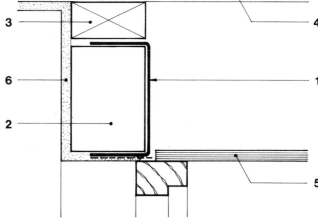

C Opening below eaves
When a window opening is positioned just below the eaves, a galvanized steel lintel may be used to support the roof construction. For normal loading a lintel 150 mm deep is suitable for a clear span up to 3000 mm. The lintel is carried on the inner leaf and has a minimum end bearing of 150 mm on sides of the opening.

1 Hot-dip galvanized steel lintel
2 Concrete block
3 Timber wall plate
4 Timber ceiling joist
5 Plywood soffit
6 Plaster 13 mm thick

D Opening in brickwork partition
When a door opening is required in a brickwork partition, a galvanized steel lintel with a trough profile may be used to support the brickwork over the opening. The head of the door frame is supported by the jambs.

1 Hot-dip galvanized steel lintel
2 Brickwork
3 Timber door head
4 Plaster 13 mm thick

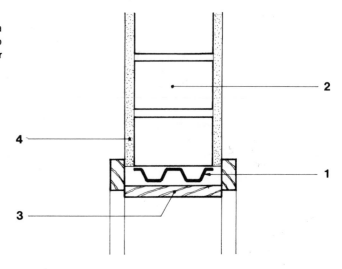

WALLS: Concrete masonry block lintels

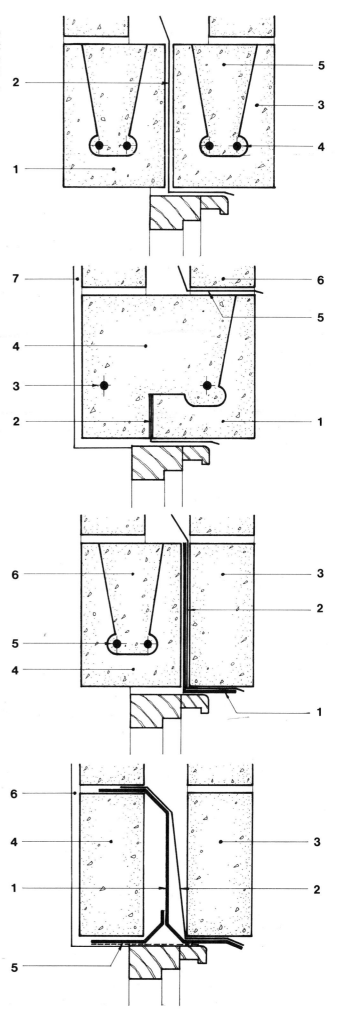

A   Concrete masonry block cavity wall 300 mm wide

For a clear span up to 1800 mm and for normal loading concrete masonry lintel blocks with reinforcement may be used to support the outer and inner leaves. A stepped damp-proof course is positioned to cross the cavity, go between the two lintels and project to form a waterbar beyond the top of the window head.

1   Concrete masonry lintel block
2   Stepped damp-proof course
3   Concrete masonry lintel block outer leaf
4   Reinforcing bar
5   Concrete infill 1 : 3 : 2 cement : sand : aggregate by volume

B   Concrete masonry block cavity wall 250 mm wide

For a clear span exceeding 1800 mm and depending on the loading a suitably reinforced in situ concrete lintel is formed with cut concrete masonry lintel blocks used as a shuttering on the outside. A stepped damp-proof course is positioned to cross the cavity and project beyond the top of the lintel. A damp-proof course is cast in position to form a waterbar above the head of the window.

1   Concrete cut masonry lintel block
2   Damp-proof course and waterbar
3   Reinforcing bar
4   Concrete infill 1 : 3 : 2 cement : sand : aggregate by volume
5   Stepped damp-proof course
6   Weephole 80 mm high, 10 mm wide at 800 mm centres
7   Plaster 13 mm thick

C   Concrete masonry block cavity wall 250 mm wide

For a clear span up to 1800 mm, an alternative lintel is formed by means of a hot-dip galvanized mild steel angle to support the outer leaf and reinforced concrete masonry lintel blocks to support the inner leaf. A stepped damp-proof course is positioned to cross the cavity, go between the angle and the outer leaf, and project to form a waterbar beyond the top of the window head.

1   Hot-dip galvanized mild steel angle
2   Damp-proof course
3   Concrete masonry block
4   Concrete masonry lintel block
5   Reinforcing bar
6   Concrete infill 1 : 3 : 2 cement : sand : aggregate by volume

D   Concrete masonry block cavity wall 250 mm wide

For a clear span up to 1800 mm and for normal loading, an alternative lintel is formed by means of a hot-dip galvanized mild steel lintel that is designed to support both leaves of the wall. A stepped damp-proofed course is positioned to cross the cavity, go on the outside of the lintel and project to form a waterbar beyond the top of the window head.

1   Hot-dip galvanized steel lintel with 150 mm bearing at both ends
2   Stepped damp-proof course
3   Concrete masonry block outer leaf
4   Concrete masonry block inner leaf
5   Expanded metal welded to lintel
6   Plaster 13 mm thick

WALLS : Clay tile and brick sills

A Roofing tiles

When a window sill is formed of clay roofing tiles a continuous flexible or semi-rigid damp-proof course is laid across the cavity. The first course of tiles crosses the cavity and is laid on a mortar bed to the required slope. The second course of tiles is laid with the joints between tiles placed over the centre of the tiles in the first course.

1 Brick outer leaf
2 Damp-proof course
3 Mortar bed
4 Clay roofing tile

B Bricks on edge

When a window sill is formed of bricks laid on edge, a continuous flexible or semi-rigid damp-proof course is first laid across the cavity. The bricks, which require to be frost-resistant and durable, are cut at one end to the required slope of the sill and laid on a mortar bed on the outer leaf. A metal flashing is provided at both ends of the sill to stop water running off each end down the face of the wall.

1 Brick outer leaf
2 Damp-proof course
3 Mortar bed
4 Brick-on-edge
5 Metal flashing

C Sill bricks with no projection

When the facing brick has a low water absorption, there is no projection of the brick sill, When a window sill is formed of special sill bricks, a continuous flexible damp-proof course is first laid across the cavity and up the back of the sill. The sill bricks, which require to be frost-resistant and durable, are specially shaped and sized to fit between the reveals. The damp-proof course projects beyond the face of the outer leaf and extends at both ends beyond the reveals.

1 Brick outer leaf
2 Damp-proof course
3 Mortar bed
4 Sill brick
5 Non-setting mastic pointing

D Sill bricks with projection

When the facing brick has a high water absorption the brick sill projects beyond the face of the wall to shed rainwater clear of the facing brick. A course of engineering bricks is laid to project 20 mm beyond the face of the wall. A continuous flexible damp-proof course is laid across the bricks and up the back of the sill bricks. Specially cut engineering bricks are laid to form the sill.

1 Engineering brick-on-edge
2 Damp-proof course
3 Mortar bed
4 Engineering brick sill
5 Non-setting mastic pointing

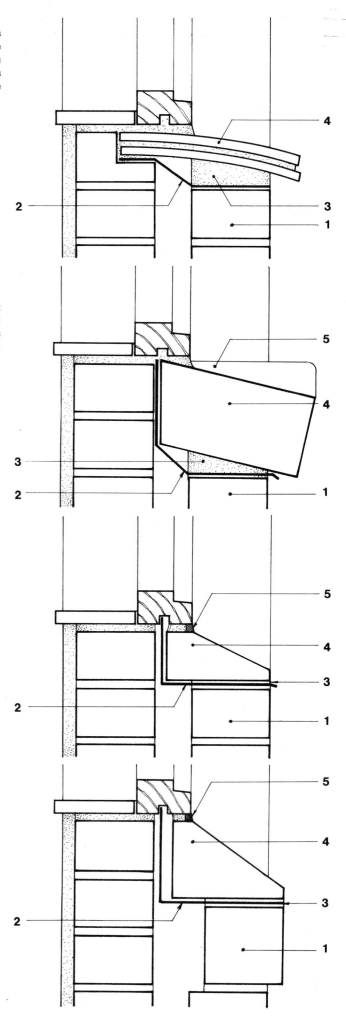

WALLS: Cast concrete and natural stone window sills

A With timber window frame in forward position
When a cast concrete or natural stone sill is used with a timber window frame set in a forward position, the sill is stepped, weathered, throated and provided with stooling at both ends. A groove is provided along the top of the sill to take a waterbar. A damp-proof course is positioned below and at the back of the sill.

1 Brick wall outer leaf
2 Mortar bed 12 mm 1:1:6 cement:lime:sand
3 Damp-proof course
4 Cast concrete or natural stone sill
5 Galvanized steel waterbar in mastic
6 Timber window frame

B With timber window frame in back position
When a cast concrete or natural stone sill is used with a timber window frame set in a back position, the sill is stepped, weathered, throated and provided with stooling at both ends. A groove is provided along the top of the sill to take a waterbar. A damp-proof course is positioned below and at the back of the sill.

1 Brick wall outer leaf
2 Mortar bed 12 mm 1:1:6 cement:lime:sand
3 Damp-proof course
4 Cast concrete or natural stone sill
5 Galvanized steel water bar in mastic
6 Timber window frame

C With metal window frame in forward position
When a cast concrete or natural stone sill is used with a metal window frame set in a forward position, the sill is rebated to give a support for the window board. The sill is weathered, throated, and provided with a stooling at both ends. A damp-proof course is positioned below and at the back of the sill.

1 Brick wall outer leaf
2 Mortar bed 12 mm 1:1:6 cement:lime:sand
3 Damp-proof course
4 Cast concrete or natural stone sill
5 Plug
6 Metal window frame

D With metal window frame in back position
When a cast concrete or natural stone sill is used with a metal window frame set in a back position, the sill is stepped, weathered, throated, and provided with a stooling at both ends. A damp-proof course is positioned below and at the back of the sill.

1 Brick wall outer leaf
2 Mortar bed 12 mm 1:1:6 cement:lime:sand
3 Damp-proof course
4 Cast concrete or natural stone sill
5 Plug
6 Metal window frame

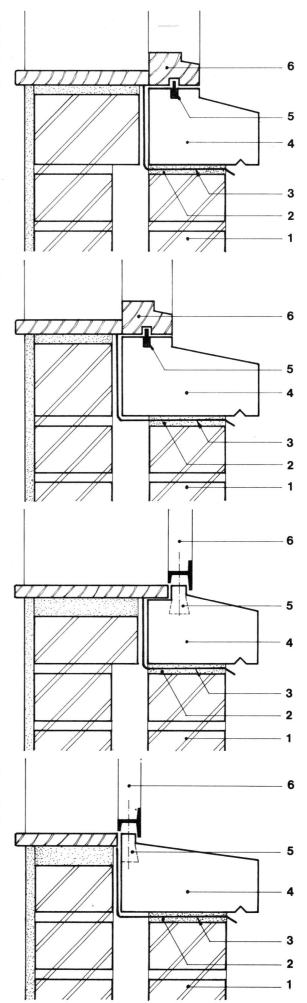

WALLS : Slate sills

A With timber window frame in forward position

When a slate sill is used with a timber window frame set in a forward position, it is normally stepped, weathered and throated. It is serrated on the underside to form a key for the mortar bed. The sill is grooved 12 mm deep to take a waterbar. The ends of the sill may be provided with a stooling.

1 Brick wall outer leaf
2 Mortar bed 12 mm 1 : 1 : 6 cement : lime : sand
3 Slate sill
4 Galvanized steel waterbar bedded in mastic
5 Timber window frame

B With timber window frame in back position

When a slate sill is used with a timber window frame set in a back position, it is throated and serrated on the underside. It is bedded to slope outwards and a weatherbar is fitted between the sill and the window board which is also made of slate in this example.

1 Brick wall outer leaf
2 Mortar bed 1 : 1 : 6 cement : lime : sand
3 Slate sill 20 mm thick
4 Slate window board
5 Galvanized steel waterbar bedded in mastic
6 Timber window frame

C With metal window frame in forward position

When a slate sill is used with a metal window frame set in a forward position the sill is rebated to take a hardwood bead which is bedded in mastic and fastened from the underside with brass countersunk screws. The sill is weathered and throated. The underside of the sill is serrated to form a key for the mortar bed.

1 Brick wall outer leaf
2 Mortar bed 12 mm 1 : 1 : 6 cement : lime : sand
3 Slate sill
4 Mastic bed
5 Hardwood bead 40 mm x 18 mm
6 Countersunk brass wood screw 37 mm long
7 Metal window frame

D With metal window frame in back position

When a slate sill is used with a metal window frame set in a back position, one method is to use a combined external and internal sill. The sill is grooved in the position required for the window and a hardwood bead is bedded in mastic in the groove and fastened from the underside with brass screws. The sill is weathered and throated, and is serrated on the underside to provide a key for the mortar beds.

1 Brick wall outer leaf
2 Mortar bed 12 mm thick 1 : 1 : 6 cement : lime : sand
3 Slate sill
4 Mastic bed
5 Hardwood bead 40 mm x 18 mm
6 Countersunk brass wood screw 37 mm long
7 Metal window frame

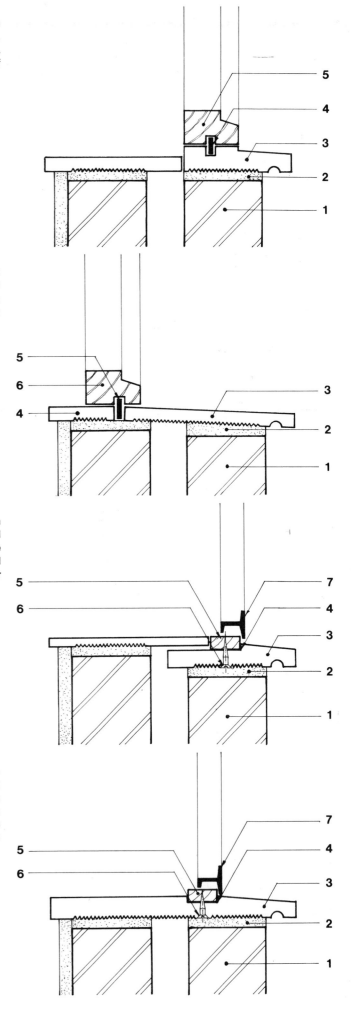

A Concrete masonry block cavity wall 250 mm wide
The sill for a concrete masonry block cavity wall 250 mm wide is formed with a special sill block 140 mm wide and having a cut face which slopes downwards at 45 degrees. A damp-proof course is positioned at the back and along the underside of the sill and projects beyond the outer face of the wall.

1 Concrete masonry block outer leaf
2 Damp-proof course
3 Dense concrete masonry sill block 140 mm wide
4 Concrete masonry block inner leaf

B Concrete masonry block cavity wall 300 mm wide
The sill for a concrete masonry block cavity wall 300 mm wide is formed with a special sill block 190 mm wide and having a cut face which slopes downwards at 45 degrees. A damp-proof course is positioned at the back and along the underside of the sill and projects beyond the outer face of the wall.

1 Concrete masonry block outer leaf
2 Damp-proof course
3 Dense concrete masonry sill block 190 mm wide
4 Concrete masonry block inner leaf

C When the course height of the blockwork is 200 mm and the window height is an odd multiple of 100 mm coordination can be achieved with a sill unit having a height of 100 mm.

1 Concrete masonry block outer leaf
2 Damp-proof course
3 Dense concrete masonry sill block
4 Concrete masonry block inner leaf
5 Timber inner lining

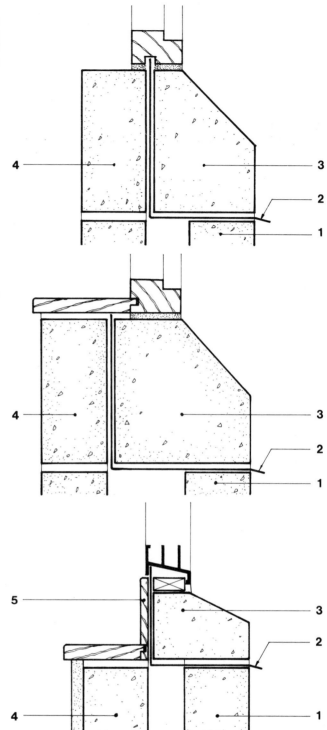

WALLS: Brick and clayware copings

A Brick copings are normally in the form of bricks laid on edge. A damp-proof course is essential and is usually placed in the second joint below the top of the coping brick. The following alternative forms of brick coping are shown:

1 Brick wall
2 Damp-proof course
3 Engineering brick-on-edge

1 Brick wall
2 Damp-proof course
3 Bull nosed brick-on-edge

1 Brick wall
2 Damp-proof course
3 Tile creasing
4 Brick-on-edge coping
5 Mortar fillet

1 Brick wall
2 Damp-proof course
3 Tile creasing
4 Brick-on-edge coping

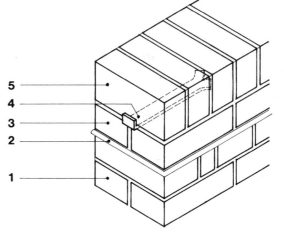

B At the end of a brick wall there is a tendency for the last brick of the coping to be displaced by impact on the corner or movement of the coping bricks. Additional support for the coping bricks at the end of the wall is provided by means of a galvanized steel or non-ferrous cramp with a fish-tailed end at one end of the bar and a right-angled bend at the other end.

1 Brick wall
2 Damp-proof course
3 Course of bricks
4 Galvanized steel or non-ferrous metal cramp
5 Brick-on-edge coping

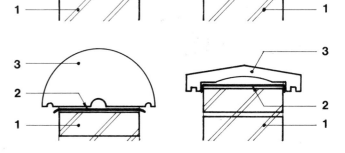

C Clayware copings are bedded directly on a damp-proof course laid on the top of the wall. The joint between adjoining coping units is strengthened by means of a dowel, cramp or mortar joggle. Flat-bottomed coping units not intended to be fixed by cramps should weigh not less than 28 kg/m run. The following alternative forms of clayware coping units are shown:

1 Brick wall
2 Damp-proof course
3 Splayed coping

1 Brick wall
2 Damp-proof course
3 Saddleback coping

1 Brick wall
2 Damp-proof course
3 Half round coping

1 Brick wall
2 Damp-proof course
3 Clip type coping

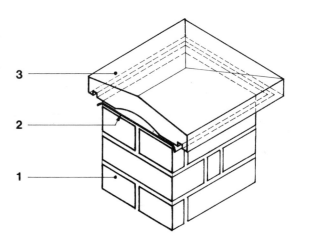

D Special coping units are made to suit the end of a wall, corners, and 3-way junctions. The saddleback coping unit is usually hipped at the end of the wall as shown and the drip is continued across the end. The drip is 12 mm wide x 8 mm deep and not less than 16 mm from the edge of the coping unit.

1 Brick wall
2 Damp-proof course
3 Clayware hipped stopped end saddleback coping

WALLS : Cast concrete, natural stone and slate copings

A Cast concrete and natural stone copings should always be bedded on a damp-proof course set on the top of the wall Coping units not held down by cramps should weigh not less than 28 kg/m run to minimise displacement by impact, pressure of a ladder or wind loading. Dowels, cramps or joggled mortar joints are used to connect the ends of adjoining coping units and should be of copper, brass, bronze or a steel that is resistant to corrosion. The cross-section of two forms of cast concrete coping and two of natural stone are shown.

1 Brick wall
2 Damp-proof course
3 Splayed cast concrete coping

1 Brick wall
2 Damp-proof course
3 Saddleback cast concrete coping

1 Brick wall
2 Damp-proof course
3 Splayed stone coping

1 Brick wall
2 Damp-proof course
3 Saddleback stone coping

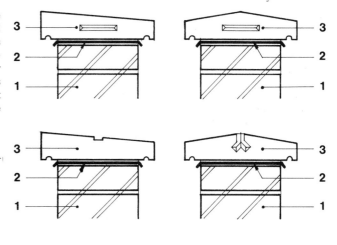

B Both types of coping unit are made with special units for the end of a wall, corners and 3-way junctions. The stone saddleback coping is shown with a joggle for the mortar joint between adjoining units and the drip that is carried around across the end of the wall. The drip is 12 mm wide, 8 mm deep and not less than 16 mm from the edge of the coping unit.

1 Brick walling
2 Damp-proof course
3 Stone hipped stopped end saddleback coping

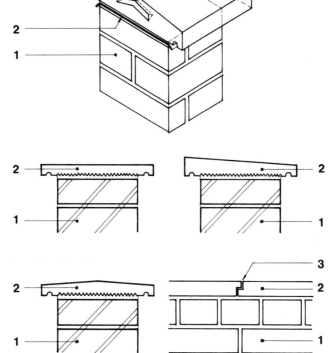

C Slate coping units are laid directly on the top of a wall as a damp-proof course is not needed. The joint between adjoining units is usually rebated with a minimum overlap of 12 mm and a clearance of 1 mm to 2 mm which is filled with a sealing compound able to accommodate movement. Holes provided in the joint face of adjacent units to take dowels must register with one another. Dowels are of copper, brass, bronze, or a steel that is resistant to corrosion. The cross-section of three alternative copings are shown and the rebated joint between adjoining coping units.

1 Brick wall
2 Slate flat coping

1 Brick wall
2 Slate splayed coping

1 Brick wall
2 Slate saddleback coping

1 Brick wall
2 Slate flat coping
3 Rebated joint

D Each type of coping unit is made with a range of special units for ends, corners, and three-way junctions. The slate flat end coping is shown. The drip is carried round across the end of the wall and is normally 10 mm wide x 8 mm deep. It should be not less than 16 mm from the edge of the coping unit.

1 Brick wall
2 Slate flat end coping
3 Rebated joint

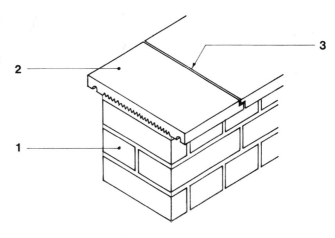

A Vertical-twist wall tie

The drip of the wall tie is placed centrally in the cavity or near the outer leaf. The tie is embedded in the mortar joint of each leaf of the wall for a width of at least 50 mm. The ties are staggered and evenly distributed in the wall. The spacing is varied to suit the loading on the wall, the thickness of the leaves, and the width of the cavity. For non-load bearing brickwork or blockwork, ties are normally placed at intervals of 900 mm horizontally and 450 mm vertically.

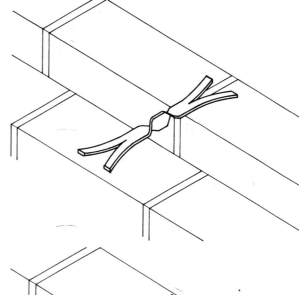

B Fish tail masonry anchor wall tie

The twist in the strip is placed centrally in the cavity and the fishtail is embedded in the mortar joint of the inner leaf of the wall. The hook of the anchor is placed in a vertical slot in the top of the stone facing slab. The ties are made in copper or phosphor bronze.

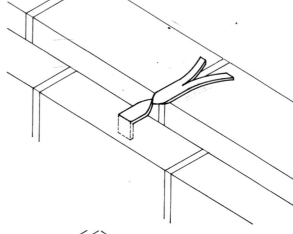

C Butterfly wall tie

The butterfly wall tie is placed centrally and laid with the drip downwards. The tie is embedded in the mortar joint and extends not less than 50 mm into each leaf of the wall. The wire tie is less likely to hold mortar droppings than the twisted strip type of tie but is more likely to corrode in conditions of severe exposure.

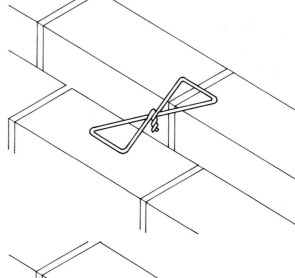

D Double-triangle wall tie

The double-triangle wall tie is placed centrally and laid with the drip upwards so as to form a drip groove. The tie is embedded in the mortar joint and extends not less than 50 mm into each leaf of the wall.

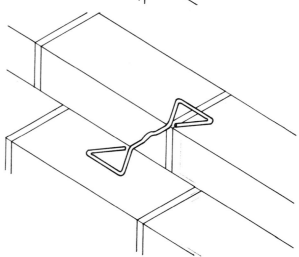

WALLS : Pitch polymer damp-proof courses

A Internal corner between flat roof and walls
One method of forming a damp-proof course at the junction of a flat roof with an internal corner of a wall or parapet is by means of a preformed cloak made of pitch polymer to the shape and sizes required. It is laid on an even bed of mortar. Overlaps of 100 mm are sealed with one part synthetic rubber/resin mixture contact adhesive. Each surface to be bonded is coated with adhesive and after drying the two are pressed firmly together. The cloak is used in conjunction with an external cloak.

1 Roof
2 Wall
3 Pitch polymer preformed cloak 2 mm thick

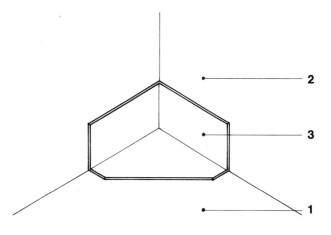

B External corner between flat roof and walls
The junction of a flat roof with the external corner of a wall or parapet may be formed by means of a preformed cloak, factory welded to the shape and sizes required to suit the given situation. The cloak is laid on an even bed of mortar and bonded to the roofing and adjoining DPC's with contact adhesive. The cloak is used in conjunction with an external cloak.

1 Roof
2 Wall
3 Pitch polymer preformed cloak 2 mm thick

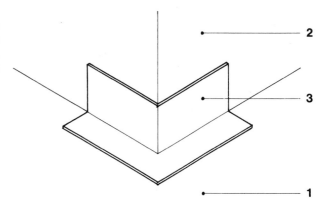

C Internal corner of cavity wall
At the internal corner of a cavity wall a stepped damp-proof course may be formed by means of a preformed cloak, factory welded to the shape and sizes required to fit the width of cavity and the thickness of the inner and outer leaves of the wall. The adjoining damp course is lapped 100 mm and bonded to the cloak with contact adhesive.

1 External leaf of wall
2 Inner leaf of wall
3 Pitch polymer preformed cloak 2 mm thick

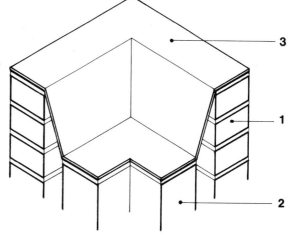

D External corner of cavity wall
The preformed cloak which is shaped for use at the internal corner of a cavity wall can be inverted and used to fit an external corner of a similar wall.

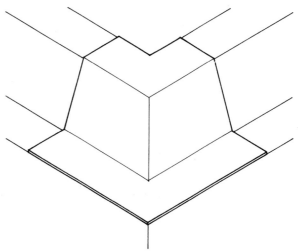

109

WALLS: Protected steel trough sheeting

A Eaves

The joint between a wall and roof covered with protected steel trough sheeting is made with an eaves flashing that covers the wall cladding for a height of 125 mm and is positioned under the roof sheeting for a distance up the slope of 225 mm. The flashing is fixed, together with the end of the cladding to an angle purlin by means of a high tensile steel hook bolt.

1 Steel angle purlin
2 Protected steel trough vertical cladding
3 Eaves flashing
4 High tensile steel hook bolt with square nut
5 Protected steel trough roof sheeting

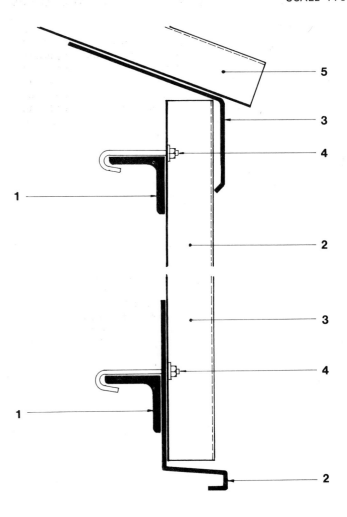

B Sill

At sill level the joint between the wall cladding and the top of the site slab or plinth is made with a specially formed sill flashing 225 mm high that is fastened to the angle purlin, together with the lower end of the vertical cladding, by means of a high tensile steel hook bolt.

1 Steel angle purlin
2 Sill flashing
3 Protected steel trough vertical cladding
4 High tensile steel hook bolt with square nut

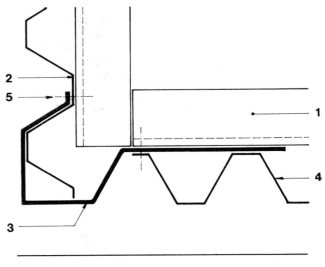

C External corner

The joint at the external corner between two lengths of vertical cladding is made with a specially formed cover flashing designed to fit the trough of the sheeting and fastened to the sheeting at 400 mm centres with a pan head type A self-tapping screw 6 mm diameter 20 mm long.

1 Steel angle purlin
2 Protected steel trough vertical cladding
3 Cover flashing
4 Protected steel trough vertical cladding
5 High carbon steel bright zinc plated self-tapping screw

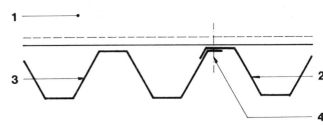

D External lap

The joint between two adjacent vertical cladding trough sheets is a side lap 19 mm wide that is fastened by self-tapping screws 6 mm diameter 20 mm long at 400 mm centres positioned centrally in the turn-down edge of the side lap and not less than 40 mm from the end of a sheet.

1 Steel angle purlin
2 Protected steel trough vertical cladding
3 Protected steel trough vertical cladding
4 High carbon steel bright zinc plated self-tapping screw

WALLS : Aluminium profiled cladding

SCALE 1 : 2

A Fixing to timber purlin through trough
The trough profiled sheeting is lapped and fixed along the valley of a trough with dome-headed buttress ring nails driven into the timber purlins which must be not less than 70 mm thick. The nail must be driven in squarely to ensure a satisfactory seal by means of the integral aluminium polychloroprene washer.

1 Timber purlin
2 Aluminium troughed sheeting
3 Dome-head buttress ring nail with integral washer

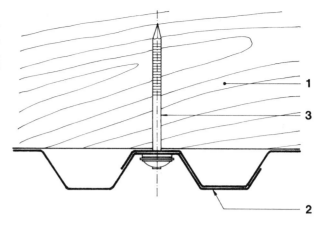

B Fixing to steel purlin
The trough profiled sheet is lapped and fixed along the valley of a trough with stainless steel self-tapping screws screwed into pre-drilled holes in the steel purlins.

1 Steel purlin
2 Aluminium troughed sheeting
3 Stainless steel washer with polychloroprene seal
4 Stainless steel self-tapping screw

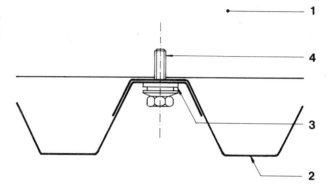

C Fastening of side lap
The trough profiled sheeting is fastened along the side of the lap with rivets positioned at 500 mm centres in pre-drilled holes. A light pressure is applied to the overlapping sheeting when drilling and riveting.

1 Purlin
2 Aluminium troughed sheeting
3 Aluminium dome-headed rivet

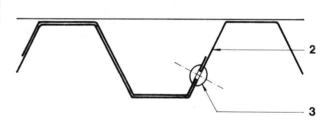

D Fixing to timber purlin through crown
When the profile of the sheeting does not permit a double lap, the overlapping sheet is fixed through the crown of the corrugation to the timber purlins. The sheeting is drilled with holes 0.5 mm diameter under nail size and is fixed with dome-head buttress ring nails driven into the timber purlins.

1 Timber purlin
2 Aluminium profiled sheeting
3 Dome-head buttress ring nail

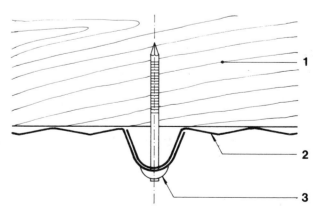

WALLS: Movement joints for brickwork

A Section of brick wall supporting reinforced concrete slab

When a brick wall is supporting a reinforced concrete slab, a slip plane is provided to permit horizontal movement of the slab. Two layers of bituminous felt are laid along the top of each leaf of wall and the slab is cast directly on these layers.

1 Brick load-bearing wall external leaf
2 Bituminous felt in two layers
3 Reinforced concrete slab

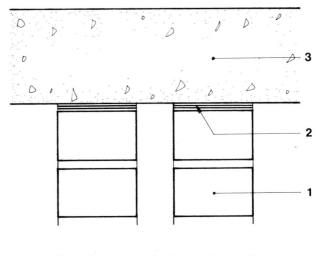

B Section of brick panel in reinforced concrete frame

When a brick wall is built in the form of a panel in a reinforced concrete frame, a movement joint is provided to allow for contraction of the concrete and expansion of the fire-clay units. The joint is packed with a compressible strip to form a back-up for the sealant which is applied to the joint externally. The depth of the sealant is half the gap width.

1 Reinforced concrete structural frame
2 Brick wall panel external leaf
3 Cellular polyethylene compressible strip back-up material
4 Sealant

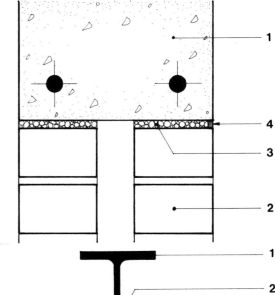

C Plan of brick wall with steel support column

When a brick wall or partition is supported between steel columns, the joint between the end of the wall and the column is formed with a compressible strip and dowels. The dowels, not more than 6 mm diameter, are lubricated or wrapped with a plastic sheath to allow for movement of the brickwork and are positioned in three or more places in the horizontal joints over the height of the storey.

1 Steel support column
2 Cellular preformed compressible strip
3 Brick wall
4 Galvanized steel dowel 6 mm diameter
5 Brick wall

D Plan of expansion joint in brick external wall

When external brick walls of clay-fired units exceed about 12 m in length, a movement joint is provided every 12 m to allow for expansion of the brickwork. The joints are not less than 10 mm wide and are filled with cellular preformed compressible strip which also serves as a back-up material for the sealant. Sealant is applied to the joint externally to a depth of half the gap width.

1 Brick wall external leaf
2 Cellular preformed compressible strip
3 Brick wall external leaf
4 Sealant

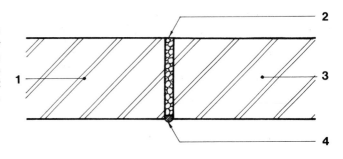

WALLS: Movement joints in blockwork

A There are a number of alternative ways of forming movement joints in blockwork. In the first method, the blocks are bonded and laid to give a continuous vertical joint which is filled with mortar as the work proceeds. The mortar is then raked out on both sides of the joint to a depth of 20 mm and the gap is filled with a sealing compound. The movement joints are spaced at 6 m centres for normal blockwork without openings.

1 Concrete block
2 Portland cement : lime : sand 1 : 1 : 6 mortar
3 Polysulphide sealing compound

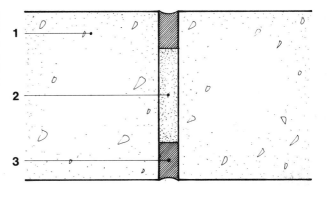

B Another method of forming a movement joint is to bond and lay the blockwork so as to form a continuous vertical open joint 10 mm wide. The centre of the joint is then filled with a compressible filler, such as cellular polyethylene or cellular polyurethane, which serves as a back-up material for the sealing compound which is used to fill the gap on both sides of the joint.

1 Concrete block
2 Cellular polyethylene back-up material filler
3 Polysulphide sealing compound

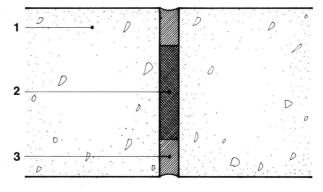

C A third method of forming a movement joint is used for completed blockwork. The blockwork is constructed in the normal manner. At the position required for the vertical movement joint, a groove 10 mm wide by 20 mm deep is cut with a chasing tool on both sides of the blockwork. The chase is then filled with a sealing compound.

1 Concrete block
2 Polysulphide sealing compound

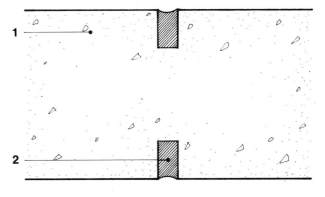

D In the case of internal blockwork which is unplastered and does not require to be weather-resistant the joint may be pointed with a weak mortar instead of being filled with a sealing compound.

1 Concrete block
2 Portland cement : lime : sand 1 : 1 : 6 mortar
3 Portland cement : lime : sand 1 : 2 : 9 mortar pointing

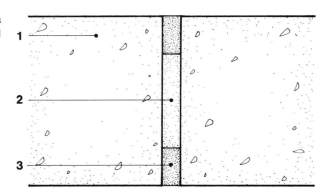

WALLS: Precast concrete panels

A Section of horizontal joint between panels

The horizontal joint between two precast concrete panels which form part of an open-drained joint is formed with a loosely fitting flexible PVC baffle in the vertical grooves and a preformed gasket in the horizontal gap between the panels at the back of the joint. The gaskets are compressed between the panels and are self-adhesive.

1 Precast concrete lower panel
2 Extruded flexible PVC baffle
3 Cellular polychloroprene preformed gasket with adhesive coating
4 Precast concrete upper panel

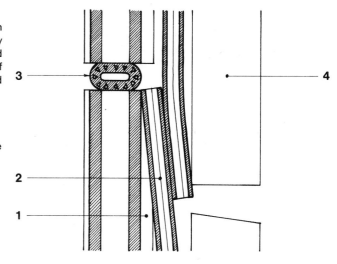

B Plan of vertical joint between panels

The open vertical joint between precast concrete panels has a clearance of 20 mm. The vertical gasket at the back of the joint adheres to the horizontal gasket and is compressed between the joint faces of the two panels. The PVC baffle is narrower than the minimum distance between the bottom of the opposing grooves to permit ease of insertion, and of sufficient width to bridge the gap so as to prevent displacement. It is stiffened by the central hollow section and the longitudinal ridges, thus enabling it to be pushed into position after the two adjacent panels have been positioned.

1 Precast concrete panel
2 Cellular polychloroprene preformed gasket with adhesive coating
3 Precast concrete panel
4 Extruded flexible PVC baffle

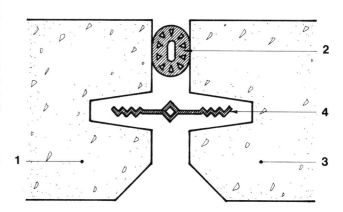

C Intersection between horizontal and vertical joint

The 4-way joint between the horizontal and vertical gaskets at the back of the panel must be effectively made and may be formed by a cruciform junction piece or by vertical gaskets stuck to a continuous horizontal gasket. The vertical baffles overlap by at least 50 mm and are set back from the panel face a distance of 50 mm.

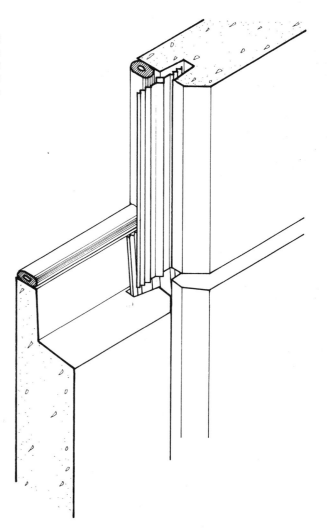

114

WALLS : Precast concrete cladding panel

A One form of joint between precast concrete cladding panels is a drained joint that incorporates a loose baffle. The baffle hangs loosely in the precast grooves and is fixed at the top edge of each panel. A flashing is fitted over the rebate at the top of the lower panel. A continuous sealant is applied along the top ledge and is held in position by the upper panel. The upper panel is assembled to give a minimum clearance between the upper and lower panels of 10 mm.

1 Precast concrete lower panel
2 Plastic baffle 40 mm wide
3 Flashing 100 mm wide sealed to back of panels
4 Sealant strip
5 Precast concrete upper panel
6 Plastic baffle 40 mm wide

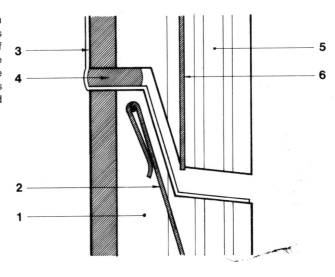

B The joint profile of the vertical edge of the panel is shaped to provide a groove for the baffle, a weather check and a splay to prevent spalling of the concrete at the outer edge. Adjacent panels are assembled to give a minimum clearance of 10 mm. The width of the baffle is in practice related to the actual clearance on site. After the panels have been fixed a vertical sealant strip is inserted at the back of the joint.

1 Precast concrete panel
2 Precast concrete panel
3 Loose hanging plastic baffle
4 Sealant strip

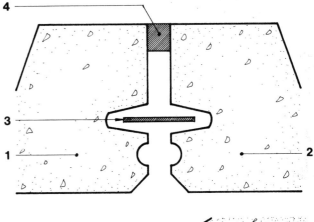

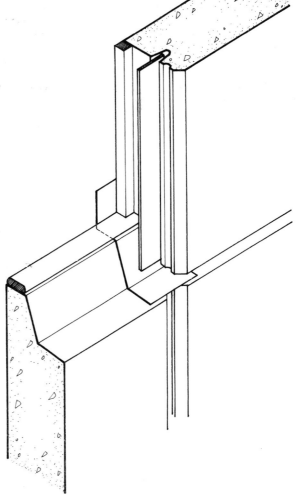

WALLS : Precast concrete panels

A   Section through horizontal joint

The horizontal joint between two precast concrete panels in the form of an open-drained joint is made with a seal at the back of the joint and a baffle positioned not less than 50 mm from the front of the panel. In this example, the seal consists of cellular foam strip compressed and fixed with adhesive. The baffle consists of two synthetic rubber strips positioned in the two grooves of the adjacent panels and lapped at the joint.

1   Precast concrete lower panel
2   Vulcanized synthetic rubber baffle
3   Polychloroprene flashing strip with adhesive coating
4   Cellular foam synthetic rubber strip with adhesive coating
5   Precast concrete upper panel
6   Vulcanized synthetic rubber baffle

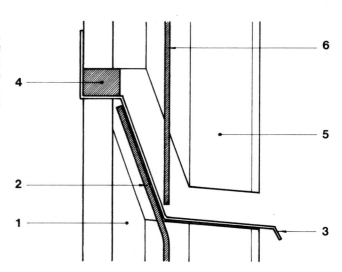

B   Plan of vertical joint

The groove cast in the edge of each panel is designed to take the vertical baffle and accommodate the maximum permissible tolerance on the gap width. A flashing is fitted across the joint over the sill of the lower panel and behind the back of the upper panel. The vertical gap at the back is filled with a compressed foam synthetic rubber strip that is fixed to the joint face of the panels with adhesive and also bonded to the horizontal seal to ensure an air-tight joint.

1   Precast concrete panel
2   Precast concrete panel
3   Cellular foam synthetic rubber strip with adhesive coating
4   Vulcanized synthetic rubber baffle

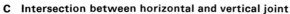

C   Intersection between horizontal and vertical joint

The 4-way joint at the back of the panels consists of a junction between the two vertical sealing strips and the horizontal strip. This joint is further protected by the flashing which is turned up the back face of the panels. The flashing also serves to throw water clear of the vertical joint at each panel height and so lessen the quantity of water that flows down the baffle and the vertical grooves.

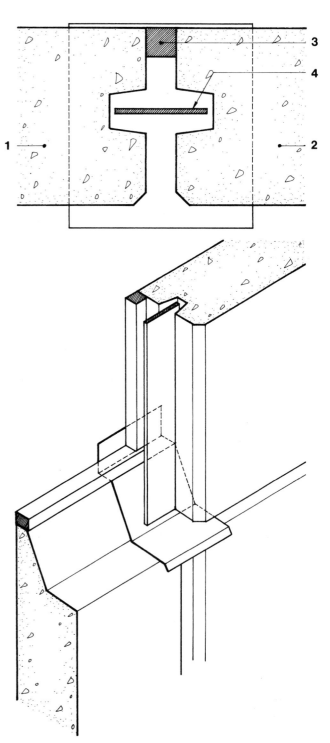

WALLS: Precast concrete panels

A One form of joint between precast concrete cladding panels is a drained joint that incorporates a cruciform weather-seal. It is essential that the clearance is maintained between a minimum of 10 mm and a maximum of 20 mm for a cruciform section that measures 40 mm across the diagonal. The horizontal joint has a flashing and is sealed as for the drained joint with the loose baffle.

1 Lower precast concrete panel
2 Plastic weather strip of cruciform cross-section
3 Flashing 100 mm wide sealed to back of panels
4 Sealant strip
5 Upper precast concrete panel
6 Plastic weather-seal of cruciform cross-section

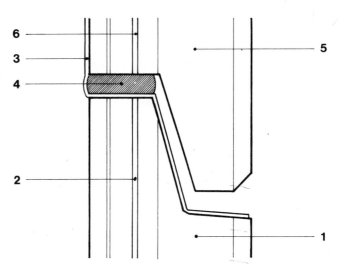

B The joint profile of the vertical edge of the panel is shaped at the back accurately to provide a recess to take a leg of the cruciform weather strip. At the front a splay is made to prevent spalling of the outer edge. The weather strip is compressed when inserted and exerts continuous pressure against the edges of both panels.

1 Precast concrete panel
2 Precast concrete panel
3 Plastic weather strip of cruciform cross-section

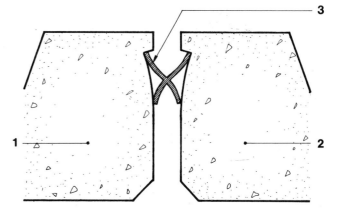

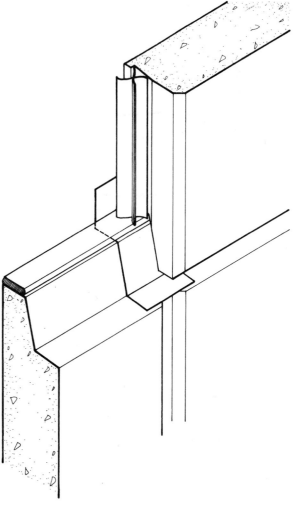

117

WALLS : Precast concrete panels

SCALE 1 : 2

A Section across panels at horizontal joint

The joint is made by means of a gun applied one part sealant. The clearance between the two adjacent panels is 15 mm. The gap is first packed firmly with a foam polyethylene strip that is positioned to provide a square pocket for the sealant. The sealant is based on acrylic polymer which has excellent characteristics. The surfaces of the concrete joint profiles must be clean, dry and free from dirt or grease before application of the sealant.

1 Precast concrete lower panel
2 Precast concrete upper panel
3 Foam polyethylene compressible backing strip
4 One-part gun applied sealant

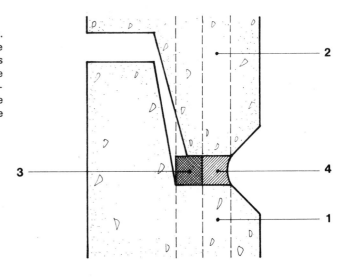

B Plan of vertical joint

The construction of the vertical joint is similar to that of the horizontal. The front edges of the concrete panels are splayed to prevent spalling of the concrete, provide a weather check, and set back the face of the sealant. A width to depth ratio of 1 : 1 is recommended for the sealant with a minimum width of 6 mm and a maximum of 18 mm. The sealant will accommodate movement up to 20 per cent of the initial joint width.

1 Precast concrete panel
2 Precast concrete panel
3 Foam polyethylene compressible backing strip
4 One-part gun applied sealant

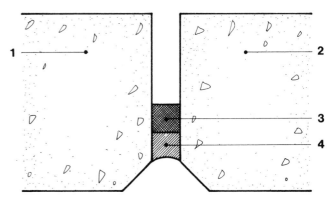

C Intersection between horizontal and vertical joint

The four-way joint at the intersection of the horizontal and vertical sealant is fully symmetrical. The sealant must be applied so as to avoid voids and entrapment of air.

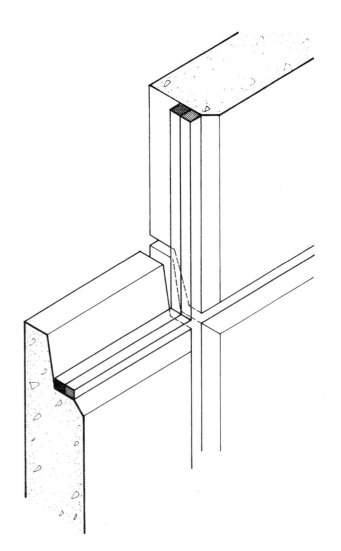

118

WALLS : Concrete panel sealed joints

A Plan of vertical joint with a single gasket
The continuous gasket is in the form of a strip of circular cross-section with a cellular polychloroprene core and an outer sleeve of waterproof self-adhesive composition. The strip is pressed against the joint face of a panel during erection and is compressed by the positioning of the adjacent panel. A clearance of 20 mm is recommended for a gasket 25 mm in diameter.

1 Concrete wall panel
2 Polychloroprene gasket 25 mm diameter before compression
3 Concrete wall panel

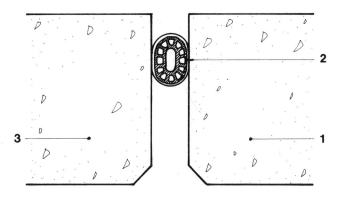

B Plan of vertical joint with a sealant and joint filler
The gap between the two panels is filled with a preformed strip designed as a backfilling to support the sealant. The sealant is applied cold with a trowel or gun. The optimum width is twice the depth, but this shape is only suitable for gap widths not less than 25 mm.

1 Concrete wall panel
2 Concrete wall panel
3 Polyethylene joint filler with closed cell structure
4 Polysulphide rubber sealant

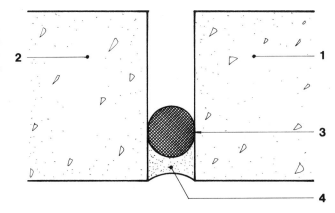

C Plan of vertical joint with gasket and grout filling
The joint face of the concrete panel is first treated with a priming adhesive. The hollow gasket is then driven into the gap by means of a rubber or plastic hammer. The gasket is then driven further with a caulking tool to the required depth. The gap on the inner side of the gasket is filled with grout. The clearance shown of 30 mm is the mean distance between the maximum and minimum gap width.

1 Concrete wall panel
2 Concrete wall panel
3 Priming butyl-based solvent adhesive with resin additions
4 High grade polychloroprene or other synthetic rubber gasket
5 Grout

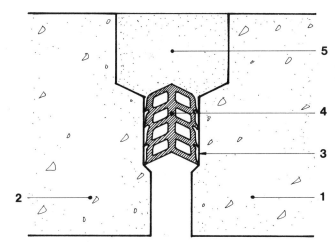

D Arrangement of 4-way junction
At the intersection of a vertical and a horizontal gasket, a U-shaped section is cut out of each gasket but on opposite sides. The two gaskets are then locked together so that they remain in the same plane. After being placed in position the intersection is bonded and sealed with a polychloroprene or polyurethane based bonding compound.

1 Vertical gasket
2 Horizontal gasket
3 Bonding compound

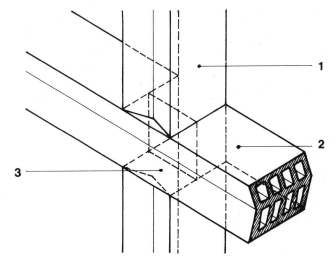

A Panel supported at the top: upper connection

A flange along the top of the concrete panel is located on the structural support and is positioned by means of non-ferrous dowels which are grouted in. A backing strip is inserted at the back of the bed joint which is packed with a continuous solid mortar bed.

1 Concrete structural support
2 Non-ferrous dowel
3 Grout
4 Closed cell foamed polyethylene backing strip
5 Mortar bed joint
6 Concrete panel

B Panel supported at the top: lower fastening

The flange along the lower edge of the concrete panel is fastened to the top of the panel below by means of cleats which are packed out as required and bolted with set screws to socket anchors. The gap between the two panels is filled with a backing strip and sealed with a gun-grade sealant.

1 Concrete panel below
2 Socket anchor
3 Non-ferrous cleat
4 Packing plates
5 Concrete panel
6 Set screw and washer
7 Closed cell foamed polyethylene backing strip
8 Gun-grade sealant

C Panel supported at the bottom: upper fastening

A flange along the top of the panel contains socket anchors. The panel is fastened back to the upper supporting structure by means of cleats and set screws. Packing plates are used as required to position the panel laterally.

1 Concrete structural support above
2 Socket anchor
3 Concrete panel
4 Socket anchor
5 Packing plates
6 Non-ferrous cleat
7 Set screw and washer

D Panel supported at the bottom: lower connection

The lower flange of the panel is supported on the supporting structure below on a solid mortar bed. The back of the bed joint is filled with a backing strip. The panel is positioned and connected by means of a non-ferrous dowel which is grouted in position. The joint between the two wall panels on the external face is designed as a compression joint: it is filled with a backing strip and sealed with a gun-grade sealant.

1 Concrete structural support
2 Non-ferrous dowel
3 Grout
4 Closed cell foamed polyethylene backing strip
5 Mortar bed joint
6 Concrete panel
7 Gun-grade sealant

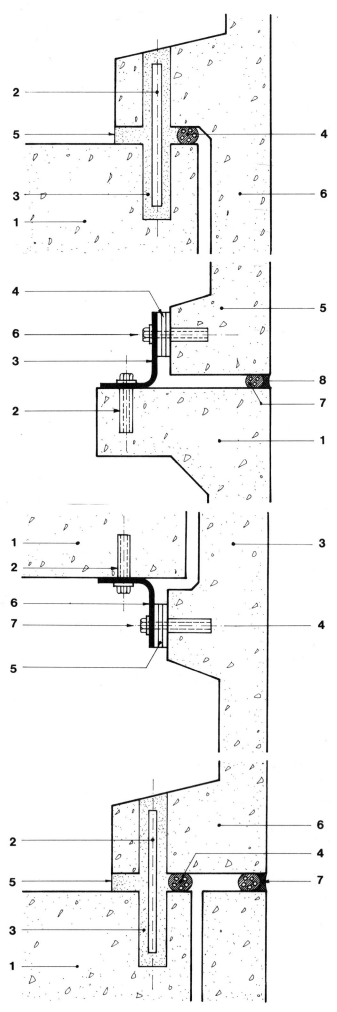

WALLS: Aerated structural concrete slabs

A Longitudinal joint between slabs

The aerated structural concrete slabs are laid horizontally outside the structural frame and extend from the centre-line of one column to the centre-line of the next. Galvanized steel dowels are driven into the vertical preformed holes in the slabs to maintain alignment during erection. The longitudinal joint is formed by two preformed compressible strips laid along the outer edges of the top of each slab.

1 Aerated structural concrete slab 150 mm thick
2 Galvanized mild steel dowel
3 Preformed compressible strip
4 Aerated structural concrete slab

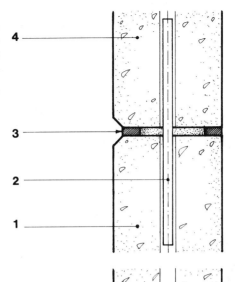

B Longitudinal joint between slab and foundation

The concrete ground slab is cast with an edge beam, the outer face of which is positioned accurately. A damp-proof course is placed along the top edge of the slab. Galvanized mild steel dowels are driven into position to take the first slab of the wall, which is bedded on two preformed compressible strips laid along both sides of the damp-proof course.

1 Concrete ground slab and foundation beam
2 Galvanized mild steel dowel
3 Damp-proof course
4 Preformed compressible strip
5 Aerated structural concrete slab 150 mm thick

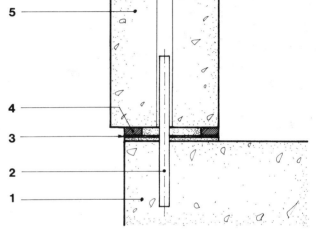

C Vertical joint between slabs and column

The slabs are lowered into position with their back face against the outer face of the column. The clearance between adjacent slabs is 25 mm. The slabs are attached to the column by means of a cover strip and bolts.

1 Concrete structural column
2 Aerated structural concrete slab
3 Aerated structural concrete slab
4 Expansion anchor
5 Cover strip and bolt

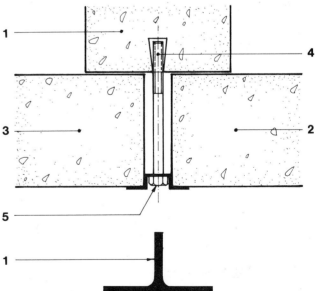

D Vertical joint between slabs and stanchion

When the slabs are used in conjunction with a structural steel frame, threaded sleeve pieces are welded to the external flange and on the centre-line of the stanchion. A clearance of 25 mm is maintained between the ends of adjacent slabs which are attached to the stanchion by means of a cover strip and bolts.

1 Rolled steel stanchion
2 Threaded sleeve piece welded to stanchion
3 Aerated structural concrete slab
4 Aerated structural concrete slab
5 Aluminium cover strip and bolt

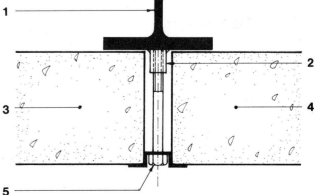

WALLS: Timber frame and plywood

A Window head

In light timber framed wall construction, the lintel over window and door openings normally consists of two 100 mm x 50 mm joists. The window unit is nailed to the studs and the external face of the studding is covered with exterior plywood siding fixed with galvanized nails 50 mm long at 150 mm centres around the perimeter of the sheets and at 300 mm centres on intermediate studs. The inner lining is of plasterboard.

1 Timber lintel
2 Window frame
3 Exterior plywood siding 12 mm
4 Metal plasterboard stop
5 Plasterboard

B Window sill

The wall studding is trimmed with two horizontal joists to support the window sill which is grooved to take the top of the exterior plywood siding and to provide a drip. The sill is nailed to the support joist, as is the top of the exterior plywood siding, with galvanized nails 50 mm long. The inner lining is of plasterboard.

1 Timber plate
2 Window sill
3 Exterior plywood siding 12 mm
4 Metal plasterboard stop
5 Plasterboard

C Window jamb

Each side of the window opening is constructed with two vertical studs. The window is placed in the opening and nailed to the studs. The exterior plywood siding is positioned to cover the gap between the window frame and the stud, the vertical edge of the siding being sealed with an exterior type sealer before assembly. The inner lining is of plasterboard.

1 Timber stud at 400 mm centres
2 Window jamb
3 Exterior plywood siding 12 mm
4 Metal plasterboard stop
5 Plasterboard

D Vertical joint and external corner

The exterior corner is constructed with three vertical studs arranged to provide edge support for the exterior plywood siding and for the plasterboard lining. A vertical damp-proof course 100 mm wide is fixed to the corner and the joint between the plywood sheets with a clearance of 5 mm is filled with sealant. Two cover strips 50 mm x 25 mm are nailed to the corner to give additional protection to the joint at the corner.

1 Timber stud
2 Damp-proof course
3 Exterior plywood siding 12 mm
4 Sealant
5 Plasterboard
6 Cover strip

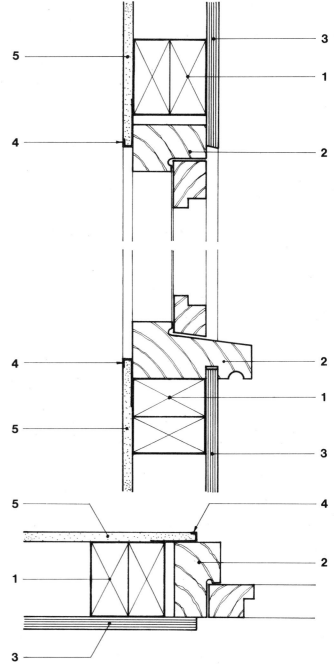

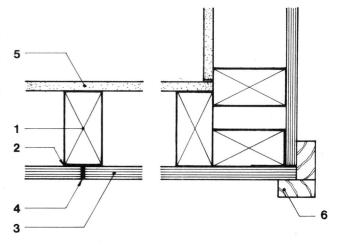

WALLS : Timber cladding

A There are a number of alternative methods used to give an external timber finish to wood frame construction. Horizontal boarding is nailed through the plywood sheathing directly to the vertical studs that are normally at 400 mm or 600 mm centres. The minimum recommended thickness for weather-boarding is 16 mm or, if feather-edge, it may be 8 mm thick at the thinner edge and 16 mm thick at the thicker edge.

1 Timber stud 100 mm x 50 mm
2 8 mm waterproof plywood
3 Breather type building paper
4 Timber board laid horizontally
5 Feather-edge board laid horizontally
6 Aluminium or double-dipped galvanized nail

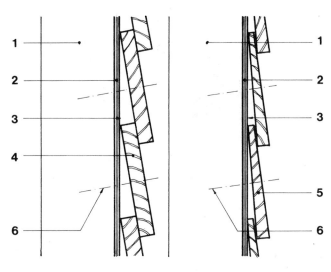

B Another method of timber cladding is the use of boards fixed vertically nailed to horizontal nogging between the studs. The gap between the boards is covered with a vertical batten, or alternatively covered by the use of rebated boards.

1 Timber stud
2 Timber nogging fixed horizontally
3 8 mm waterproof plywood
4 Breather type building paper
5 Board fixed vertically
6 Aluminium or double-dipped galvanized nail
7 Timber batten

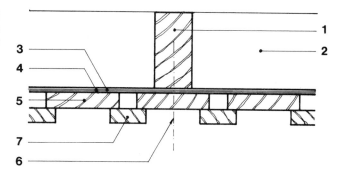

C The use of rebated boards fixed vertically affords a means of taking up shrinkage and movement in the timber. It also allows for alternative widths, depths and profiles for the rebates formed at both edges of the board.

1 Timber studs
2 Timber nogging fixed horizontally
3 8 mm waterproof plywood
4 Breather type building paper
5 Rebated timber board
6 Aluminium or double-dipped galvanized nail

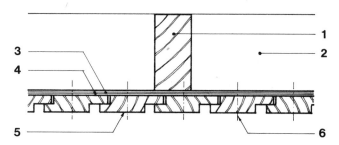

D Another kind of timber wall finish is the use of plywood as a combined sheathing and cladding. A clearance of 2 mm is left between adjacent sheets and the gap is covered by a vertical batten not less than 50 mm wide. The plywood and the battens are nailed to the studs.

1 Timber studs
2 15 mm waterproof plywood
3 Timber batten 50 mm x 25 mm
4 Aluminium or double dipped galvanized nail

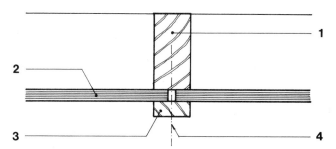

WALLS : External plywood panels

A The joint between external waterproof plywood panels is designed to protect the edges of the panel, to accommodate movement, and to resist weather. The plywood panel is bedded on sealing compound on the support batten and positioned to give a clearance of 10 mm between the edges of both panels. The cover batten is bedded on sealing compound on the plywood or screwed directly to the support batten.

1 Timber batten
2 Sealing compound
3 Surfaced waterproof plywood panel 12 mm
4 Sealing compound
5 Hardwood cover batten
6 Wood screw and pellet

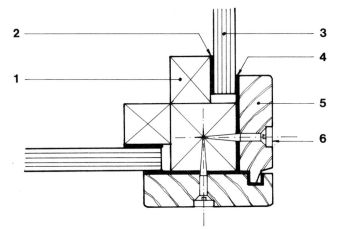

B The joint between external waterproof plywood panels at an external corner is similar in principle to the joint shown in A above. A corner batten is used to maintain the 5 mm margin between the edge of the plywood and the joint reference plane, and to provide support for the two cover battens.

1 Timber batten
2 Sealing compound
3 Surfaced waterproof plywood panel 12 mm
4 Sealing compound
5 Hardwood cover batten
6 Wood screw and pellet

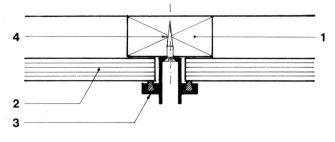

C An alternative form of straight joint is made by means of a special aluminium section with two flanges that incorporate continuous polychloroprene seals. The section is screwed to the timber support batten so that the seals are compressed against the face of the plywood panels and protect their edges.

1 Timber batten
2 Surfaced waterproof plywood panel 12 mm
3 Aluminium section with polychloroprene seals
4 Aluminium wood screw

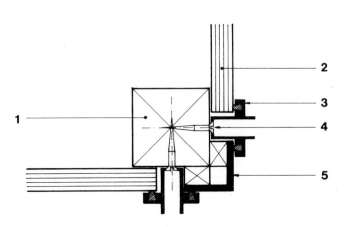

D The alternative form of joint between external waterproof plywood panels at an external corner, which corresponds to the joint shown in C above, is by means of two aluminium sections combined with an aluminium angle at the external corner. Accurate setting out is required as the positional tolerance is small.

1 Timber batten
2 Surfaced waterproof plywood panel 12 mm
3 Aluminium section with polychloroprene seals
4 Aluminium wood screw
5 Aluminium angle

WALLS: Lightweight cladding sheet

A The cladding sheet is a composite material reconstituted from natural slate and stone fillers with a resin binder and glass fibre reinforcement. The sheet is pre-drilled for fixing with screws which are placed at a minimum distance of 20 mm from the edge of the sheet. A clearance of 10 mm is provided between adjacent sheets and the gap between the sheet and the timber batten is sealed by the compression of a special neoprene gasket.

1 Timber batten 100 mm x 38 mm
2 Neoprene gasket
3 Cladding sheet 7 mm thick
4 Non-ferrous screw with plastic-capped screw or countersunk non-ferrous screw with filler

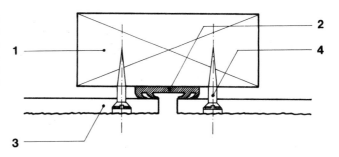

B An alternative method of forming the vertical joint on timber framing is to fix the sheet to aluminium alloy angle brackets. A clearance of 10 mm is provided between adjacent sheets and the gap is filled with a foam strip back and a gunned sealant.

1 Timber framing stud 100 mm x 50 mm
2 Aluminium alloy bracket 50 mm x 50 mm x 3 mm
3 Cladding sheet 10 mm thick
4 Fixing anchor
5 Foam strip backing
6 Gun grade sealant

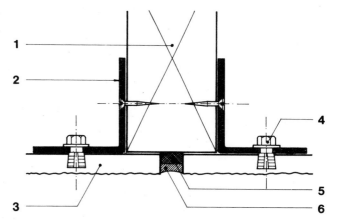

C Another method of fixing is designed to avoid perforation of the sheet by drilling of holes for screws. Rebated timber battens are bonded to the edge of the sheet and have aluminium alloy fixing angles with slotted holes. The angle is screwed to the vertical wall batten with a non-ferrous screw to give a clearance of 10 mm between adjacent sheets. The gap is then filled with foam strip backing and sealed with gun grade sealant.

1 Timber batten 50 mm x 50 mm
2 Cladding sheet 7 mm bonded to rebated timber batten
3 Aluminium alloy angle with slotted hole
4 Non-ferrous screw
5 Foam strip backing
6 Gun grade sealant

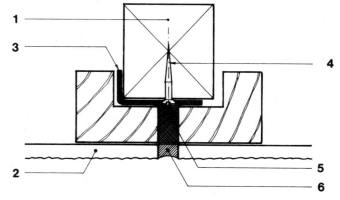

D When the structural framing is of aluminium alloy, the cladding sheet is bonded to an insulating board and a backing sheet to form a prefabricated panel. The panel is bedded in butyl mastic against a rebate on the mullion and held in position by a fixing bead. A silicone or polysulphide-based sealant may also be used, but an oil-based sealant should be avoided to prevent edge staining of the cladding sheet.

1 Aluminium alloy support mullion
2 Butyl bedding
3 Cladding sheet with insulating board and backing sheet
4 Fixing bead

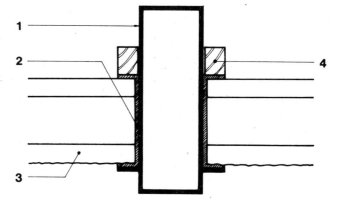

WALLS: Slate cladding slabs

A The slate cladding slabs are usually square or rectangular, roughened on the back face to give a key for bedding and finished slab are drilled to take cramps and S hooks. The cramps are fixed to the support wall by means of expanding bolts. The slab is bedded on mortar dabs: one to each corner of the slab and one in the centre.

1 Support wall
2 Mortar dab 12 mm bed joint
3 Slate slab 25 mm thick
4 Phosphor bronze cramp 4 mm diameter
6 S hook 4 mm diameter
7 Foam strip backing and polysulphide sealant

B For large wall areas and where the lower course of slabs is not directly supported, supports are provided at each 3 m level. One form of support is a phosphor bronze angle fixed to the support wall with two 7 mm expanding bolts. Slots are cut in the back face of the slab and the slab is bedded on mortar dabs 12 mm thick arranged at each corner and in the centre of the slab.

1 Concrete support wall
2 Phosphor bronze support angle
3 Expanding bolt 7 mm diameter
4 Mortar dab 12 mm bed joint
5 Slate slab 25 mm thick

C Another method of supporting slate slabs is to use a corbel in the form of copper, bronze, or phosphor bronze plates set into pockets in the support wall which are then filled with mortar. A slot is cut in the back face of the slate slab to take the corbel plate and the slab is bedded on mortar dabs.

1 Support wall
2 Phosphor bronze corbel plate
3 Cement mortar
4 Mortar dab 12 mm bed joint
5 Slate slab 25 mm thick

D The vertical joint between two slabs is made with a foam strip backing and polysulphide sealant. At an external corner it is common to form a birdsmouth joint with a clearance of 6 mm to take the sealant and backing material.

1 Support wall
2 Mortar dab 12 mm bed joint
3 Slate slab 25 mm thick
4 Foam strip
5 Slate slab 25 mm thick
6 Polysulphide sealant 6 mm square

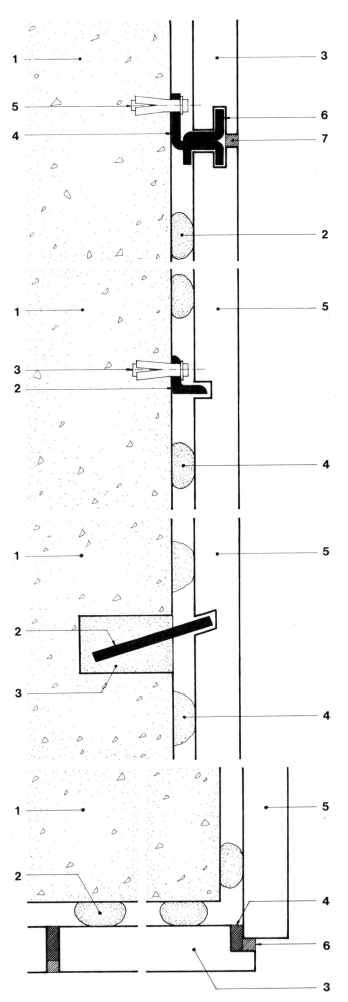

WALLS: Granite cladding units

A   Section through corbel plate and compression joint

The granite cladding units are normally not less than 40 mm thick with slots cut in the back face to take the corbel plates. A minimum void of not less than 20 mm is maintained between the face of the support wall and the back of the cladding units. The horizontal compression joint is designed mainly to accommodate the shrinkage of a reinforced concrete frame. The minimum clearance between adjacent cladding units is 13 mm, assuming a joint at each floor level.

1   Concrete support wall
2   Phosphor bronze corbel plate
3   Cement mortar 1 : 2 Portland cement : sand
4   Granite cladding unit
5   Expanded rubber or polyethylene back-up material
6   Two-part polysulphide gun sealant

B   Section through shelf angle and compression joint

An alternative method of fixing granite cladding units to a concrete frame is by means of a continuous shelf angle which is attached to the support wall with anchor bolts. The horizontal compression joint is placed immediately below the support angle. A minimum void of not less than 20 mm is maintained between the face of the support wall and the back of the cladding units.

1   Concrete support wall
2   Phosphor bronze shelf angle
3   Anchor bolt
4   Granite cladding unit
5   Expanded rubber or polyethylene back-up material
6   Two-part polysulphide gun sealant

C   Plan through vertical joint

A normal vertical joint between granite cladding units is filled and pointed as the work proceeds. The clearance between adjacent cladding units is not less than 5 mm or more than 13 mm. The front and back edges of the units must be buttered before the gap is filled with grout to prevent grout escaping into the void or outside.

1   Concrete support wall
2   Void 20 mm wide
3   Granite cladding unit 40 mm thick
4   Cement : sand mortar 1 : 4

D   Plan through vertical movement joint

Vertical movement joints are provided to accommodate movements in the length of the building. The joint is carried through the cladding units. The clearance is calculated to be sufficient to take account of the several dimensional changes that will occur. The gap is thoroughly cleaned out and packed with a compressible back-up material. The front of the joint is then pointed with a sealant able to accommodate the expected movement.

1   Concrete support wall
2   Void 20 mm wide
3   Granite cladding unit 40 mm thick
4   Expanded rubber or polyethylene back-up material
5   Two-part polysulphide gun sealant 20 mm wide

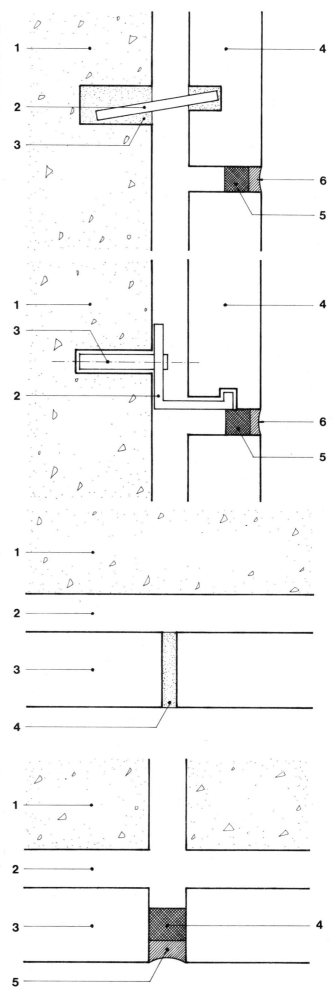

WALLS : Glass channel units

A Head

The aluminium head channel is placed in position on a strip of pitch polymer. The screw hole is filled with sealing compound and the screw screwed home. Gun grade sealing compound is applied to the gap between the face of the channel and the lintel internally and externally. The glass unit is placed in position and supported by a polychloroprene gasket externally. A polystyrene block is inserted to support the aluminium clip with a wedging strip that forms an internal bead.

1 Concrete lintel
2 Pitch polymer packing strip
3 Aluminium channel
4 Zinc plated steel screw 50 mm x 10 g at 300 mm centres
5 Gun grade sealing compound
6 Polychloroprene periphery gasket
7 Glass unit
8 Polystyrene block
9 Polychloroprene wedging strip and aluminium clip

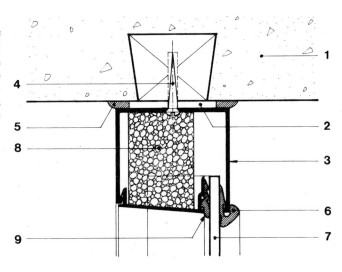

B Sill

At floor level or sill level an aluminium channel is positioned on a strip of pitch polymer and screwed through a hole filled with sealing compound. Two PVC setting blocks per unit are placed in the channel to support the glass. Weepholes are drilled at the bottom of the external flange of the channel. The glass unit is supported by a polychloroprene periphery gasket on the outer flange of the channel and a polychloroprene wedging strip attached to the internal clip.

1 Structural support slab
2 Pitch polymer packing strip
3 Aluminium channel
4 Zinc plated steel screw 50 mm x 10 g at 300 mm centres
5 Gun grade sealing compound
6 PVC setting block 50 mm x 12 mm x 5 mm
7 Weephole
8 Polychloroprene periphery gasket
9 Glass unit
10 Polychloroprene wedging strip and aluminium clip

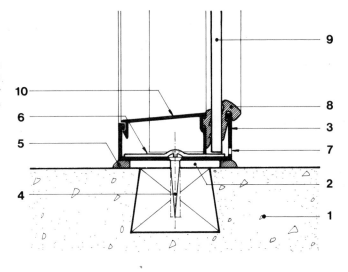

C Jamb

The junction between a glass unit and a wall is made with the standard aluminium channel as used at the head of an opening. The minimum recommended clearance between the face of the flange of the glass and the inside face of the channel is 6 mm. A spacer of expanded polystyrene strip is inserted between the flange of the unit and the web of the channel.

1 Structural wall
2 Pitch polymer packing strip
3 Aluminium channel
4 Zinc plated steel screw 50 mm x 10 g at 300 mm centres
5 Gun grade sealing compound
6 Polychloroprene periphery gasket
7 Glass unit
8 Expanded polystyrene strip
9 Polychloroprene wedging strip and aluminium clip

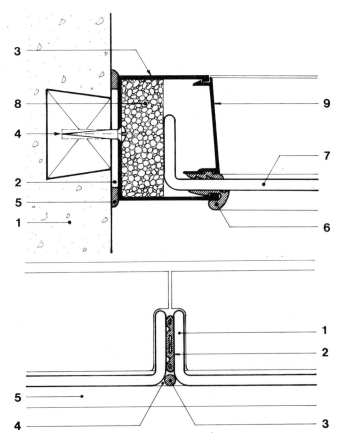

D

The vertical joint between two glass units is the polychloroprene jointing strip cut to a length approximately 25 mm longer than the glass unit. A small strip hook is inserted in the strip about 25 mm from the top and hooked over the top of one flange. The strip is straightened but not stretched. The second glass unit is offered up to it and the two flanges are clamped together using special flange clamps at about 600 mm centres to ensure a recommended clearance. The clamps must remain in position until jamb joints are wedged in position.

1 Glass unit
2 Polychloroprene gasket
3 Polychloroprene plug
4 Silicone mastic to cap plug
5 Polychloroprene periphery gasket

WALLS : Side wall patent glazing

A Head

When patent glazing bars are used to form side wall glazing, the joint at the head is made by means of a channel section that is screwed to fixing plugs in the lintel. A slotted aluminium fixing plate is bolted to the leg of the channel and retains the flanges of the glazing bar which is thereby able to move freely when subject to changes of temperature.

1 Concrete lintel
2 Fixing plug
3 Sealing compound
4 Aluminium head channel
5 Wood screw round head
6 Aluminium alloy fixing plate
7 Aluminium alloy glazing bar
8 Glass 6 mm thick

B Sill

The joint at the sill is made by means of an aluminium sill section that is bedded on the concrete base and screwed to fixing plugs. The glazing bar is retained by a slotting fixing plate which is bolted to the upstand flange of the sill. The weight of the glass is taken directly on the sill through a small rubber channel section.

1 Concrete base
2 Fixing plug
3 Bedding mortar
4 Aluminium sill
5 Wood screw countersunk head
6 Aluminium fixing plate
7 Aluminium alloy glazing bar
8 Rubber channel section
9 Glass 6 mm thick

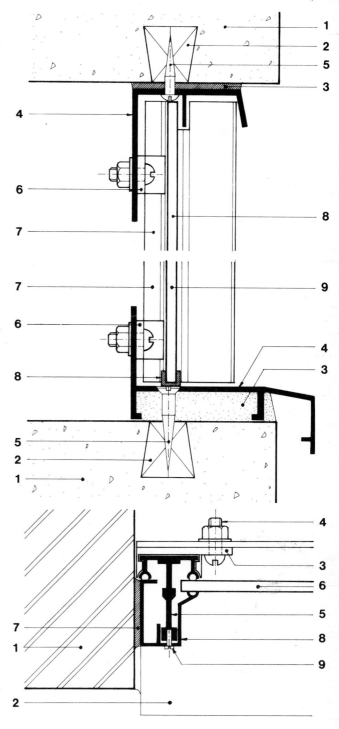

C Abutment

The joint at one end of a run of glazing that abuts a wall is made by means of a special fixing plate to suit the end condition and a special capping. The clearance between the end face of the brick and the capping is filled with sealing compound.

1 Brick wall
2 Aluminium sill section
3 Aluminium fixing plate
4 Bolt
5 Aluminium alloy glazing bar
6 Glass 6 mm thick
7 Sealing compound
8 Extruded aluminium capping
9 Stainless steel self-tapping screw

D Mullion

The intermediate glazing bar is made in a number of different profiles to suit the span of the bar. It is held at the upper and lower ends by fixing plates. The glass is bedded on greased asbestos fitted into a groove in the glazing bar, and is held in position by an extruded aluminium capping that is screwed to the top flange of the bar by stainless steel pan head self-tapping screws.

1 Aluminium sill section
2 Aluminium fixing plate
3 Bolt
4 Aluminium alloy glazing bar
5 Greased asbestos cord
6 Glass 6 mm thick
7 Extruded aluminium capping
8 Stainless steel self-tapping screw

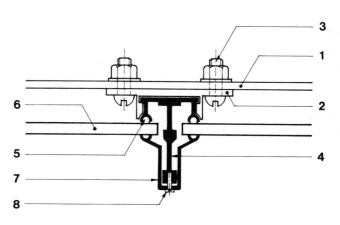

WALLS : Ceramic tile cladding

A The surface of the wall must be stable, clean, true, and otherwise suitable. A slurry is applied to act as a bonding agent. The bedding mortar is applied to average 15 mm in thickness. During tiling and before the bedding mortar sets, the joints are raked out to a depth of 10 mm. When the bedding mortar is set, jointing mortar is well filled in.

1 Support wall
2 Slurry 1 : 2-3 Portland cement : sand
3 Bedding mortar 1 : 4-5 Portland cement : sand
4 Ceramic tile with 10 mm joint clearance
5 Jointing mortar

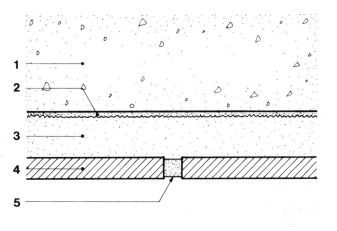

B Movement joints in the tile cladding must be provided at the main movement joints of the building and elsewhere to limit the area of tiling. The bedding mortar is fully raked out at the joint and the space filled with a movement joint filler. The clearance between the tiles is then filled with a pointing sealant.

1 Support wall
2 Slurry 1 : 2-3 Portland cement : sand
3 Bedding mortar 1 : 4-5 Portland cement : sand
4 Ceramic tile with 10 mm joint clearance
5 Movement joint filler
6 Pointing sealant

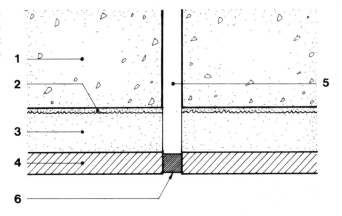

C Movement joints in the tile cladding are required at all internal and external angles of the building. At external corners, tiles are arranged to allow for a movement joint and the bedding mortar is raked out to provide for a movement joint filler that separates the mortar on the adjacent walls. An alternative form of corner is to use a special corner tile, as shown.

1 Support wall
2 Slurry 1 : 2-3 Portland cement : sand
3 Bedding mortar 1 : 4-5 Portland cement : sand
4 Ceramic tile with 10 mm joint clearance
5 Movement joint filler
6 Pointing sealant

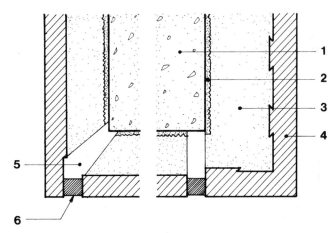

D Movement joints are also required at window and door openings and at positions where there is a change of material. The bedding mortar must be fully raked out so that the movement joint filler separates entirely the mortar from the adjoining materials. The pointing sealant should normally fill a space with a clearance of 10 mm and a depth of 10 mm

1 Brickwork
2 Timber frame
3 Support wall
4 Slurry 1 : 2-3 Portland cement : sand
5 Bedding mortar 1 : 4-5 Portland cement : sand
6 Ceramic tile with 10 mm clearance
7 Movement joint filler
8 Pointing sealant

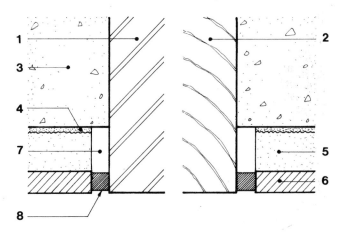

WINDOWS : Glazing into timber frames

A Rebate without bead glazed with putty

The rebate must be clean, dry and free from frost and grease. Softwood frames are primed. Absorbent hardwoods require no preparation. For small panes with putty glazing in low exposure conditions the minimum rebate depth is 12 mm and rebate width 19 mm. The minimum edge clearance is 3 mm. The bed putty is applied by hand or knife. The glass is positioned and secured with glazing sprigs spaced not more than 350 mm apart. The front putty is then applied and painted within 28 days.

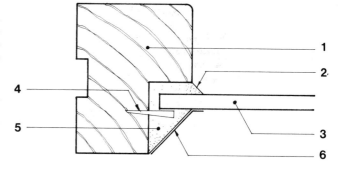

1 Absorbent hardwood or primed softwood frame
2 Bed putty
3 Glass 4 mm thick
4 Glazing sprig
5 Front putty
6 Paint

B Rebate with external bead glazed with non-setting compound

The surfaces of the rebate must be sealed with a timber sealer. Setting blocks at the sill and location blocks at the jambs and head are positioned to maintain an even edge clearance. Distance pieces are positioned to maintain a face clearance of 3 mm on both sides of the glass, opposite each other, and not more than 300 mm apart. The non-setting compound is used as a bed for the glass and for the external timber bead. The bead is fixed with panel pins or screws.

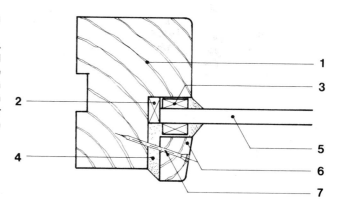

1 Sealed timber frame
2 Location block
3 Distance piece
4 Non-setting compound
5 Glass 4 mm thick
6 Sealed timber bead
7 Panel pin

C Rebate with internal bead glazed with non-setting compound

The surfaces of the rebate must be sealed with a timber sealer. Setting blocks at the sill and location blocks at the jambs and head are positioned to maintain an even edge clearance. Distance pieces are positioned to maintain a face clearance of 3 mm on both sides of the glass, opposite each other, and not more than 300 mm apart. The glass is bedded on non-setting compound. The internal bead is bedded against the glass also on non-setting compound and is fixed to the frame with panel pins or screws.

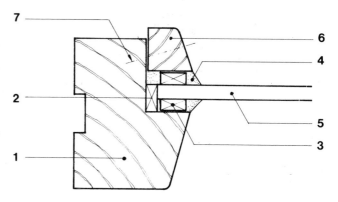
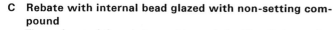

1 Sealed timber frame
2 Location block
3 Distance piece
4 Non-setting compound
5 Glass 4 mm thick
6 Sealed timber bead
7 Panel pin

D Rebate with internal bead and glazing channel

The rebate must be clean, dry and free from grease. The depth and width of rebate are made to suit the sizes of the standard range of glazing channel sections that vary to fit the thicknesses of single sheets of glass and double glazed units. The gasket channel in rectangular form is fitted round the perimeter of the glass unit and held in compression by the bead which is screwed to the frame.

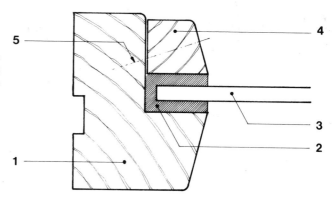

1 Hardwood frame
2 Polychloroprene glazing channel
3 Glass 4 mm thick
4 Hardwood bead
5 Wood screw

A Head

The opening light of this horizontally pivoted high performance timber window is fitted with a continuous black polychloroprene weather strip that is paint and water repellent and is fixed with non-rusting staples. The joint profile of the head section and of the combined head drip are provided with effective drips.

1 Timber head section ex 75 mm x 63 mm
2 Timber opening light section ex 63 mm x 50 mm
3 Continuous black polychloroprene weather strip
4 Non-rusting staple

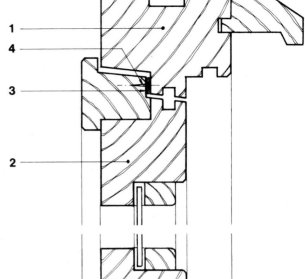

B Sill

The sill section is machined on the back face to take the stop for the pivotted opening light and the tongue of a window board. The front face is machined to provide a steeply sloping sill and a rebate for a timber sub-sill section.

1 Timber sill section ex 75 mm x 75 mm
2 Timber opening light section ex 63 mm x 50 mm
3 Continuous black polychloroprene weather strip
4 Non-rusting staple

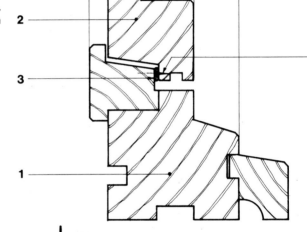

C Jamb

The basic jamb section is the same both above and below the pivot, but the rebated stop that is fixed to the opening light above the pivot is slightly modified in cross section and fixed to the jamb below the pivot. The weather strip is fixed to the stop above the pivot and to the frame of the opening light below the pivot.

1 Timber jamb ex 75 mm x 63 mm
2 Timber opening light ex 63 mm x 50 mm
3 Timber stop ex 50 mm x 44 mm
4 Continuous black polychloroprene weather strip

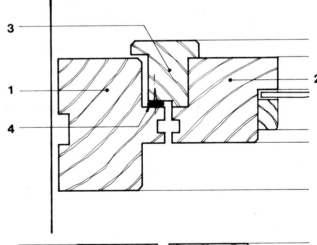

D Mullion

Windows may be coupled to form composite units and also maintain modular coordinating sizes. They are linked with a special polychloroprene compressible gasket that provides a clearance of 5 mm. The projecting flanges of the gasket fit into a central groove in the back face of each jamb. Separate head drips and sub-sills are fitted to ensure continuous protection across the separate windows.

1 Timber jamb ex 75 mm x 63 mm
2 Polychloroprene compressible gasket to give 5 mm clearance
3 Timber jamb ex 75 mm x 63 mm

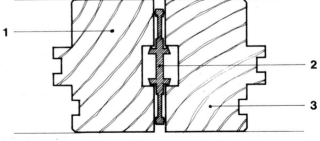

WINDOWS : Domestic vinyl sheathed timber

A Head

The timber sections of the frames and sashes are encased in a layer of PVC 1 mm in thickness. The top hung sash is hung on cranked rustproofed steel hinges that are concealed within the gap between the sash and the head member. The gap at the back is closed by a weather strip secured to the rebate of the head.

1 Head member
2 Sash
3 Rustproofed steel hinge
4 Wood screw
5 Weather strip

B Sill

The sill section of the window frame is grooved to fit over a separate projecting sill. There is a gap between the frame of the sash and the sill that is open to the outside air at the front. At the back it is closed by a weather strip secured to the rebate of the sill. The channel drip that runs around the frame is covered along the sill with a polychloroprene filler strip.

1 Sill member
2 Sash
3 Polychloroprene filler strip
4 Weather strip

C Jamb

The joint between the sash and the jamb is similar to the joint at the head of the frame. The gap between the two frame members is closed at the back by the weather strip and open to the outside air at the front, thereby forming an air pressure chamber. The continuous weather strip at the back is secured to the rebate of the jamb.

1 Jamb
2 Sash
3 Weather strip

D Mullion

The joint between two windows placed side by side is formed by means of a timber batten that fits the grooves in the back of the frames thereby providing alignment and a standard clearance between the two frames of 6 mm. The two frames are fastened together with a bolt. The gap at the front and at the back is closed with a PVC strip that clips into position.

1 Window jamb
2 Timber batten
3 Bolt
4 PVC strip

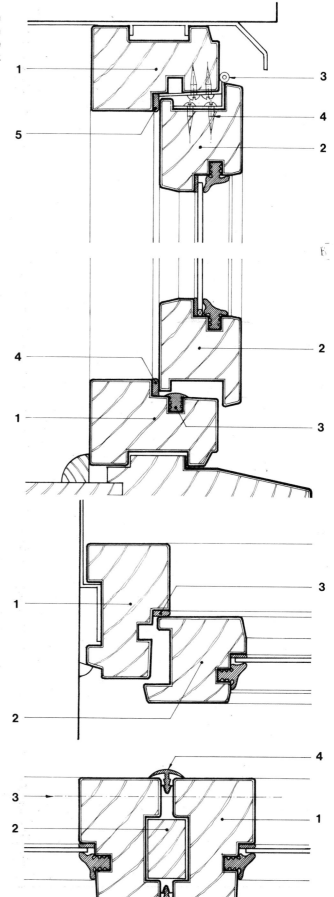

WINDOWS: Steel casements in brickwork

A Head

Windows constructed of galvanized hot rolled steel sections can be built directly into masonry openings. At the head of the window an adjustable fixing lug is screwed to a plug in the lintel. The window frame is positioned to give the recommended clearance of 3 mm and secured to the lug with a countersunk screw. Mastic pointing is applied on the outside to seal the gap between the frame and the lintel.

1 Concrete lintel
2 Adjustable fixing lug of galvanized steel
3 40 mm pan head passivated wood screw
4 Window frame
5 6 mm diameter countersunk screw and nut
6 Waterproof cement fillet
7 Mastic pointing

B Sill

At the sill a fixing lug is screwed to the top of the wall and connected to the window frame with a countersunk screw. The pressed galvanized steel sill is bedded on a waterproof cement fillet and the gap between the lower flange of the window frame and the top flange of the sill is pointed with mastic pointing.

1 Brickwork wall
2 Fixing lug
3 40 mm countersunk wood screw
4 Window frame
5 12 mm countersunk screw and nut
6 Galvanized pressed steel sill
7 Mastic pointing

C Jamb

At the junction between the window and the side of the window opening the window frame is connected to the wall with an adjustable fixing lug. A waterproof cement fillet fills the gap between the frame section and the wall. Mastic pointing is then applied on the outside to seal the gap between the flange of the section and the wall.

1 Wall
2 Adjustable fixing lug
3 40 mm pan head passivated wood screw
4 Window frame
5 6 mm diameter countersunk screw and nut
6 Waterproof cement fillet
7 Mastic pointing

D Mullion

1 Galvanized hot rolled steel window frame section
2 Steel coupling section
3 Polystyrene filler strip
4 Countersunk head rustproof coupling screw
5 Countersunk nut
6 Bedding compound

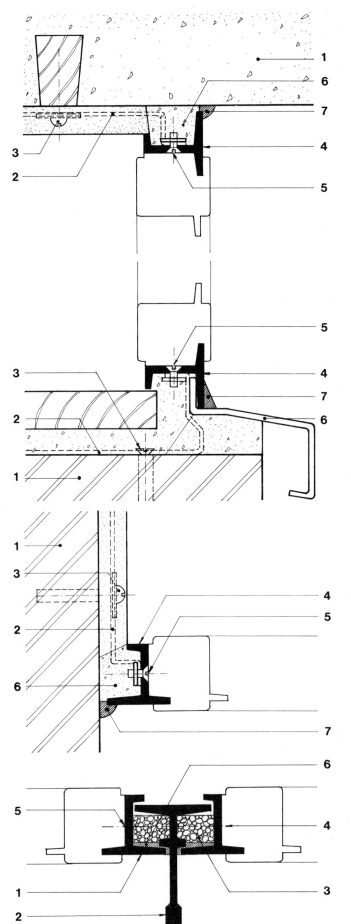

WINDOWS : Steel

A Transom

When steel window units are assembled one above the other the coupling bar is in the form of a steel transom section. The top member of the lower window unit is filled with a continuous filler strip of polystyrene which is packed with bedding compound. The transom is then placed in position. A filler strip and bedding compound are packed along the top of the transom and the upper window unit is positioned and fastened to the lower unit with coupling screws and nuts.

1 Steel window frame
2 Bedding compound
3 Polystyrene continuous filler strip
4 Steel transom
5 Rustproofed coupling screw with countersunk head

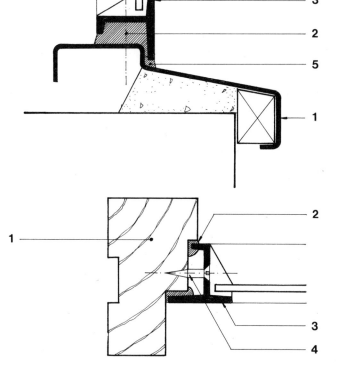

B Sill

When a steel window is used with a standard pressed steel sill, the lower channel of the window section is packed with bedding compound and positioned with its flange overlapping the rebate of the sill. The window is fastened to the sill with a coupling screw and the gap between the flange of the window and the sill is sealed with bedding compound or a gun grade mastic sealant.

1 Pressed steel sill
2 Bedding compound
3 Steel window frame
4 Rustproofed coupling screw with countersunk head
5 Bedding compound or gun grade mastic sealant.

C Jamb

When a steel window is used in conjunction with a timber subframe bedding compound is applied to the rebates of the sub-frame to take the two legs of the window section. The window section is then fastened to the timber subframe with rustproofed wood screws.

1 Timber sub-frame
2 Bedding compound
3 Steel window frame
4 Rustproofed wood screw countersunk head

D Mullion

When two steel window units are assembled side by side the coupling bar is in the form of a steel mullion section with a projecting leg sized to suit the height of the window. Bedding compound is packed against the outer leg of the section and a continuous filler strip is inserted. The coupling mullion is then positioned and the second widow unit is positioned and fastened to the first window unit with coupling screws and nuts.

1 Steel window frame
2 Bedding compound
3 Polystyrene continuous filler strip
4 Coupling mullion
5 Rustproofed coupling screw with countersunk head

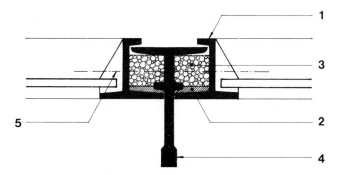

WINDOWS: Metal casements in masonry

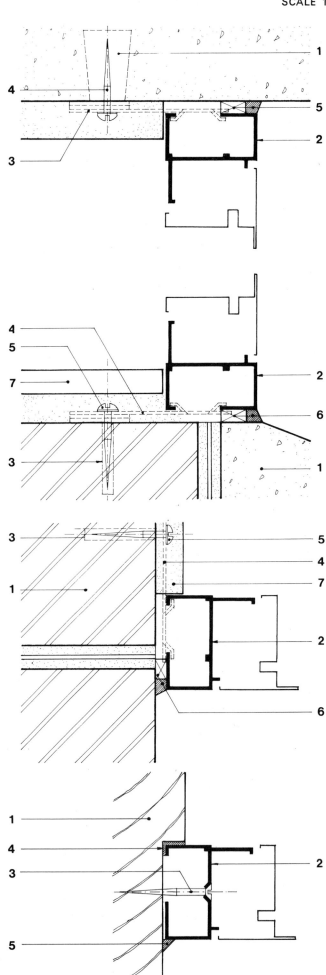

A Head

The jointing of an aluminium window frame to a concrete lintel consists in first placing the window in the opening and ensuring a minimum clearance of 6 mm between the joint face of the window and that of the underside of the lintel. An adjustable lug that clips in the window frame section is screwed to a plug cast in the lintel. The external joint is then packed with a backing strip and the joint is pointed. The internal joint is masked by the plaster or other finish.

1 Plug cast in concrete lintel
2 Aluminium window frame
3 Adjustable lug
4 Round head rustproof wood screw 36 mm long
5 Backing strip and pointing

B Sill

When an aluminium window is jointed to a concrete sill it is advantageous to place the window centrally over the joint between the external wall and the inner lining. A minimum clearance of 6 mm between the top face of the sill and the joint face of the window should be maintained and the window is fixed by means of an adjustable lug that clips into the window frame and is screwed to an insert plug. The external joint is packed with a backing strip for the pointing that is applied to seal the joint. The inner joint is masked by the bedding for the tile sill.

1 Concrete sill
2 Aluminium window frame
3 Plug
4 Adjustable lug
5 Round head rustproof wood screw
6 Backing strip and pointing
7 Tile sill on mortar bed

C Jamb

The jointing between the aluminium window frame and the brickwork jamb is similar to that used at the lintel. A minimum clearance of 6 mm is recommended between the joint face of the brickwork and the back face of the window frame. The adjustable lug is clipped to the frame and screwed to a plug in the brickwork inner leaf. The external joint is packed with a backing strip to support the pointing. The inner joint is covered with the plaster reveal.

1 Brickwork jamb
2 Window frame
3 Plug
4 Adjustable lug
5 Round head rustproof wood screw
6 Backing strip and pointing
7 Plaster

D Jamb

An alternative method of making the joint between the window frame and the brickwork jamb is to provide a rebated timber surround frame. The window frame rebate is 12 mm wide and the recommended clearance between the surround frame and the window is 1.5 mm. The bedding compound is applied to the end of the rebate. The window frame is screwed to the timber with a countersunk head wood screw. The external joint is pointed with a sealant.

1 Timber surround frame jamb
2 Aluminium window frame
3 Countersunk head rustproof wood screw
4 Bedding compound
5 Sealant

WINDOWS: Aluminium casements

A Head

The hinged joint between the outward opening top hung vent and the window frame is made by means of two interlocking extrusions at the head of the vent and the window frame. The extrusion for the vent is also shaped so as to provide channels for the weather stripping and the glazing gasket and a flange to serve as a rebate for the glass.

1 Aluminium window frame
2 Aluminium top hung vent frame
3 Continuous polychloroprene weather strip

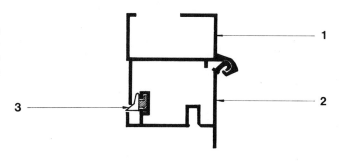

B Transom

The joint between windows placed one above the other is made by means of a transom in the form of an aluminium extrusion with or without a projecting sill. The transom is fitted over the lower window with a bedding compound applied to the external joint. The upper window is positioned against the back flange. The assembly is then fixed together with a pan head screw and a specially shaped fixing clip. The external joint is sealed with a polyethylene backing strip and pointing sealant.

1 Lower window frame
2 Bedding compound
3 Aluminium transom section
4 Upper window frame
5 Fixing clip
6 Pan head screw 25 mm long
7 Polyethylene strip 6 mm x 6 mm
8 Pointing sealant

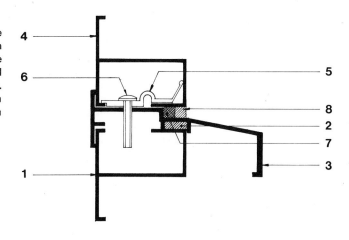

C Jamb

The joint between the opening vent frame and the window frame combines an open joint and a weather strip. The adjoining sections are shaped to provide a zone between the two frames that is connected to the outside by an open joint. The gap width is wide enough to prevent capillary action. The inner flange of the vent section incorporates a groove designed to take a specially shaped continuous polychloroprene section that provides a seal against air and water.

1 Aluminium window frame
2 Aluminium top hung vent frame
3 Continuous polychloroprene weather strip

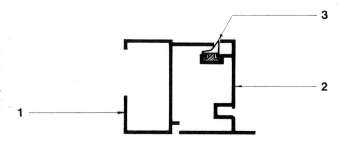

D Mullion

The joint between windows placed side by side is made with a mullion in the form of an aluminium extrusion designed to take the fixing internally and the seals externally. The head of a bolt engages in a groove at the end of the mullion. A nut on this bolt clamps a clamping bracket against the window frames and a mullion cover is then fitted. Externally the channel on both sides of the mullion is filled with a foam backing strip and a pointing sealant.

1 Aluminium mullion
2 Bolt
3 Aluminium window frame
4 Clamping bracket
5 Hexagonal nut
6 Mullion cover section
7 Polyethylene strip
8 Pointing sealant

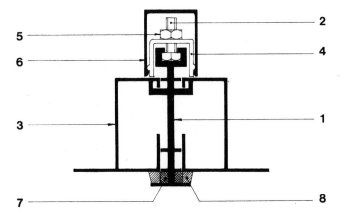

WINDOWS: Joints for glazing

A Glazing into steel window frames is normally done on site. The rebate section must be thoroughly clean, dry and free from grease. The glazing cleat is screwed to the frame section with a flat head rustproof screw. Metal casement putty is applied to the back face of the angle seating. Distance pieces are positioned to suit the thickness of glass and the metal casement putty is finished at the required slope to the edge of the rebate.

1 Steel window frame section
2 Glazing cleat
3 Flat head rustproof screw
4 Metal casement putty, bed putty
5 Glass 4 mm thick
6 Distance piece
7 Metal casement putty, front putty

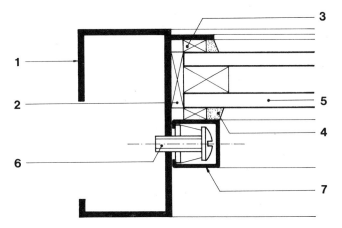

B An alternative method of glazing on site is to use glazing beads. With aluminium window frames, location blocks and distance pieces are used to position the glass unit which is bedded in non-setting glazing compound. The compound is also used to bed the bead which is held by means of a bead stud and a pan head rustproof screw 12 mm long. Setting blocks are used to carry the weight of the glazing unit on the lower horizontal section.

1 Aluminium window frame jamb section
2 Location block
3 Distance piece
4 Non-setting glazing compound
5 Double glazed unit
6 Pan head rustproof screw and bead stud
7 Aluminium bead

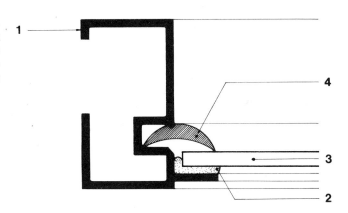

C An alternative and more recent method of glazing into an aluminium window frame is by means of a PVC glazing strip. A special window frame extrusion contains a channel formed to engage the shaped PVC glazing strip which is clipped into position after the glass has been bedded on a non-setting glazing compound.

1 Aluminium window frame jamb section
2 Non-setting glazing compound
3 Glass 4 mm thick
4 PVC glazing strip

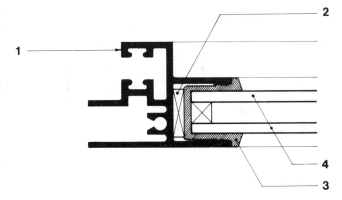

D Another method of glazing into an aluminium window frame is to use a glazing gasket. In this case, the window is glazed in the factory and the corners of the glazing gasket are sealed with gun-grade sealing compound of a colour to match the gasket. Other sections of gasket are used to take different glass thicknesses and double glazing units. For double glazing, setting blocks are required at the bottom of the channel of the sill section to take the weight of the glass.

1 Aluminium window frame jamb section
2 Distance piece
3 Glazing gasket
4 Double glazing unit

A   Single glazing bedded in sealant

One method of glazing directly into a precast concrete panel is by means of a sealant. Distance pieces are positioned at intervals of 400 mm starting at 75 mm from the corner of the rebate. The glass is placed on setting blocks. The sealant is gunned in so as to completely fill the gap and is tooled to a smooth triangular fillet on both sides of the glass.

1   Concrete panel
2   Setting block
3   Distance piece
4   Glass 6 mm thick
5   2-part polysulphide rubber sealant
6   Mortar bed
7   Slate sill

B   Single glazing with structural gasket

Another method of glazing into a precast concrete panel is by means of a structural gasket. A rigid PVC channel section is cast into the panel so as to frame the opening. The finned spline of the structural glazing gasket is fitted into the groove of the channel to retain the lips of the gasket against the frame face. The glass is then positioned on setting blocks in the groove of the gasket and is sealed by means of a lock strip inserted continuously along the inside of the gasket and mitred at the corners.

1   Concrete panel
2   PVC channel
3   Rubber compound structural glazing gasket
4   Setting block
5   Glass 12 mm thick
6   Rubber compound lock strip

C   Single glazing with tape and metal bead

The opening in the precast concrete panel must be square and plumb and have a rebate 33 mm wide x 21 mm high. The rebate is cleaned and coated with primer. Tape is placed round the opening with corners butt jointed. Setting blocks are positioned and the glass positioned and pressed home. Sealant is gunned around the edge of the glass. The aluminium angle bead is positioned to clear the inside face of the glass by 3 mm and the cover plate is snapped on. Vision strip is compressed into the gap between the bead and the glass. A sealant is gunned into the gap above the tape externally.

1   Concrete panel
2   Primer
3   Tape bedding compound
4   Setting block
5   Sealant 1-part gun applied
6   Glass 6 mm thick
7   Aluminium angle bead
8   Aluminium cover strip
9   Vision strip
10   Sealant 1-part gun applied

D   Double glazing with tape and metal bead

The method of fixing double glazing is similar to that used for single glazing. The rebate required is 45 mm wide and 21 mm high. The aluminium angle bead is screwed to plastic blocks cast into the concrete 75 mm from each corner and at 200 mm centres.

1   Concrete panel
2   Primer
3   Tape bedding compound
4   Setting block
5   Sealant 1-part gun applied
6   Double glazed unit 18 mm overall thickness
7   Aluminium angle bead
8   Aluminium cover strip
9   Vision strip
10   Sealant 1-part gun applied

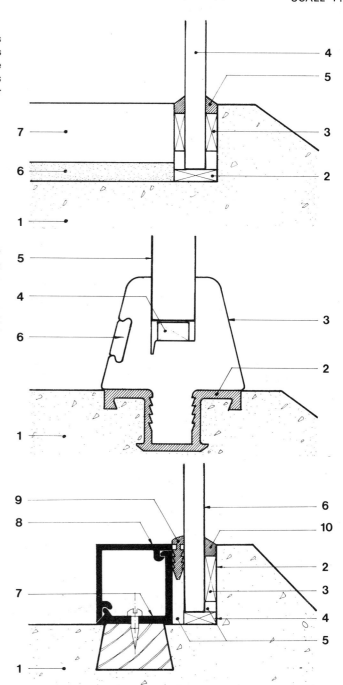

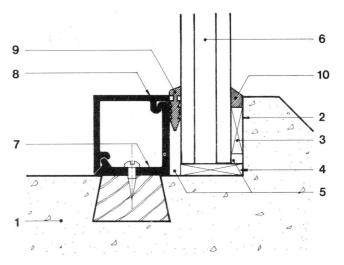

A Head

It is customary good practice to fix standard domestic steel windows into timber surround frames. A clearance of 1.5 mm is allowed between the steel sections and the timber rebate. A bedding compound is applied to the back and front legs of the steel section. The window section is screwed to the frame with countersunk rustproof wood screws.

1 Timber head
2 Bedding compound
3 Steel window frame
4 Countersunk rustproof wood screw 32 mm long

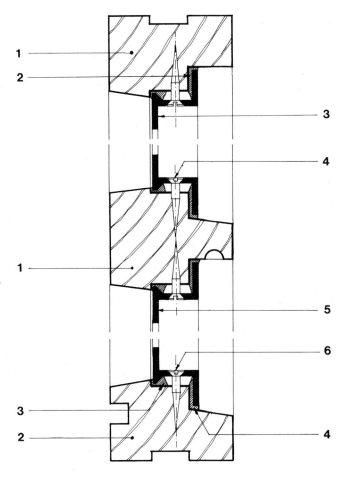

B Transom and Sill

The same method of fixing is used at the transom and sill. The surface of the timber must be clean, dry and free from dust and grease.

1 Timber transom
2 Timber sill
3 Bedding compound
4 Bedding compound
5 Steel window frame
6 Countersunk rustproof wood screw 32 mm long

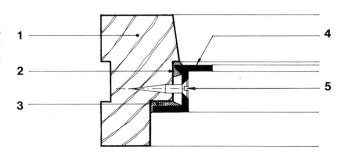

C Jamb

The joint between the steel window frame and the timber jamb is the same as that used at the head of the window and has a minimum clearance of 1.5 mm. The minimum clearance between the timber surround frame and the wall opening is 3 mm.

1 Timber jamb
2 Bedding compound
3 Bedding compound
4 Steel window frame
5 Countersunk rustproof wood screw 32 mm long

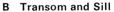

D Mullion

The timber mullion is designed to provide for the same method of jointing as elsewhere. In this example, the width of the mullion is such that the use of a single mullion does not permit modular coordinating sizes to be used for the steel windows as well as the timber surround frame simultaneously.

1 Timber mullion
2 Bedding compound
3 Bedding compound
4 Steel window frame
5 Countersunk rustproof wood screw 32 mm long

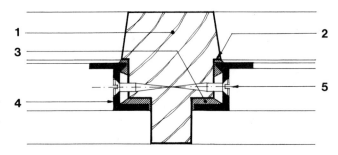

WINDOWS : Curtain wall glazing

A Head

The windows are formed of three pieces of clear polished plate glass mounted in a frame made of special aluminium extrusions. At the head of the opening the plate glass is held in position between a continuous polychloroprene spacer at the front and a continuous polychloroprene rope at the back. The channels formed externally and internally are sealed with silicone sealant.

1 Aluminium extrusion
2 Continuous polychloroprene face spacer
3 Continuous polychloroprene rope
4 Clear polished plate glass 22 mm thick
5 Silicone sealant

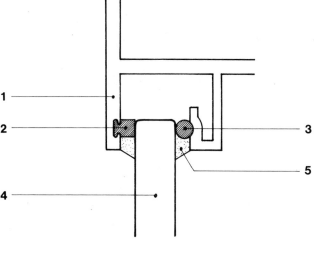

B Sill

The weight of the glass is transmitted to the support frame through polychloroprene setting blocks. The glass is located between polychloroprene spacers held in the frame. The channels formed externally and internally are sealed with silicone sealant.

1 Aluminium extrusion
2 Polychloroprene setting block
3 Polychloroprene face spacer
4 Continuous polychloroprene rope
5 Clear polished plate glass 22 mm thick
6 Silicone sealant

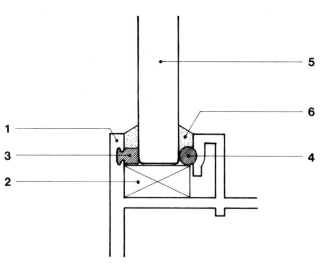

C Glass-to-glass vertical joint

The joint between adjacent pieces of glass is without a mullion. A clear vinyl tube is placed centrally between the two pieces of glass and the channel internally and externally is filled with clear silicone sealant.

1 Clear polished plate glass 22 mm thick
2 Clear polished plate glass 22 mm thick
3 Clear vinyl tube 8 mm diameter
4 Clear silicone sealant
5 Clear silicone sealant

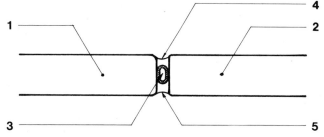

D Jamb

The joint between the plate glass and the aluminium support frame at the jamb is made in the same way as at the head, described in A above.

1 Aluminium extrusion
2 Continuous polychloroprene face spacer
3 Continuous polychloroprene rope
4 Clear polished plate glass 22 mm thick
5 Silicone sealant

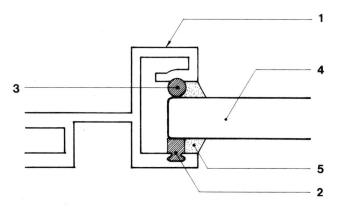

WINDOWS: Glazing into patent glazing bars

A Glazing with extruded aluminium wings

There are several alternative methods used to retain glass on patent glazing bars. With an extruded aluminium patent glazing bar having an external web the glass is bedded on greased asbestos cord. Extruded aluminium wings which contain greased asbestos cord are placed on both sides of the web and held firmly in position by means of round head screws and nuts.

1 Extruded aluminium glazing bar
2 Greased asbestos cord
3 Glass 6 mm thick
4 Extruded aluminium wing
5 Round head screw and nut

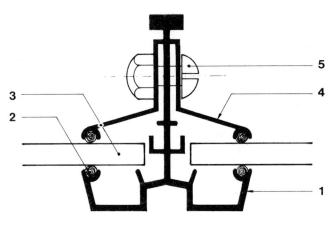

B Glazing with extruded aluminium external cap

With an extruded aluminium patent glazing bar having an internal web the glass is bedded on greased asbestos cord. Snap-on clips are positioned to form fixing pads to take the grub screws which are used to fix the extruded aluminium external cap. The cap contains greased asbestos cord that is pressed firmly against the external surface of the glass.

1 Extruded aluminium glazing bar
2 Greased asbestos cord
3 Glass 6 mm thick
4 Extruded aluminium external cap
5 Aluminium snap-on clip at 460 mm centres
6 Aluminium round head grub screw and washer

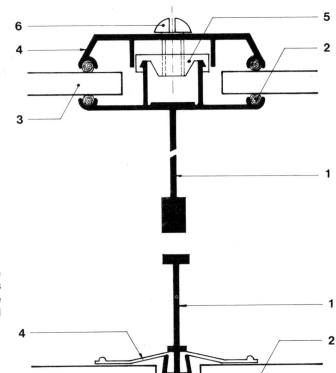

C Glazing with continuous lead wings

Another method of glazing is to use an extruded aluminium glazing bar with an external web and with special projections designed to hold a continuous lead wing on both sides of the bar. The glass is supported on greased asbestos cord and held down by the lead wings.

1 Extruded aluminium glazing bar
2 Greased asbestos cord
3 Glass 6 mm thick
4 Continuous lead wing

D Glazing with lead clothed steel glazing bar

Another form of bar is a rolled steel T section clothed in lead and having lead wings attached to the flange of the T which are used to support the glass and external lead wings attached to the web of the T to retain the glass in position. The air spaces between the pairs of lead wings form drainage channels both externally and internally.

1 Rustproofed steel glazing bar clothed in lead
2 Lead support wing
3 Glass 6 mm thick
4 Continuous lead wing

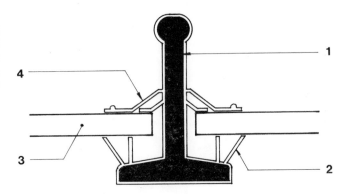

A Head

Flexible spring bronze weather strips are designed to seal and weatherproof existing external doors or new doors. The strips are nailed to the door frame at regular intervals of 25 mm so as to compress against the outer edge of the door when it is closed.

1 Door head
2 Flexible spring bronze weather strip
3 Brass nail 18 mm long at 25 mm centres
4 Timber door

B Sill

The joint at the sill is formed by means of a special interlocking sill section and hook strip combined with a weather strip. The sill is screwed to the door sill. The underside of the door is rebated to take the hook strip which is nailed at 25 mm centres. The weather strip is then separately nailed and compresses against the top of the threshold when the door is closed.

1 Hardwood sill
2 Aluminium alloy sill section
3 Aluminium wood screw at 200 mm centres
4 Bronze hook strip
5 Flexible spring bronze weather strip
6 Brass nail 18 mm long at 25 mm centres
7 Timber door

C Jamb: hinge side

The weather strip is nailed to the front edge of the jamb and the strip continues across flaps of the hinges. The spring bronze strip is tempered and has hemmed edges for contact with the timber surfaces.

1 Door jamb: hinge side
2 Flexible spring bronze weather strip
3 Brass nail 18 mm long at 25 mm centres
4 Timber door

D Jamb: lock side

On the lock side of the door jamb a special lockplate strip is fitted around the lock and connects with the continuous weather strip along the jamb.

1 Door jamb: lock side
2 Flexible spring bronze weather strip
3 Brass nail 18 mm long at 25 mm centres
4 Timber door

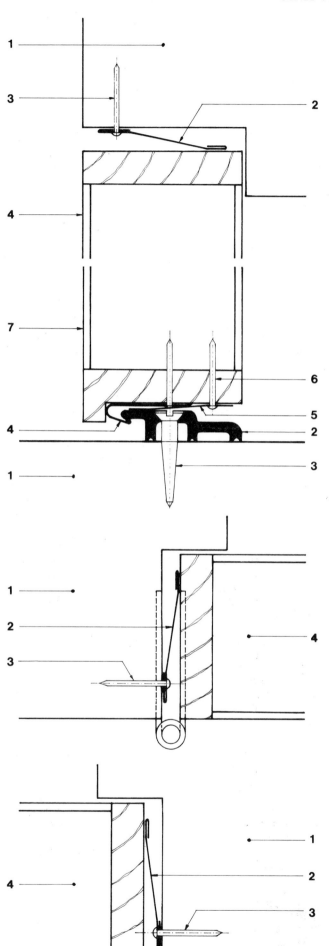

143

EXTERNAL DOORS: Aluminium sliding frames

A Head

The aluminium door frame is positioned in the opening with a minimum clearance of 3 mm between the top of the head member and the underside of the concrete head. A special adjustable lug is clipped to the flanges of the frame, 150 mm from each end and at 600 mm centres, and is screwed to a plug in the concrete. A triangular fillet of pointing is applied externally along the top of the frame to close the gap and to seal the joint.

1 Concrete head
2 Aluminium door frame head member
3 Nylon plug
4 Adjustable lug
5 Pan head rustproof wood screw 36 mm long
6 Pointing

B Sill

A sill support member is positioned on the concrete base, levelled by means of shims to give a minimum clearance of 3 mm, and screwed to a nylon plug in the concrete by rustproof wood screws. A triangular fillet of pointing is applied externally to seal the gap between the sill support and the concrete. The sill track is then screwed to the sill support member using pan head stainless steel screws.

1 Concrete base
2 Nylon plug
3 Shim
4 Aluminium sill support member
5 Pan head rustproof wood screw
6 Pointing
7 Aluminium sill track

C Concrete Jamb

At a concrete jamb, the door frame is secured with an adjustable lug 150 mm from each end and at 600 mm centres. The lug is clipped to the flanges at the back of the frame and screwed to a plug inserted in the concrete with a countersunk head rustproof wood screw. At the lock position additional fixing is provided by a countersunk stainless steel wood screw 50 mm long. The external gap is sealed with a triangular fillet of pointing.

1 Concrete jamb
2 Nylon plug
3 Adjustable lug
4 Countersunk head rustproof wood screw
5 Aluminium frame side member
6 Countersunk stainless steel wood screw
7 Pointing

D Timber Jamb

At a timber jamb, the door frame side member is secured directly to the jamb by means of a countersunk stainless steel wood screw inserted in holes provided in the frame member. Shims are used at fixing positions to maintain a minimum clearance of 3 mm between the back of the frame and the joint face of the timber. A triangular fillet is applied externally to seal the gap between the aluminium frame member and timber jamb.

1 Timber jamb
2 Aluminium door frame side member
3 Shim
4 Countersunk stainless steel wood screw
5 Pointing

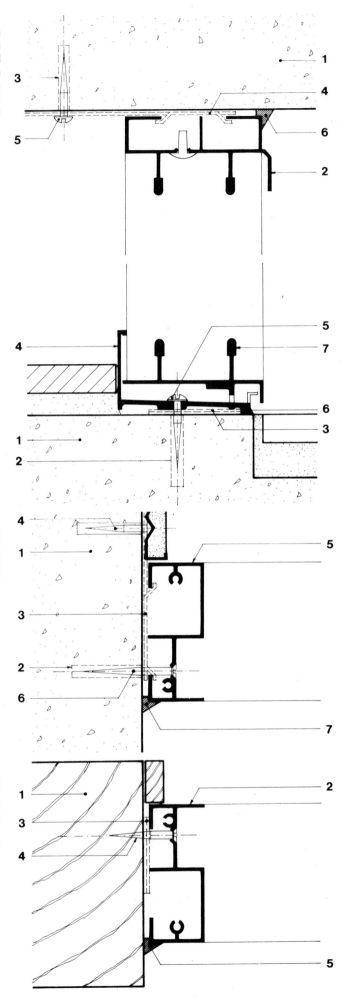

EXTERNAL DOORS : Aluminium framed sliding panels

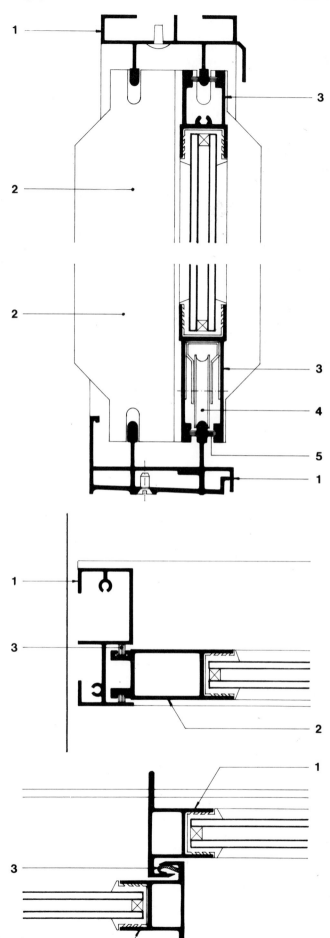

A Head

The glazed sliding aluminium framed panels are fitted to the aluminium surround frame from outside. The inner panel is lifted up at an angle so that its upper channel is positioned astride the inner head track. The panel is then lowered so that the adjustable wheel runs on the inner sill track. The outer panel is then assembled in a similar manner on the outer head and sill tracks. Each panel can be raised or lowered, to ensure that the panel is level with the sill and plumb with the jamb, by means of a pan head screw on the wheel assembly.

1 Surround frame head section
2 Inner glazed sliding aluminium framed panel
3 Outer glazed sliding aluminium framed panel

B Sill

The upper and lower channel sections of the sliding framed panels are fitted with pile weather strips on both sides. The weather strips serve as guides and run at each side of the fixed track on the head and on the sill of the surround frame. Water that collects in the sill drains into the sill support channel and out through drainage slots cut in its outer flange.

1 Surround frame sill section
2 Inner glazed sliding framed panel
3 Outer glazed sliding framed panel
4 Adjustable wheel
5 Pile weather strip

C Jamb

The joint between a sliding framed panel and the jamb surround frame is formed by means of interlocking channels that are part of the respective panel and jamb sections. The channel of the jamb has dovetail-shaped slots on the outer sides that contain vertical pile weather strip. The weather strip fits the sides of the channel in the jamb. Any water that may collect in the channel from past the outer weather strip finds its way downwards to the sill channel and thence to the sill support drainage channel.

1 Surround frame jamb section
2 Outer glazed sliding framed panel
3 Pile weather strip

D Meeting rails

The joint between the inner and outer sliding framed panels is formed by means of two special interlocking aluminium sections that contain a continuous vertical weather strip. Each section also provides additional transverse rigidity at this position as well as providing a channel to take the gasket for the double glazing.

1 Inner glazed sliding framed panel
2 Outer glazed sliding framed panel
3 Weather strip

A Section of door set head with ceiling
The storey height door set is designed to provide a clearance of
24 mm between the top of the door set head and the ceiling.
Providing there is no deflection of the ceiling, the gap on both
sides of the frame is closed with architrave/cover strips fitted on
site. When required, the gap above the door head is filled with a
timber blocking piece.

1 Ceiling
2 Timber head of door set
3 Timber architrave

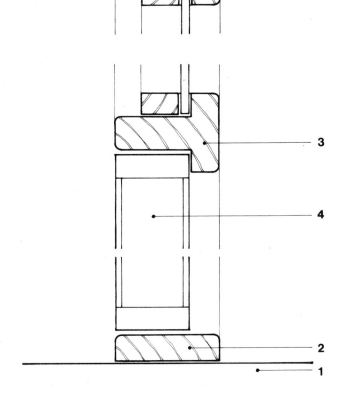

B Section of door set transom and sill
The sill of the door set is positioned so that its underside is level
with the finished floor. The sill, transom and door form an
integral part of the door set which is fixed on both sides to the
adjoining partitions.

1 Floor
2 Timber sill
3 Timber transom of door set
4 Timber door

C Door set jamb and partition 50 mm thick
The door set is fixed to the partition by means of screws at four
points in each jamb. The jambs are drilled to take wood screws
which are screwed through packing pieces into plugs in the
edge of the partition. When the thickness of the door jamb is
greater than that of the partition a rebated architrave is fixed on
one side.

1 Partition
2 Packing
3 Plug
4 Timber jamb
5 Wood screw
6 Timber architrave

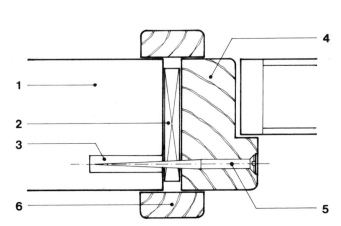

D Door set jamb and partition 70 mm thick
When the thickness of the door set is the same as that of the
finished partition, the gap between the door jamb and the
partition is closed on both sides by plain architrave sections.
The length of screw thread in the plug in the partition must not
be less than 38 mm.

1 Partition
2 Packing
3 Plug
4 Timber jamb
5 Wood screw
6 Timber architrave

INTERNAL DOORS: Timber and PVC door set

A Head

The room-height door set consists of a modular frame that is supplied complete with a door and a top panel designed to receive glass or painted hardboard. The profiles of the timber frame jamb cover different thicknesses of partition and are encased with rigid PVC. The sections of the frame have grooves in both sides to take the plastic architraves that close the gap between the frame and the ceiling.

1 Ceiling
2 Door frame head section for partition 68 mm thick
3 Glass panel
4 Timber glazing bead
5 Plastic architrave and ceiling cornice

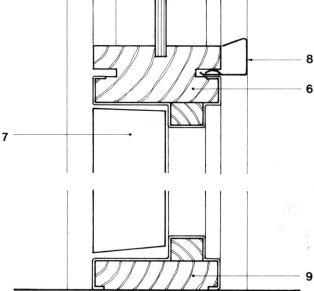

B Transom and sill

The intermediate transom is designed to take the door, the panel above and the plastic architrave sections that have a hook on one edge to fit the groove in the door frame. The sill is an integral part of the door frame and door set. It contributes to a rectilinear opening with close tolerances that provide for a well-fitting door.

6 Timber transom
7 Timber door
8 Plastic architrave
9 Timber sill

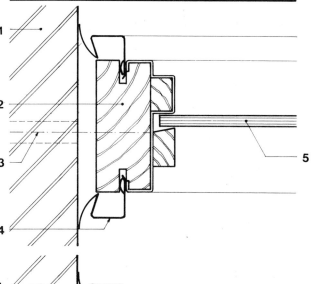

C Jamb

The door frame is screwed to the supporting wall with screws inserted in pre-drilled holes in the jambs at about 550 mm centres. A plastic pellet covers the screw and screw hole. The door frame has a groove on both sides to take a plastic architrave section that has a hook on one edge designed to fit the groove.

1 Structural wall
2 Door frame
3 Wood screw and plug
4 Plastic architrave
5 Glass panel above transom

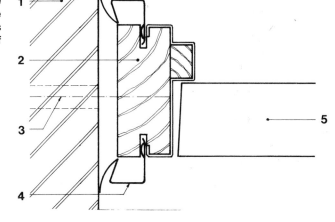

D Jamb

The joint between the door frame and a structural wall at right angles is made by screws inserted in the pre-drilled holes in the door frame jamb and screwed to plugs in the wall. The clearance of 10 mm is closed with the special plastic architrave that fits the groove in the door jamb and is sprung against the face of the wall.

1 Structural wall
2 Door jamb
3 Wood screw and plug
4 Plastic architrave
5 Door

INTERNAL DOORS: Timber fire-resisting and fire check doors

SCALE 1:2

A One-hour fire-resisting door

The door is not less than 54 mm thick and of composite construction consisting of an impregnated timber frame with a core of blockboard or compressed straw or cork covered on both sides with asbestos insulating board 6.4 mm thick. The door stop rebate is not less than 25 mm deep cut from the solid frame. The joint is sealed with intumescent strips 10 mm x 2 mm set in both the edge of the door and the door jamb. The clearance between the door frame and jamb must be not greater than 3 mm.

1 Timber door frame jamb
2 Intumescent strip 10 mm x 2 mm
3 Fire-resisting door
4 Intumescent strip 10 mm x 2 mm

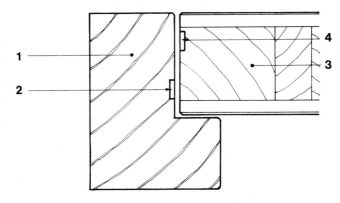

B Half-hour fire-resisting door

The door is not less than 45 mm thick and constructed of solid timber or timber framed with a core of compressed straw, or chipboard, or cork. The door stop with a rebate not less than 25 mm deep is screwed to the frame, or glued and pinned. One intumescent strip is required set in the edge of the door or, alternatively, in the edge of the door jamb. The clearance between the door and jamb must be not greater than 3 mm.

1 Timber door frame jamb
2 Timber stop
3 Wood screw
4 Fire-resisting door
5 Intumescent strip 10 mm x 2 mm

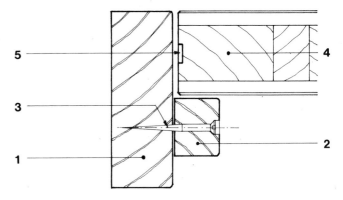

C One-hour fire check door

The door is not less than 54 mm thick and is of composite construction consisting of an impregnated timber frame with a core of blockboard or compressed straw or cork, covered on both sides with asbestos insulating board. The door stop rebate is not less than 25 mm deep cut from the solid frame. No intumescent strip is required provided that the clearance between the edge of the door and the edge of the door jamb is not greater than 2 mm.

1 Timber door frame jamb
2 Fire-resisting door
3 Clearance not greater than 2 mm

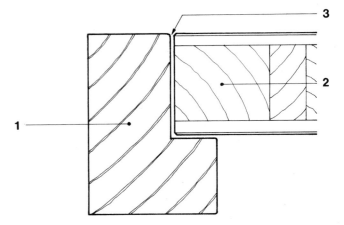

D Half-hour fire check door

The door is not less than 45 mm thick and is of composite construction consisting of an impregnated timber frame with a core of blockboard or compressed straw or cork, covered on both sides with asbestos insulating board. The door stop is glued and pinned to the frame, or alternatively screwed. The clearance between the edge of the door and the edge of the frame is not greater than 3 mm.

1 Timber door frame jamb
2 Glue
3 Timber door stop
4 Pin
5 Fire-resisting door
6 Clearance not greater than 3 mm

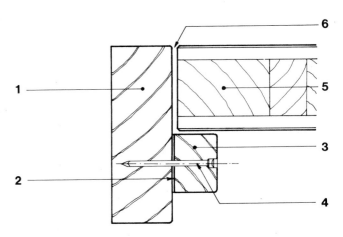

INTERNAL DOORS: Fire-resisting

A Swing doors without rebated meeting stiles

The clearance between the two doors is 4 mm. The fire check channel is screwed to the edge of the door frame on intumescent mastic bedding and the groove in the channel is filled with intumescent mastic and a draught strip. The joint between the channel and its frame is given additional protection with a hardwood bead or by extending the hardwood facing on the door. The fire resistance to collapse is 60 minutes.

1 Door framework 50 mm square section
2 Hardwood facing 10 mm thickness
3 Intumescent mastic bedding
4 Fire check channel 50 mm wide
5 Countersunk wood screw 38 mm long at 200 mm centres
6 Hardwood bead
7 Countersunk wood screw
8 Intumescent mastic and woollen felt draught strip in groove

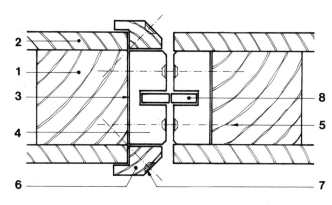

B Glazing in fire-resisting door (half-hour fire check)

Glazing of a fire-resisting door to give a fire resistance to collapse time of 30 minutes is effected by setting wired glass in a fire check channel screwed to a door with a softwood carcase of 44 mm minimum square section.

1 Softwood door carcase 44 mm square section
2 Fire check channel 44 mm wide
3 Countersunk wood screw 38 mm long at 200 mm centres
4 Georgian wired or diamond wired glass 6 mm thickness

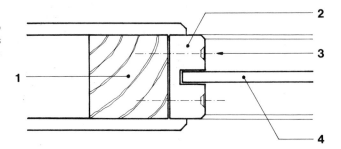

C Glazing in fire-resisting door (one-hour fire resistance)

Glazing of a fire-resisting door for one hour fire resistance is done with wired glass set in a fire check channel 50 mm wide screwed to a softwood carcase of 38 mm square section with countersunk wood screws at 200 mm centres. The door carcase is covered on both sides with 6 mm asbestos composition sheet fixed with countersunk wood screws 25 mm long.

1 Softwood door section 38 mm x 38 mm
2 Fire check channel 50 mm wide
3 Countersunk wood screw 38 mm long at 200 mm centres
4 Georgian wired or diamond wired glass 6 mm thickness
5 Asbestos composition sheet 6 mm thickness
6 Countersunk wood screw 25 mm long

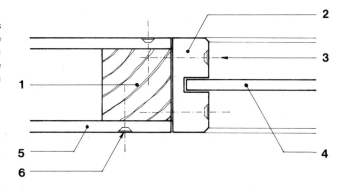

D Glazing in fire-resisting door (one-hour fire resistance)

An alternative way to achieve a one hour fire resistance is to use a softwood carcase of 50 mm square section on both sides with hardwood cladding 10 mm thick that extends so as to protect the joint between the edge of the carcase and the fire check channel.

1 Softwood door section 50 mm x 50 mm
2 Fire check channel 50 mm wide
3 Countersunk wood screw 38 mm long at 200 mm centres
4 Georgian wired or diamond wired glass 6 mm thickness
5 Hardwood cladding 10 mm thickness
6 Countersunk wood screw 25 mm long

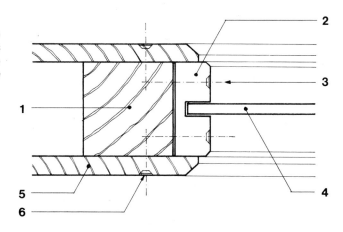

INTERNAL DOORS: Seals

A Sill of a new or an existing door
A separate aluminium alloy strip is screwed to the sill so as to provide a level surface for the seal. The seal consists of a poly-chloroprene tubular gasket that is contained in an anodized aluminium section. The section is screwed to the face of the bottom of the door with self-tapping mushroom headed screws through holes drilled oversize to permit adjustment in the location of the section.

1 Sill
2 Anodized aluminium strip
3 Countersunk screw
4 Timber door
5 Anodized aluminium section containing polychloroprene gasket
6 Self-tapping mushroom headed screw

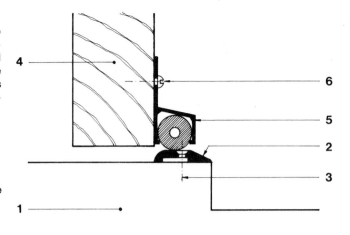

B Sill of a sliding door
The weight of the door when sliding and at rest is taken on a nylon strip fixed to the underside of the door that rests on a nylon tube that is in turn supported by a polychloroprene tubular gasket. The gaskets are contained in a U-shaped anodized aluminium holder that is recessed into the floor. The underside of the door is rebated to take a nylon guide strip.

1 Anodized aluminium sectional holder containing gaskets
2 Polychloroprene tubular gasket
3 Black nylon tube
4 Black nylon strip
5 Wood floor
6 Black nylon guide strip
7 Timber door

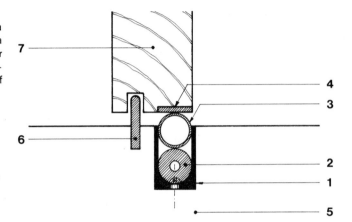

C Jamb of a new or an existing door
The compression seal may also be used with a door stop. The polychloroprene gasket closed cell is inserted into the rectangular anodized aluminium alloy section. The section is screwed into a rebate in the door stop or, alternatively, may be screwed to the side of the door stop facing the door. The edge of the door stile should be rounded on the hinge end.

1 Door frame
2 Door
3 Door stop with rebate
4 Anodized aluminium alloy section with polychloroprene gasket
5 Mushroom head screw

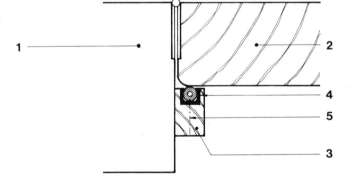

D Jamb of a new or an existing door
An alternative form of door seal makes use of a compression seal and is designed as a door stop. It may be used on all four sides of the door. The stop consists of an anodized aluminium alloy section formed to take a closed cell polychloroprene tube. The section is screwed with countersunk screws to the door frame. The edges of the door stiles should be rounded.

1 Door frame
2 Door
3 Anodized aluminium alloy section containing polychloroprene tube
4 Countersunk screw

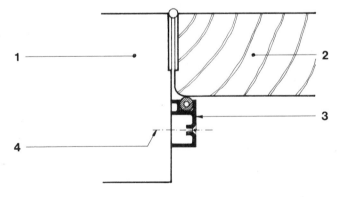

INTERNAL DOORS : Floor seals

A Timber pivoted door
The gap between the underside of an internal door and the finished floor level can be closed with a compression seal. The seal consists of a polychloroprene closed cell tubular gasket contained within an anodized aluminium alloy channel section that is fitted in a slot in the floor and screwed to the floor. The closing edge of the door rail should be slightly rounded to prevent damage to the gasket.

1 Floor
2 Anodized aluminium alloy channel section containing poly-chloroprene closed cell tubular gasket
3 Screw
4 Door

B Timber pivoted door
An alternative method of closing the gap between the underside of an internal door and the finished floor level is especially applicable to timber pivoted doors. A specially shaped hollow black polychloroprene section is held in position in an anodized aluminium alloy section that is screwed directly to the finished floor with self-tapping stainless steel screws. Both bottom edges of the door rail should be slightly rounded.

1 Floor
2 Mastic
3 Anodized aluminium alloy section containing hollow poly-chloroprene gasket
4 Stainless steel self-tapping screw
5 Door

C Armour plate pivoted door
The method, used in B above, is also applicable to pivoted armour plate doors. Both of the lower edges of the door should be slightly rounded. The sill is bedded in compound and extends the full width of the door opening over the floor pivot spring cover plate to the edge of the pivot. The section is cut at the edge of the cover plate so that the end piece can be removed when the springs have to be serviced. The gasket, however, is not cut.

1 Floor
2 Bedding compound
3 Anodized aluminium alloy sill
4 Hollow polychloroprene gasket
5 Stainless steel screw
6 Armour plate glass door

D Armour plate pivoted door
An alternative form of sill for an armour plate pivoted door or a pair of doors is to use a sill that contains a compression seal. The sill is screwed to a recess in the flooring with stainless steel screws. The hollow polychloroprene closed cell tube is then inserted and runs between the pivot box plates. Half round pieces of polychloroprene are fitted over the pivot boxes and may be removed when the springs have to be serviced.

1 Floor
2 Anodized aluminium sill
3 Rawlplug
4 Stainless steel screw
5 Black polychloroprene gasket
6 Armour plate glass door

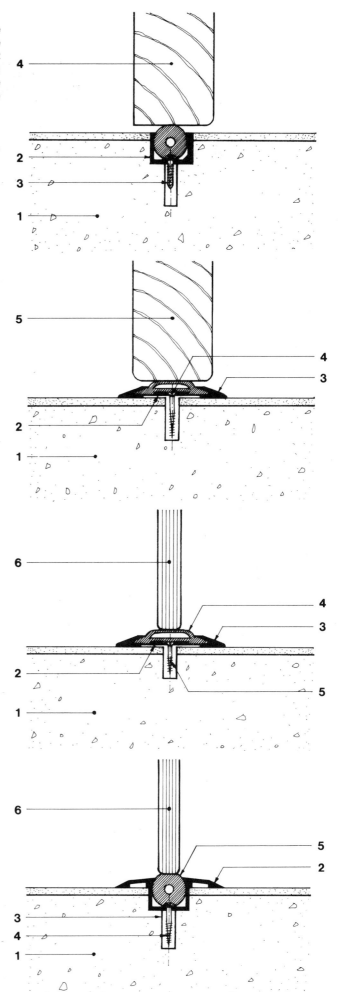

151

INTERNAL DOORS : Timber sound-resistant

A Sound-resistant door in an existing door frame
The door has a core of chipboard and is faced on both sides with hardwood veneer. When fitted to an existing door frame the joint between the frame and the door is sealed by means of a continuous polychloroprene rubber tubular seal which is held in an extruded aluminium strip screwed to the side of the door frame so that the rubber is compressed against the face of the door on all four sides.

1 Timber door frame
2 Door with chipboard core 35 mm and with veneered faces
3 Aluminium strip with polychloroprene rubber gasket
4 Aluminium screw

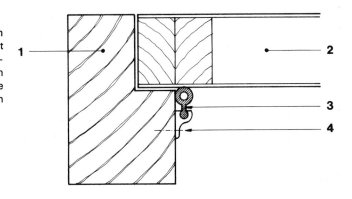

B Sound-resistant door in a new door frame
The door lining is grooved to take splines which accommodate a tolerance of 10 mm on the overall width of the partition. The edge of the door is rebated and the gap between the face of the end of the door and the edge of the door lining is sealed with a continuous tubular rubber seal that is shaped to fit a groove in the edge of the door lining.

1 Partition
2 Timber door lining
3 Rubber gasket
4 Timber spline
5 Timber architrave
6 Door with chipboard core 42 mm overall thickness

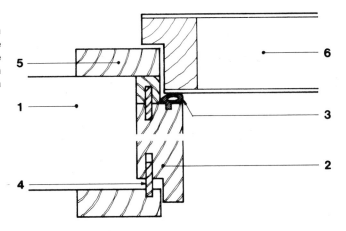

PARTITIONS: Plasterboard panel

A Head

This single-leaf partition consists of prefabricated panels of gypsum wallboard bonded on both sides. A 37 mm x 19 mm timber batten is fixed to the ceiling and the rebate at the edge of the panel fits over the batten.

1 Ceiling
2 Timber head batten 37 mm x 19 mm
3 Gypsum wallboard panel
4 Galvanized nail 30 mm x 2 mm diameter at 230 mm centres

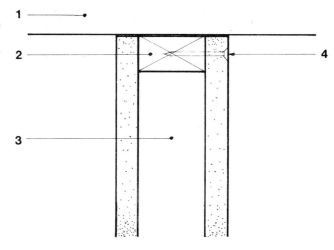

B Sill

A timber sole plate of the same thickness as the panel is fixed to the floor. The panel is placed over the sole plate and a 300 mm length of 37 mm x 19 mm batten is nailed to the sole plate so as to run between adjoining panels. The panel is nailed to the batten. Skirtings are then added and nailed to skirting plugs set between the two layers of wallboard.

1 Flooring
2 Timber sole plate 63 mm x 25 mm
3 Gypsum wallboard panel
4 Timber batten 37 mm x 19 mm x 300 mm long
5 Galvanized nail 30 mm x 2 mm diameter at 230 mm centres
6 Timber skirting
7 Galvanized nail

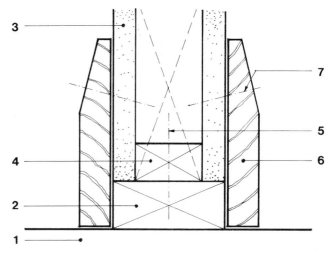

C Jamb

When a doorway is required, a small amount of panel core is removed to accept a timber batten 37 mm x 37 mm for the door frame fixing. The batten is driven flush with the edge of the panel. The door frame is then positioned and nailed to the batten. The architrave is then nailed into position.

1 Walling
2 Gypsum wallboard panel
3 Timber batten 37 mm x 37 mm
4 Timber door frame
5 Timber architrave

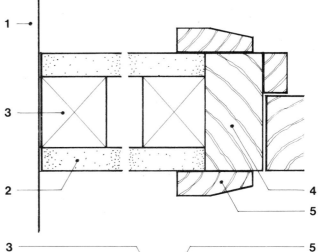

D Mullion

The vertical joint between two panels is made with a timber batten 37 mm x 37 mm fitted halfway into the core of the first panel. The panel is then nailed to the batten with galvanized nails 30 mm x 2 mm diameter at 230 mm centres. The sharp edges of battens should be planed off to ease assembly. The second panel is then placed into position over the other half of the batten and nailed to it.

1 Gypsum wallboard panel
2 Timber batten 37 mm x 37 mm
3 Galvanized nail 30 mm x 2 mm diameter
4 Gypsum wallboard panel
5 Galvanized nail 30 mm x 2 mm diameter

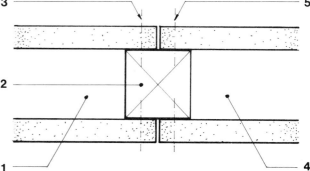

PARTITIONS : Composite board partition panels

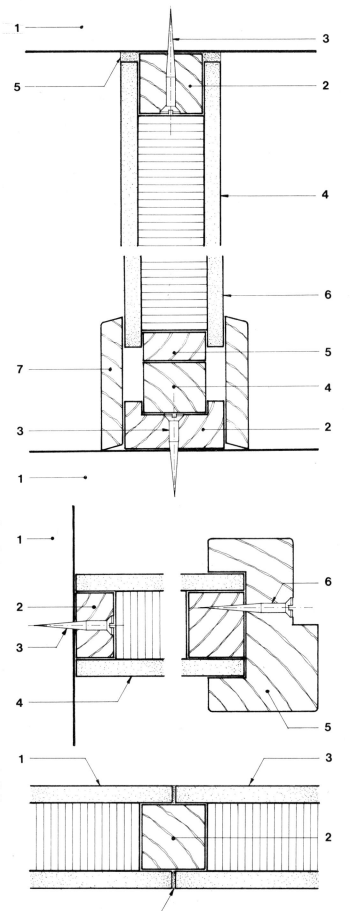

A Head

The partition is constructed of panels with a solid core of flax-board faced on both sides with plasterboard 9 mm thick to give an overall thickness of 54 mm. Around the perimeter of the panel the flaxboard is stopped short of the plasterboard to provide a recess to take timber battens. At the head of the panel a continuous timber batten is screwed to the structural ceiling and the panel is wedged up from below. The gaps between the plasterboard and the ceiling are filled with plaster.

1 Structural ceiling
2 Continuous timber batten
3 Wood screw countersunk head
4 Composite partition panel
5 Plaster filling

B Sill

A timber sill with a continuous groove is screwed to the floor in line with a ground fixed to the ceiling. The partition panel is positioned over the sill, jacked up and wedged solidly in position by means of folding wedges placed on the sill. A skirting is then fixed on both sides of the panel.

1 Floor
2 Continuous timber sill
3 Wood screw
4 Folding wedge
5 Folding wedge
6 Composite partition panel
7 Timber skirting

C Wall abutment and door jamb

The vertical joint between a panel and a wall at right angles is formed by screwing a continuous batten to the wall and fitting the end of the panel over the batten. At a door opening, the jamb of the door frame, which is rebated to take the end of the panel and provide additional stiffness at this position, is screwed to timber blocks in the edge of the panel.

1 Structural wall
2 Timber batten
3 Wood screw countersunk head
4 Composite partition panel
5 Timber door jamb
6 Wood screw

D Mullion

The vertical joint between two adjacent panels is formed by means of a timber batten which is fitted tightly into the recesses formed at the edge of both panels. The gap between adjacent sheets of plasterboard is filled and made good with plaster.

1 Composite partition panel
2 Timber batten
3 Composite partition panel
4 Plaster filling

PARTITIONS: Plasterboard on steel framing

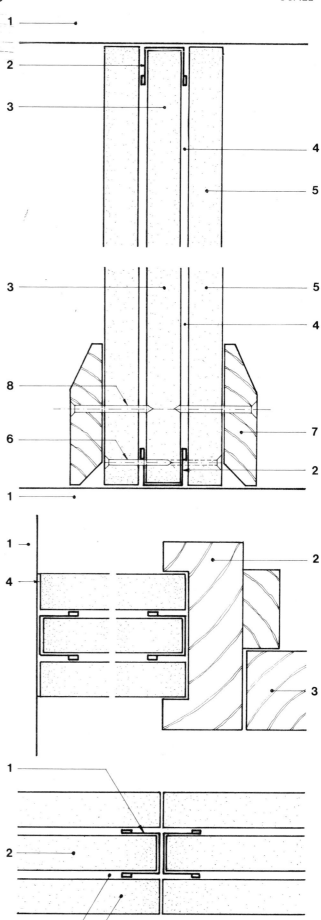

A Head

The single-leaf non-combustible laminated plasterboard partition is 65 mm thick. A metal looped box channel is fixed to the floor, ceiling and boundary walls along the centre line of the partition with fixing points 600 mm apart. Services, including outlet, are then installed. The plasterboard planks are then positioned vertically into the channels. Bonding compound is applied to the surface of the plank at 300 mm centres on both sides to take the outer planks.

1 Ceiling
2 Metal looped box channel section galvanized rolled mild steel
3 Plasterboard plank 19 mm thick
4 Bonding compound
5 Plasterboard plank 19 mm thick

B Sill

The outer boards are pressed into position on bonding compound and screwed at 300 mm centres into the box channel at the top, bottom and adjacent walls with 36 mm dry wall screws. Joints between boards of separate layers should be staggered. The skirting is screwed to a short length of looped box channel inserted at the edges of boards.

1 Flooring
2 Metal looped box channel, 0.7 mm thick, galvanized rolled mild steel
3 Plasterboard plank 19 mm thick
4 Bonding compound
5 Plasterboard plank 19 mm thick
6 36 mm dry wall screw
7 Timber skirting
8 45 mm dry wall screw

C Jamb

Door frames and window frames can be incorporated into the partition where required. The door frame shown is rebated to take the partition thickness and to provide a stop for the wood skirtings. Acoustical sealant or acrylic caulk should be used at the perimeter of the partition and to seal gaps around service outlets and other openings.

1 Wall
2 Timber door frame
3 Timber door
4 Acrylic caulk sealant

D Mullion

Where a partition 65 mm thick exceeds 7200 mm in length, H sections formed of two lengths of looped box channel fixed back to back are inserted vertically at intervals of 3600 mm to support the partition. The lengths of channel are fitted from floor to ceiling on to the centre planks at a joint.

1 Metal looped box channel galvanized rolled mild steel
2 Plasterboard plank 19 mm thick
3 Bonding compound
4 Plasterboard plank 19 mm thick

PARTITIONS: Demountable fire-resisting

A Head

A high performance demountable partition with combinations of solid and glazed panels and ducts to take services. The joint at the head consists of an aluminium channel bedded on foam strip and screwed to plugs in the structural ceiling through steel liner and inner support channels that provide the fire-resisting supporting framework. The outer faces of the solid partition are plasterboard and the core may be filled with fibreglass quilt.

1 Structural ceiling
2 Foam strip
3 Anodized aluminium channel
4 Steel liner channel section
5 Steel inner channel section
6 Countersunk head wood screw 30 mm long in plug
7 Steel vertical stud channel section
8 Plasterboard 12.5 mm

B Sill

The joint at floor level has a timber floorplate that is screwed to the structural floor. A steel inner channel is placed centrally on the floorplate and screwed to it with a countersunk wood screw 30 mm long. Vertical steel channel sections are fitted between top and bottom inner channels. Plasterboard panels are placed on the wall plate and held by means of plastic skirtings screwed to the inner channel with countersunk screws 30 mm long.

1 Structural floor
2 Timber floorplate
3 Countersunk wood screw 30 mm long in plug
4 Steel inner channel section
5 Steel vertical stud channel section
6 Plasterboard 12.5 mm
7 Plastic skirting 100 mm high
8 Countersunk screw 30 mm long

C Jamb

The joint between the partition and a structural wall is similar in construction to that at the head of the partition. The special aluminium door frame section has a steel liner and both are screwed to the vertical stud. The door has the same fire resistance as the partition.

1 Structural wall
2 Foam strip
3 Aluminium channel
4 Steel liner channel section
5 Steel inner channel section
6 Plasterboard 12.5 mm
7 Steel vertical stud channel section
8 Aluminium door frame section with steel side liner
9 Door

D Mullion

The vertical joint between panels alongside one another is formed by means of a structural steel stud that supports the plasterboard panel on both sides. The plasterboard is fixed with self-tapping screws and special buttons and washers that enable the aluminium cover strip to be clipped on as a finish.

1 Steel vertical stud channel section at 600 mm centres
2 Non-slump adhesive
3 Plasterboard 12.5 mm
4 Washer, button, and self-tapping screw at 300 mm centres
5 Aluminium cover strip

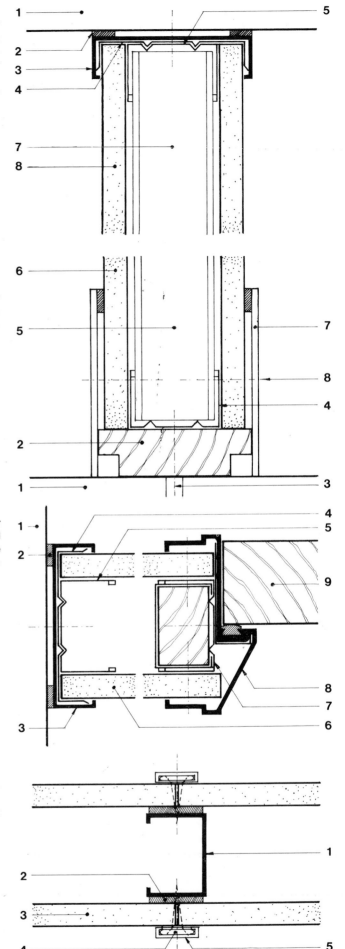

156

PARTITIONS: Demountable plasterboard on steel framing

A Head

A fully demountable office partitioning system that consists of a galvanized steel framework that is fixed to the floor and ceiling by insulated channel sections designed to minimise the transfer of sound and vibration from the building structure to the partitioning. The ceiling track is attached to the ceiling by means of a twist clip. Telescopic vertical members are placed in position to carry the windows, doors, panels and hatches.

1 Ceiling
2 PVC strip
3 Galvanized steel ceiling track
4 Twist clip
5 Horizontal framing of galvanized steel
6 Plasterboard panel 12 mm

B Sill

The floor track with PVC strips on the underside is located in line with the ceiling track and rests on the floor finish. Vertical members are then placed in position and support the plasterboard panels mounted on both sides of the framework. Where a high degree of sound absorption is required, the air-space between the panels is filled with sound-absorbent quilting. A PVC skirting clips to the base of the panels.

1 Flooring
2 PVC strip
3 Galvanized steel floor track
4 Horizontal framing channel of galvanized steel
5 12 mm plasterboard
6 PVC skirting

C Jamb

At the junction with a wall, a wall track channel with PVC strips is fastened to the wall. A telescopic stud is fixed in position and the jamb of the door frame fitted complete with door, door stop and fittings.

1 Wall
2 Channel wall track with PVC strips
3 Telescopic stud
4 Door jamb galvanized steel finished in stove enamel
5 Door stop anodized aluminium
6 Polychloroprene buffer strip
7 Door hinge
8 Timber door

D Mullion

The junction between panels of all kinds is effected by means of a telescopic stud designed to support window or door frames or plasterboard panels. The gap between adjacent panels is covered with an aluminium profiled section and finished with a PVC cover strip.

1 Telescopic stud
2 Window frame in zinc or steel finished in enamel
3 PVC glazing bead
4 Glass 4 mm thick
5 PVC glazing bead clip
6 Plasterboard panel 12 mm
7 Aluminium section
8 PVC cover strip

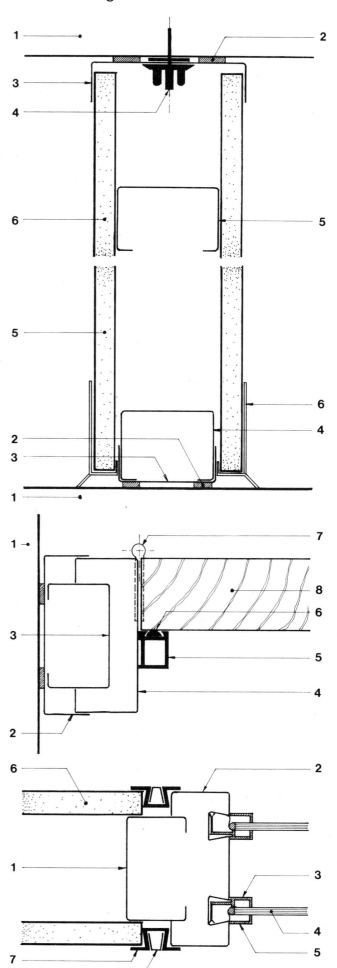

157

A Head

A demountable system of partitioning comprising galvanized rolled steel framing members that support any combination of facing panels, single or double glazing and single or double doors. At the head two channel sections are fastened to the ceiling and patented. X section vertical studs are located to support horizontal bridgings and provide panel fixings.

1 Structural ceiling
2 Head trim channel section
3 Top track channel section
4 Bridging channel section
5 Gypsum plasterboard panel 13 mm thick

B Sill

At the floor a channel section supports the vertical studs that carry the plasterboard panels and T section cover strips that also act as fixing clips. The skirting of melamine is fixed to the plasterboard. Service runs are concealed within the partition and are fitted through the holes that are punched at regular intervals in the web of the vertical studs.

1 Structural floor
2 Bottom track channel section
3 X section vertical stud
4 Melamine skirting

C Jamb

At the joint between the partition and a wall, a trim channel is bedded against foam plastic strips. The timber door jamb may be positioned within the trim channel or located on the flanges of the vertical stud.

1 Structural wall
2 Foam plastic strip
3 Trim channel
4 Timber door jamb
5 Timber door

D Mullion

Vertical joints between panels occur at the position of the vertical studs. The plasterboard panel is supported by the flange of the stud and held in position by the T section cover strip that also acts as a fixing clip.

1 Galvanized steel X section vertical stud
2 Plasterboard panel 13 mm thick
3 T section cover strip

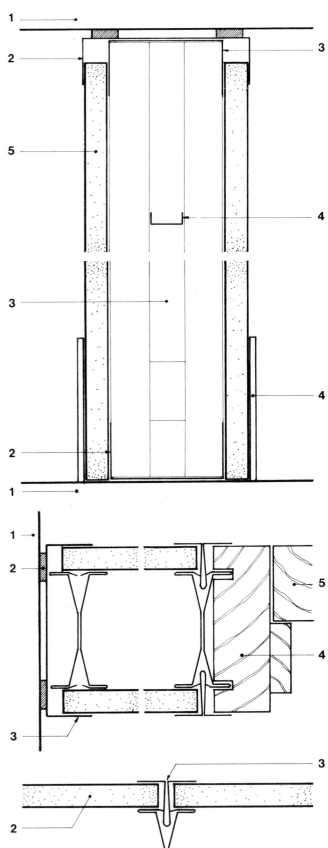

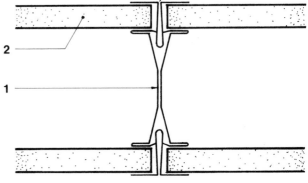

PARTITIONS: Demountable particle board

A Head

This partition is constructed of solid core panels of particle board made from flax shives amalgamated with synthetic resin. The board requires no timber lippings or separate inserts for fixings and may be grooved or cut to take service drops or runs. The board is shown faced on both sides.

1 Ceiling
2 Softwood ground
3 Wood screw
4 Flaxboard panel
5 Softwood cover strip
6 Oval lost-head nail
7 Wood screw 32 mm

B Sill

The softwood ground is first screwed to the flooring and a corresponding ground screwed to the ceiling. The panel is placed in position on the wall plate so as to leave a gap along the top of the panel that allows for variations in floor to ceiling height, possible deflection of the ceiling and tolerance on the height of the panel. Service runs are placed in the grooves provided as required. The floor skirtings and ceiling cover fillets are then nailed to the grounds and screwed to the panel.

1 Flooring
2 Softwood ground
3 Wood screw
4 Flaxboard panel
5 Softwood skirting
6 Oval lost-head nail
7 Wood screw 32 mm

C Jamb

Where the partitions meet a wall, a softwood ground is screwed to the wall, the panel is scribed to the face of the wall and a groove in the panel fits over the ground. Door openings may be pre-cut in the panels or a space allowed between panels for floor to ceiling door units. The small tolerance on the thickness of a panel allows a grooved door frame to be fitted without the need for additional architraves.

1 Wall
2 Softwood ground
3 Wood screw
4 Flaxboard panel
5 Door frame

D Mullion

The vertical joint between two adjacent panels may be made in a number of alternative ways. The method shown consists of a machined hardwood tongue that fits into a groove in the panel. The vertical edges of the facings on the panels are chamfered at 45 degrees so as to give a V-joint when assembly is complete.

1 Flaxboard panel
2 Hardwood tongue machined to fit
3 Flaxboard panel

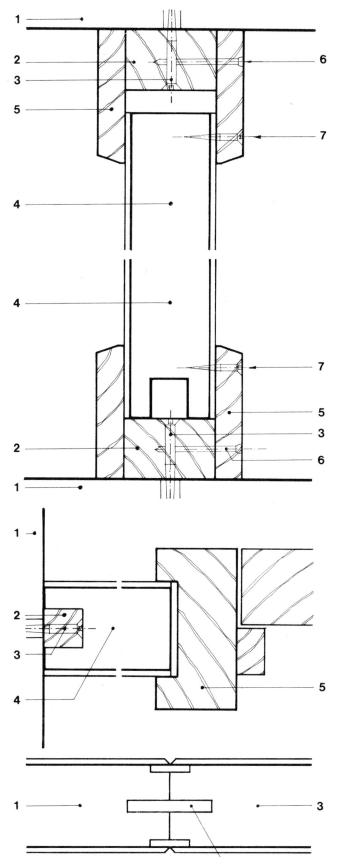

A Head

At the head of the partition an aluminium channel section is screwed to plugs in the structural ceiling. The gap is filled with foam strip to take up tolerance on the clearance and to lessen sound transmission. The partition panel consists of two layers of plasterboard on a structural core to give an overall thickness of 50 mm.

1 Structural ceiling
2 Foam strip
3 Anodized aluminium ceiling channel
4 Plasterboard 12.5 mm thick

B Sill

At the sill of the partition a special timber floorplate is screwed to a plug in the structural floor. The partition panel is placed on the floorplate and fixed in position by screws through the plastic skirting section.

1 Structural floor
2 Timber floorplate
3 Plug and wood screw 50 mm long at 600 mm centres
4 Plasterboard 12.5 mm thick
5 Plastic skirting 100 mm high
6 Wood screw 30 mm long

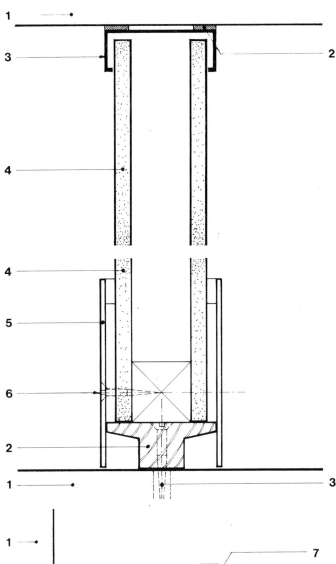

C Jamb

At the joint with a structural wall an aluminium channel is bedded on foam strip and screwed to a plug in the wall. The special aluminium door frame section is screwed to an aluminium H section upright that grips the plasterboard sides of the partition panel. The door frame is stiffened with brackets at the top and bottom.

1 Structural wall
2 Foam strip
3 Anodized aluminium channel
4 Wood screw 30 mm long in plug
5 Plasterboard 12.5 mm thick
6 Anodized aluminium door frame section
7 Wood screw 30 mm long at 450 mm centres
8 Door

D Mullion

The vertical joint between panels placed side by side is made with an aluminium H section. Alternative sections are used to provide for electrical wiring and switches or to permit a 3-way junction or to give additional strength where the floor-to-ceiling height is over 3300 mm. A special aluminium section is designed to take glazing by means of a rubber glazing section and, for double glazing, a spacer.

1 Anodized aluminium H section
2 Plasterboard 12.5 mm thick
3 Anodized aluminium insert glazing section
4 Double glazing spacer
5 Glass 6 mm thick
6 Rubber glazing section

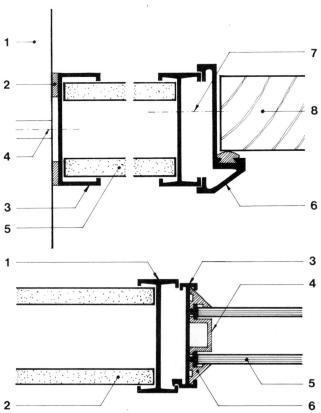

A This partition system is designed to be fully demountable. The panels or the posts are jacked up between the structural floor and ceiling. A full range of components may be inserted into the special four-way column section. A continuous rubber packing strip is placed against the ceiling and enclosed by the channel section that forms the transom.

1 Structural ceiling
2 Rubber packing strip
3 Extruded aluminium alloy anodised and etched section
4 Solid full height hardboard faced core panel

B The base jack supports the panel, is hand operated and is able to take up a tolerance of 70 mm. Skirtings are fixed on both sides and provide a continuous duct that can accommodate electric cabling and other services. Vertical drops are made within the slots of the post.

1 Floor
2 Jack support
3 Solid full height hardboard faced core panel
4 PVC skirting

C The joint between a standard post and a structural wall is made by means of rubber packing strips that are compressed in position and are slightly set back from the faces of the post. The door frame is fitted over timber inserts that are attached to the flanges of the post with toggles.

1 Structural wall
2 Rubber packing strip
3 Post of extruded aluminium alloy section anodised and etched
4 Timber insert with toggle
5 Extruded rigid PVC section or extruded aluminium door section
6 Teak veneered cellular core door

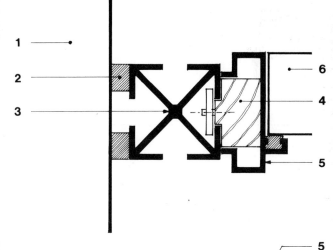

D The partition is divided into modular lengths by the standard post. Panels, door frames and glazing are fully interchangeable. A number of post and panel mounted accessories are available and are supplied with protective plastic spacers with toggle or screw fixings. Storage units form part of the system and are clipped to aluminium brackets that are secured to the posts by screws.

1 Post of extruded aluminium alloy section anodised and etched
2 Solid full height hardboard faced core panel
3 Extruded PVC bead
4 Extruded PVC bead
5 6 mm glass sheet

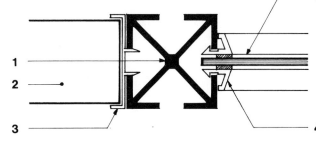

PARTITIONS: Wallboard on steel framing

A Head

The aluminium trim channel is positioned against the ceiling and supported by a steel track channel placed centrally inside and carried on steel framing studs at 600 mm centres. Both sides of the framing are covered with a wallboard that consists of a core of gypsum plasterboard, covered with a face veneer on the outside and a compensating veneer on the back.

1 Aluminium trim channel
2 Steel track channel
3 Wallboard

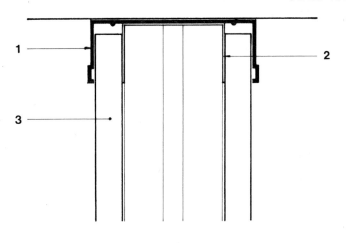

B Sill

The steel track channel is screwed to the floor. The vertical steel framing studs are placed in position and secured by intermediate bridging sections. The wallboard is positioned on both sides of the framing and held by aluminium T section cover strips that clip into the vertical studs. An aluminium skirting is fixed to both sides of the wallboard.

1 Steel track channel
2 Steel framing stud at 600 mm centres
3 Wallboard
4 Aluminium skirting

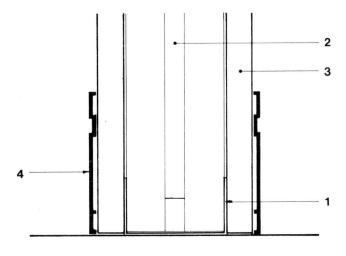

C Jamb

The joint between the partition and a structural wall is formed by means of an aluminium trim channel and a vertical stud that are both screwed to the wall. The hardwood door jamb is grooved to fit over the flanges of the stud. The wallboard is positioned and the gap between the wallboard and the door jamb is covered with an aluminium T section that clips into the vertical stud.

1 Aluminium trim channel
2 Steel stud
3 Wallboard
4 Hardwood door jamb
5 Aluminium T section

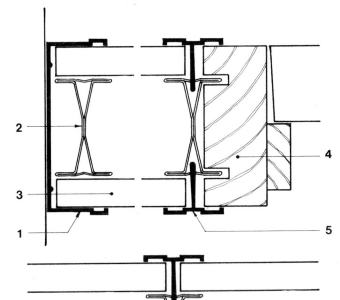

D Mullion

The partitioning system is based on vertical studs spaced at 600 mm centres. The wallboards are positioned on both sides of the steel framework and held in position by aluminium T sections that clip into the studs and also serve as a cover strip over the joint face.

1 Steel stud
2 Wallboard
3 Aluminium T section

PARTITIONS : Steel framed panel system

A Head

A system of partitioning based on the assembly of a range of sheet materials into standard sections formed from rolled steel strips that are used as framing members. At the head of the partition an H section is screwed to the ceiling. Other sections are added to complete the framing. Gaskets are fitted to all sides of a panel and the assembly is then pressed into position and eased into the channel sections with a putty knife.

1 Structural ceiling
2 Cold rolled mild steel strip folded section framing member
3 Chipboard panel
4 Plastic moulding gasket

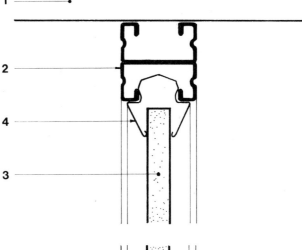

B Sill

At the sill of the partition an H section framing member is screwed to the structural floor. Electrical wiring is placed inside the channels, the flanges of which act as skirtings. The plastic moulding is designed to take any thickness of sheet or panel from 3 mm to 13 mm.

1 Structural floor
2 Cold rolled mild steel strip folded section framing member
3 Chipboard panel
4 Plastic moulding gasket

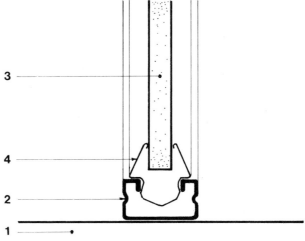

C Jamb

At a structural wall, an H section framing member is screwed to the wall and fastened to the head and sill section with special corner plates. The door frame jambs and lintel are fastened to the framing with the special self-locating nut and machine screw. The nut is placed inside the channel where it is held during assembly by the attached spring and tightened against the flanges of the channel by the screw.

1 Framing member H section
2 Self-locating nut with spring attached
3 Timber door frame
4 Machine screw
5 Door

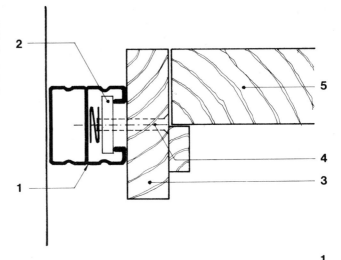

D Mullion

The joint between two panels alongside one another is made by means of the standard H section framing member. Glass sheet is fitted along four edges with the plastic moulding strip; the corners of the framing are packed with a rubber strip and the glass panel assembly is then eased into position in the channels. Panels of other materials may be assembled in the same way. The recommended clearance between the edge of the glass and framing is 8 mm. The recommended clearance for other materials is 5 mm.

1 Framing member H section
2 Glass sheet
3 Plastic moulding
4 Chipboard panel
5 Plastic moulding

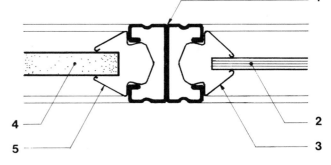

A Head

The design is for a partition subject only to small deflections of the ceiling. A timber batten is screwed to the ceiling soffit along the line of the partition. A strip of foam plastic is inserted in the groove along the top of the partition slab before it is raised into position. The ceiling finish is applied to cover the gap between the top of the partition and the structural ceiling.

1 Structural ceiling
2 Timber batten
3 Wood screw
4 Foam plastic packing
5 Lightweight aerated concrete slab
6 Ceiling finish

B Sill

The partition slab is raised to a height of about 40 mm above the floor by levers inserted under the lower edge and is fixed by means of wood wedges driven parallel to the partition. The packing at the top of the slab must not be compressed after the wedges have been driven. The space under the slab and on both sides of the wedges is filled with a 1 : 3 cement : sand mortar that is trowelled flush with the faces of the partition.

1 Structural floor
2 Lightweight aerated concrete slab
3 Timber wedge
4 Timber packing
5 1 : 3 cement : sand mortar

C Jamb

Where a slab meets a wall, the vertical edge of the slab is brushed free of any loose particles, wetted and coated with glue mortar. The slab is raised into position and pressed against the wall until adhesion is sufficient. After about half an hour, the excess glue mortar that is squeezed out along both sides is scraped off. Door frames are fixed with cut clasp nails that pass through pre-drilled holes in the frame and penetrate 50 mm into the slab.

1 Structural wall
2 Glue mortar 1.5 mm to 3 mm thick
3 Aerated concrete slab
4 Timber door frame
5 Cut clasp nails at 500 mm centres
6 Timber architrave

D Mullion

The vertical joint between two adjacent slabs is made with glue mortar applied to the edge of the slab about to be positioned. The slab is pressed home and held in position while the glue mortar is setting by three small metal shear plates that are driven across the joint about 900 mm apart and punched below the surface of the slabs. After about half an hour, the excess glue mortar which is squeezed out along both sides is scraped off.

1 Aerated concrete slab in position
2 Aerated concrete slab
3 Glue mortar

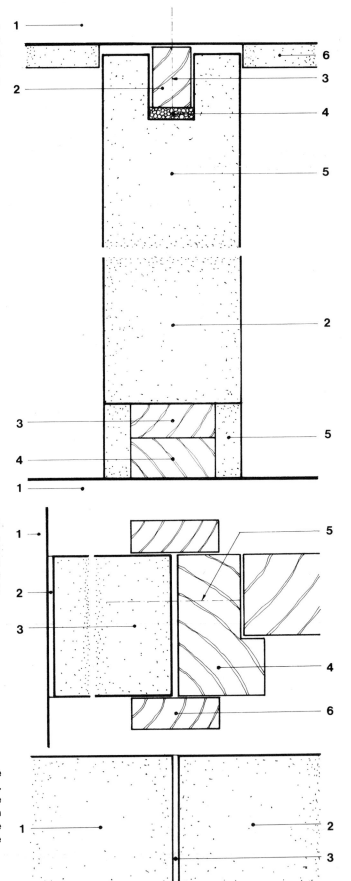

PARTITIONS: Party wall timber frame

A Head

The party wall constructed in lightweight timber framing consists of a double-leaf wall separated by a wide cavity and having a minimum weight of each leaf to give a suitable acoustic performance. It is now common practice to prefabricate the timber frames in storey-height sections, sometimes including the plasterboard linings.

1 Roof space
2 Timber frame not fixed
3 Firestop of asbestos board 12 mm thick
4 3 layers of 13 mm plasterboard
5 25 mm glass wool (or mineral wool) quilt
6 Plasterboard ceiling

B Intermediate floor

The linings for each leaf require to weigh about 25 kg/m² and may consist of three layers of 13 mm plasterboard or four layers of 10 mm. The most common type consists of two layers glued together in the factory and pre-fixed to the timber frames, with the third layer added on site with the sheets fixed at right angles to those on the frames.

1 Timber frame
2 Three layers of 13 mm plasterboard
3 25 mm glass wool (or mineral wool) quilt
4 Firestop of asbestos board, not fixed
5 Floor joist

C Sill

The width of the cavity is defined as the distance between the inner faces of the linings and should be not less than 225 mm. The cavity contains a layer of sound absorbent material in the form of a glass wool or mineral wool quilt, 13 mm to 25 mm thickness. The quilt is usually suspended in the cavity by stapling to one side of the timber frame. Two quilts, one on each side of the cavity, give additional fire resistance.

1 Ground floor concrete
2 Timber frame
3 Three layers of 13 mm plasterboard
4 25 mm glass wool quilt
5 Floor finish

D Abutment to external wall

At the junction of the party wall and the external wall, the cavity is separated from that between the inner and outer leaf of the external walling with a firestop of asbestos board.

1 Inner face of outer leaf of external wall
2 Timber frame of party wall
3 Three layers of 13 mm plasterboard
4 Inner leaf of external wall
5 25 mm glass wool quilt
6 Firestop of asbestos board 12 mm thick

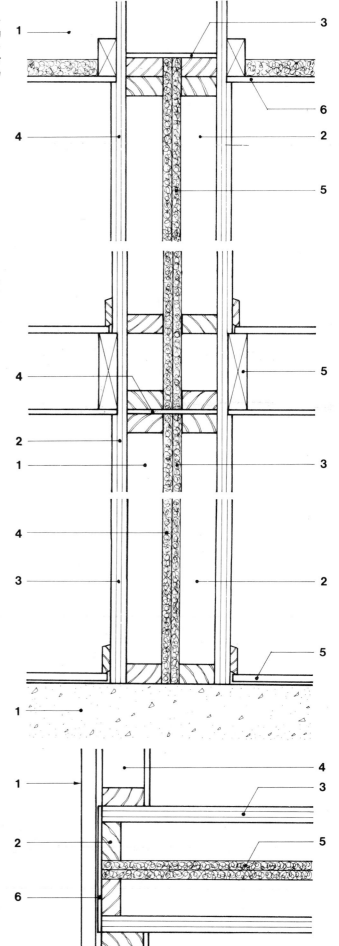

A End stop

The edge of a plastered wall finish is protected and finished by means of a galvanized steel plaster stop bead. The bead has a channel shaped end, equal in width to the thickness of the plaster, and an expanded mesh wing that rests against the wall to provide a key for the plaster. The bead is fixed to the wall with plaster dabs or, when a specially firm fixing is required, with a galvanized plasterboard nail.

1 Support wall
2 Galvanized steel plaster stop bead for 16 mm plaster thickness
3 Plaster dab
4 Plaster 16 mm

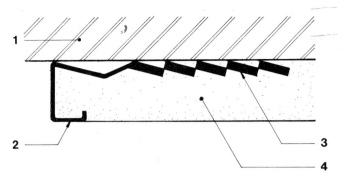

B External corner

The external corner of a plastered wall finish is protected and finished by means of a galvanized angle bead that has a circular nose and two expanded mesh wings. Plaster dabs are applied to the wall at 600 mm centres on both sides of the arris and the wings of the bead are pressed into the plaster dabs. The bead is plumbed and squared. Two coats of plaster are then applied. The finished coat is allowed to wash over the nose of the bead.

1 Support wall
2 Plaster dab
3 Galvanized steel angle bead
4 Plaster 16 mm

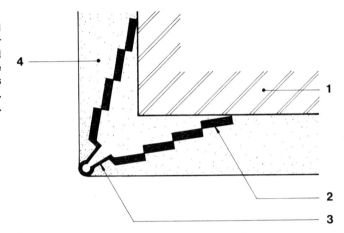

C Door jamb

The joint between the edge of a plastered wall finish and a door frame may be finished by means of a special galvanized steel architrave bead that consists of an L-shaped stop end with an expanded mesh wing. The bead is cut to fit the groove round the door frame and is fixed to the support wall with plaster dabs.

1 Support wall
2 Timber door frame
3 Galvanized steel architrave bead
4 Plaster dab
5 Plaster 13 mm

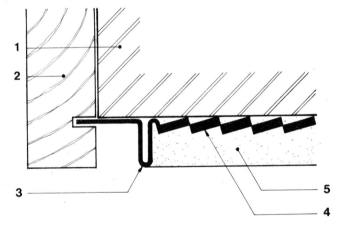

D Change of wall finish

The joint between a plastered wall finish and a different wall finish such as cement rendering may be made by means of a galvanized steel screed bead. The bead has a central U-shaped nose with an expanded mesh wing on both sides. Plaster dabs are applied to the wall at 600 mm centres on both sides of the joint and the bead is pressed into the dabs. The wall finishes are then applied to both sides of the bead.

1 Support wall
2 Plaster dab
3 Galvanized steel screed bead
4 Plaster 13 mm
5 Cement rendering

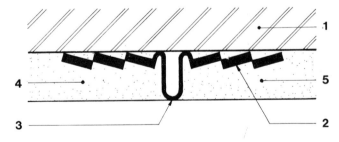

INTERNAL WALL FINISHES: Ceramic wall tiles

A Bedding of tiles with sand: cement mortar

One method of fixing ceramic wall tiles to a wall having a floated coat with a wood float finish is by means of a 1:4 cement: sand mortar. The floated coat should be completely dry before tiling commences. The bedding mortar that consists of 1:4 Portland cement: sand by volume is mixed with water within two hours of laying. Tiles are cleaned and soaked in water for at least half an hour before use. The floated coat is wetted, the tiles are evenly covered with bedding mortar and tapped firmly into position to give a bed thickness between 7 mm and 12 mm.

1 Floated coat 1:4 cement: sand
2 Bedding mortar 1:4 Portland cement: sand by volume
3 Ceramic wall tile

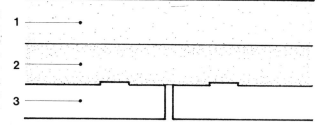

B Pointing of joints between tiles

The clearance between the tiles when laid is not less than 1.5 mm which may be obtained by using tiles with spacer-lugs or by the use of spacer pegs inserted as the work proceeds. The grout, consisting of 1:3 or 4 Portland cement: ground limestone or whiting, is mixed with clean water. The joints are wetted and the grout is applied with a brush and worked into the joints. Surplus grout is removed and the surface of the tiles polished with a dry cloth.

1 Ceramic wall tile
2 Grout 1:3 or 4 Portland cement: ground limestone or whiting

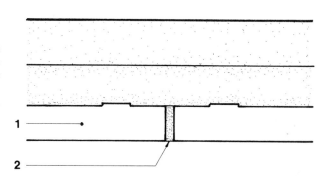

C Bedding of tiles with adhesive

When the wall tiles are not deeply keyed or frogged they may be bedded by means of a layer of cement based or mastic adhesive. A floated coat of cement: sand mortar is first applied to the wall and allowed to dry before tiling commences. The method of application of the adhesive which depends upon the type of adhesive, is specified by the manufacturer.

1 Floated coat 1:4 cement: sand
2 Cement based or mastic adhesive
3 Ceramic wall tile

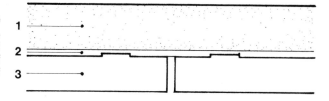

D Movement joint in tiling

When wall tiles are applied in large areas compressive stresses may be set up in the tiling due to variations in drying shrinkage. Movement joints are provided horizontally and vertically at intervals of about 4 m. The joint may be made to coincide with a structural joint in the wall. The backing strip is inserted into the gap in the floated coat and supports the sealant which must be not less than 10 mm wide.

1 Floated coat 1:4 cement: sand
2 Cement based or mastic adhesive
3 Ceramic wall tile
4 Foam backing strip
5 One-part gun-applied synthetic rubber sealant

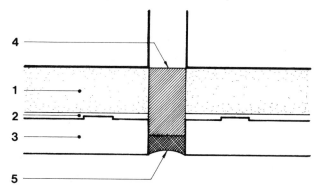

A A level screed or similar surface is prepared for the sill. The asbestos cement sill is bonded to the screed with adhesive, the sill being weighted or otherwise pressed down firmly until the adhesive is set. The edge of the sill as shown is finished with two pencil round corners.

1 Screed
2 Adhesive
3 Asbestos cement sill
4 Plaster

B Short lengths of serrated plastic T section are bonded with impact adhesive to the underside of the asbestos cement sill at 450 mm centres. The sill is then bedded on a mortar screed and weighted down until the mortar is set. The edge of the sill as shown is finished with a pencil round upper corner.

1 Mortar bed
2 Asbestos cement sill
3 Impact adhesive
4 Plastic T section 50 mm long
5 Plaster

C Self-tapping screws are fitted into holes which are blind drilled into the underside of the asbestos cement sill. The screw heads are left projecting and are bedded in a mortar screed, the sill being weighted down until the mortar is set. The edge of the sill as shown is finished with a half round. This method is only suitable when the thickness of the sill is 15 mm or more.

1 Mortar bed
2 Self-tapping screw
3 Asbestos cement sill
4 Plaster

D Holes are drilled and countersunk in the sill to take wood screws. The top surface of the wall is levelled and the sill placed in position. The top of the wall is drilled and plugged, the sill is screwed to it, and the counterholes are filled or covered with plastic caps. The edge of the sill as shown is finished with a bull nose on the top corner.

1 Asbestos cement sill
2 Plug
3 Countersunk head wood screw
4 Plaster

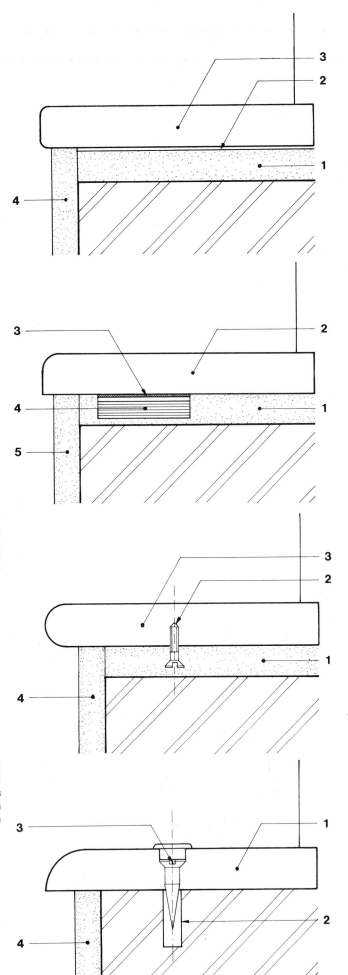

INTERNAL WALL FINISHES: Pre-surfaced plywood

A Plywood sheets are normally fixed to timber battens. Where the edges of the sheets or panels are not likely to be subject to damage, a gap is left between adjacent sheets and the screw fixings are at the back. A metal angle cleat is used to connect the sheet to the wall batten. This method is to be avoided with thin sheets.

1 Timber wall batten
2 Aluminium alloy angle cleat
3 Screw
4 Surfaced plywood panel or sheet

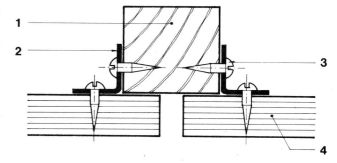

B An alternative method of fixing is to use tongued and grooved plywood panels placed directly against the batten and pinned through the tongue. Panels cannot easily be removed, however, except in a reverse sequence to assembly or by cutting through the tongue of a panel.

1 Timber wall batten
2 Tongued and grooved plywood panel
3 Pin
4 Tongued and grooved plywood panel

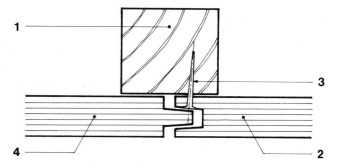

C An effective method of fixing which gives edge protection to the panel and also permits easy removal of any one panel is by means of an aluminium or plastic section which is screwed to the wall batten through holes in the central channel. Such a section can also be used to take wall brackets for shelving and fittings.

1 Timber wall batten
2 Plywood panel
3 Anodized aluminium alloy section or plastic section
4 Aluminium or stainless steel wood screw

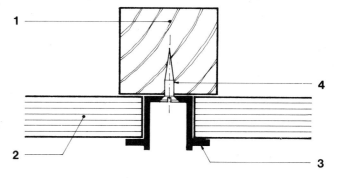

D An alternative form of capping section may be used which conceals the fixing screws. The section is first plumbed and screwed to the timber wall batten. The plywood panels are then slid into position. The method requires accurate setting out in relation to the width of sheet and the centre-line spacing of the sections.

1 Timber wall batten
2 Anodized aluminium capping section
3 Wood screw
4 Plywood panel

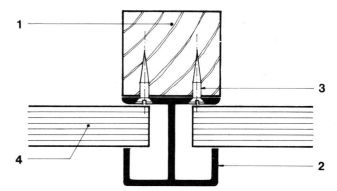

INTERNAL WALL FINISHES: Timber acoustic panels

A Head

Timber acoustic panels that are used to line walls and partitions are fixed to prevent contact with other finishes. Horizontal battens are fixed to the structural wall at 450 mm centres on packing. The acoustic panels, 600 mm wide, are fixed to the battens vertically with screws, pins, or staples. Horizontal joints between panels are either left open with a clearance of 3 mm to 6 mm or filled with a clearance of 3 mm to 6 mm or filled with a hardwood bead that may be flush or recessed.

1 Structural wall, or partition
2 Packing
3 Timber batten ex 50 mm x 25 mm
4 Timber acoustic panel 25 mm thick
5 Nail 25 mm long
6 Hardwood bead 21 mm x 6 mm

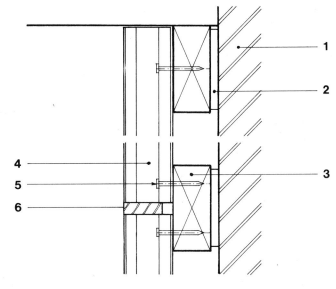

B Sill

The acoustic panels on the lower part of the walls are fixed so as not to touch the skirting. The skirting is fixed separately to its own fixing batten. An additional batten is provided to take the fixings of the acoustic panels.

1 Structural wall
2 Packing
3 Timber batten ex 50 mm x 25 mm
4 Timber skirting
5 Timber acoustic panel
6 Nail 25 mm long

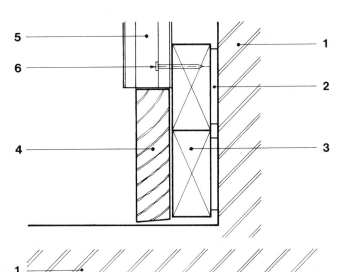

C Intermediate support

The vertical joint between the acoustic panels is arranged to ensure a continuous and regular repetition of the vertical slits. A hardboard bead with the same width as a vertical slit is pinned to the edge of a panel. The second panel is then fixed alongside. The nail is driven into the back of the panel through the slit and the nail head is punched home with a punch of uniform diameter less than the width of a slit.

1 Structural wall
2 Packing
3 Timber batten ex 50 mm x 25 mm
4 Hardboard bead
5 Timber acoustic panel
6 Nail 25 mm long

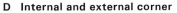

D Internal and external corner

The joint between two acoustic panels at an external corner is made by means of a hardwood batten of the same width as the panels. The joint between two panels at an internal corner is left open to give a clearance of 4 mm that matches the visible width of the vertical slits.

1 Structural wall
2 Packing
3 Timber batten ex 50 mm x 25 mm
4 Timber acoustic panel
5 Nail 25 mm long
6 Hardwood batten 25 mm x 25 mm

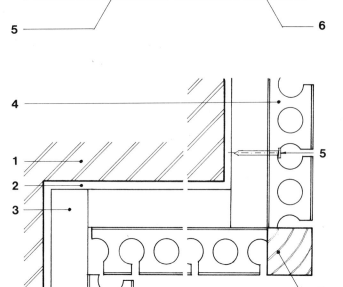

INTERNAL WALL FINISHES : Timber sound absorbent slats

A Head

Sound absorbent timber slats used as wall linings are made of tongued and grooved hardwood strips that are also grooved and slotted to control sound waves. Timber battens are fixed to the structural wall horizontally at 300 mm centres. The space between the battens is filled with glass fibre or mineral wool. The slats are placed vertically and are pinned to the battens.

1 Structural wall
2 Timber batten ex 50 mm x 25 mm
3 Glass fibre or mineral wool
4 Sound absorbent hardwood slat 15 mm thick
5 Panel pin 25 mm long

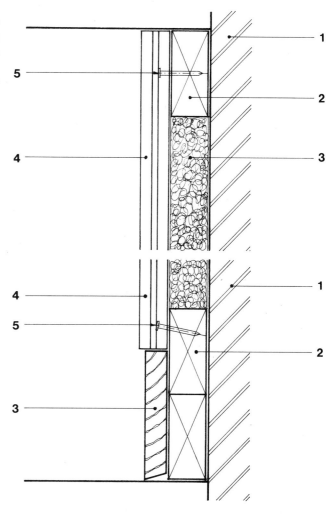

B Sill

The lower end of each slot is pinned to a horizontal batten that is independent of the batten to which the skirting is fixed. The glass fibre between the battens provides sound absorption, thermal insulation and fire protection.

1 Structural wall
2 Timber batten ex 50 mm x 25 mm
3 Timber skirting
4 Sound absorbent hardwood slat 15 mm thick
5 Panel pin 25 mm long

C Intermediate support

The slat is pinned to the timber battens through its tongue and the pins are then concealed by being within the groove of the adjacent panel.

1 Structural wall
2 Timber batten ex 50 mm x 25 mm
3 Sound absorbent hardwood slat 15 mm thick
4 Panel pin 25 mm long

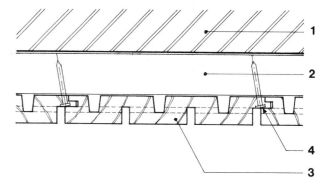

D Internal and external corner

The joint between two slats at an external corner is made by means of a hardwood batten rebated to take the thickness of the panel. When the slats are cut, the pins are fixed through a vertical groove and driven home with a narrow headed punch of uniform diameter less than the width of the groove.

1 Structural wall
2 Timber batten ex 50 mm x 25 mm
3 Sound absorbent hardwood slat 15 mm thick
4 Panel pin 25 mm long
5 Hardwood batten 18 mm x 18 mm

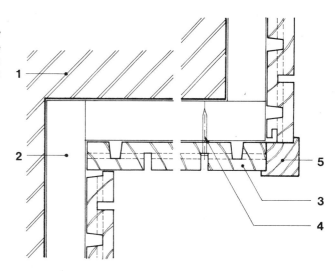

A The long edges of the wood fibreboard sheet 12 mm thick are bevelled with a bevel of about 2 mm and are positioned with a clearance between adjacent boards of about 3 mm. The boards are fixed to the support battens at 610 mm centres with rustproofed round plain head nails 40 mm long at 75 mm centres around the perimeter of the board and at 150 mm centres across intermediate supports. The nails are punched home and the holes filled.

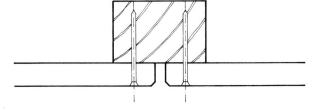

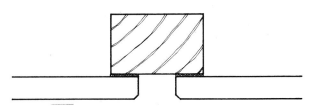

B The boards are positioned with a clearance of 20 mm and the edges bevelled with a bevel of about 2 mm. As an alternative to nails, the boards are fixed with adhesive.

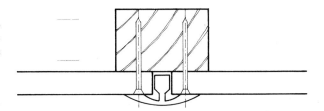

C The boards are positioned with a clearance of 10 mm and are fixed with rustproofed nails, as described in A above. The gap between the board is covered with a plastic T section which is fixed with adhesive.

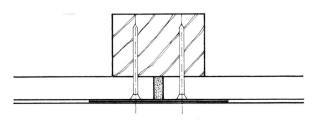

D The boards are positioned with a clearance of 3 mm and the gap is filled with a cellulose filler. A glass fibre scrim not less than 75 mm wide is pressed on to a PVA adhesive over the length of the joint. When hard and dry the surface is lightly sanded and then sized prior to the application of wallpaper.

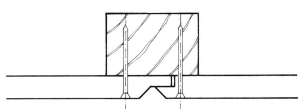

E The long edges of the board are specially machined to provide a profile that permits movement and conceals the support batten.

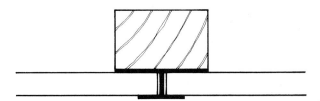

F An aluminium H section is screwed to the support batten and also serves as a cover strip that locates the boards and permits their movement.

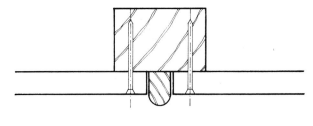

G A timber bead is pinned to the support batten and the edge of each board is positioned against the bead and fixed with pins which are punched home and filled.

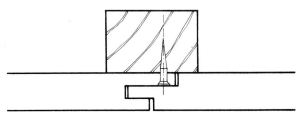

H The edges of the boards are tongued and grooved in such a way as to conceal the screws that are used to fix the first board. The joint permits movement of each board and shows on the face of the wall as a narrow gap.

A Tapered-edge boards

The joint between tapered-edge plasterboards is intended to achieve a continuous smooth plastered wall finish. When fixed to metal studs, the edge of each board is fixed with self-drilling and tapping screws. The shallow trough between the boards is filled with a joint filler into which is pressed a specially designed paper tape. The tape is covered with more joint filler made flush with the surface of the board. A joint finish is then applied as a band 200 mm wide, followed by a slurry of the same material.

1 Metal stud
2 Tapered-edge plasterboard
3 Self-drilling and tapping screw 22 mm long
4 Plaster joint filler
5 Paper joint tape 45 mm wide
6 Plaster joint finish

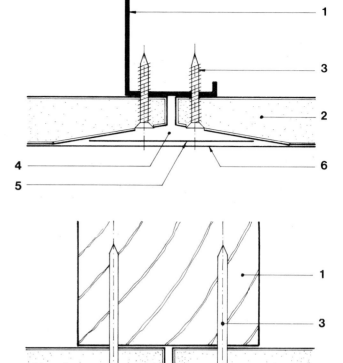

B Bevelled-edge boards

The joint between bevelled-edge plasterboards is intended to appear as a decorative V-joint. When fixed to timber studs the edge of each board is nailed with galvanized clout nails 40 mm long. The base only of the V-joint is filled with joint finish and a slurry of the same material is applied over the entire surface of the board.

1 Timber stud
2 Bevelled-edge plasterboard
3 Galvanized clout nail 40 mm long, 2 mm diameter
4 Plaster joint finish

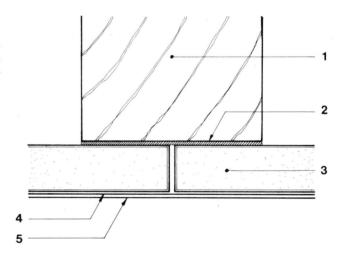

C Square-edge boards

At intermediate supports, the plasterboard is fixed with a gap-filling PVA adhesive. Nails are used at the edges. Square-edge plasterboard sheets are close-butted and the joint between them is covered with jute scrim bedded in plaster. The entire surface of the plasterboard is then covered with a plaster skim coat.

1 Timber stud
2 Adhesive with gap-filling properties (PVA)
3 Square-edge plasterboard
4 Jute scrim 90 mm wide strip
5 Plaster skim coat

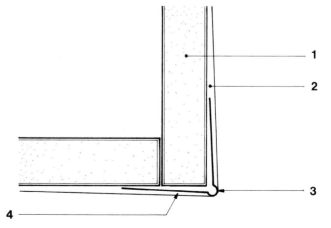

D External angle between boards

The joint between two sheets of plasterboard which meet at an external corner is made by a perforated galvanized steel angle strip with an arris formed by a quarter-round metal bead which is left exposed. A layer of joint filler is applied to both sides of the corner and the angle strip is pressed firmly into place. When the joint filler has set, another layer is applied and feathered out to the face of the plasterboard. A plaster joint filler is then applied and when set, another layer is applied and feathered out.

1 Plasterboard 13 mm thick
2 Plaster joint filler
3 Angle strip 25 mm x 25 mm
4 Plaster joint finish

A The joint between the edge of a plasterboard sheet and its supporting wall is finished and protected by means of a galvanized steel plasterboard edging bead. The perforated flange of the bead is nailed to the wall with masonry nails. The plasterboard is then pressed into the channel of the bead which provides a spring fit.

1 Supporting wall
2 Galvanized steel plasterboard edging bead
3 Masonry nail
4 Plasterboard 13 mm

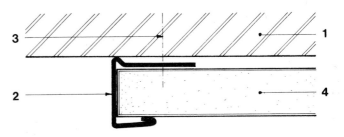

B When the plasterboard is finished with a skim coat of plaster, the edging bead is fitted first around the edge of the plasterboard with the perforated flange on the outside. The bead is nailed to the support wall through the plasterboard with a plasterboard nail. The skim coat of plaster is then applied to give a smooth finish and to cover both the bead and nails.

1 Supporting wall
2 Plasterboard 13 mm
3 Galvanized steel plasterboard edging bead
4 Plasterboard nail
5 Plaster skim coat 6 mm

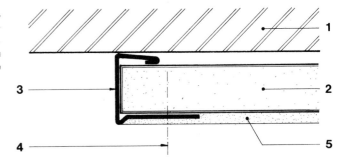

FLOOR FINISHES : Plywood panels

A   Finished plywood panel to timber floor joist

A number of alternative methods are used to fix plywood
tongued and grooved panels used as flooring. When the plywood
panels are to be the finished flooring without an overlay, the
joint is placed along the centre of the support joist and the panel
is secret nailed through the tongue with one lost-head nail in
each panel. A metal angle guard is used to prevent damage to
the joint profile during driving. The next panel is tapped home to
ensure a tight fit at the joint.

1   Timber floor joist
2   Finished plywood tongued and grooved panel 15 mm thick
3   Lost-head nail 37 mm long
4   Plywood tongued and grooved panel

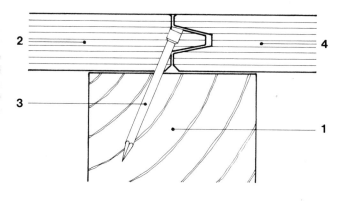

B   Underlay plywood panel to timber floor joist

When the plywood panels are used as an underlay, each panel
is nailed to the floor joist with at least one square twisted shank
flat head nail. The edge and end distance must not be less than
10 mm. The next panel is tapped home to ensure a tight fit at the
joint. A small offcut of the grooved section may be used to
protect the joint profile.

1   Timber floor joist
2   Underlay plywood tongued and grooved panel 15 mm thick
3   Square twisted shank flat head nail 37 mm long
4   Plywood tongued and grooved panel 15 mm thick
5   Floor finish overlay

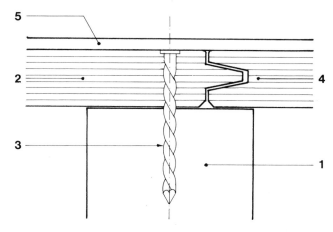

C   Underlay plywood panel to concrete floor

When the plywood panels are used over a concrete floor to serve
as an underlay, they are fixed with masonry nails driven directly
into the concrete. A synthetic resin adhesive is used as a gap-
filler between the concrete and the plywood panels. When the
concrete is not properly dried out, a vapour barrier must be
used on top of the concrete.

1   Concrete floor slab
2   Gap-filling synthetic resin adhesive
3   Underlay plywood tongued and grooved panel 15 mm thick
4   Masonry nail 40 mm long
5   Underlay plywood tongued and grooved panel 15 mm thick
6   Floor finish overlay

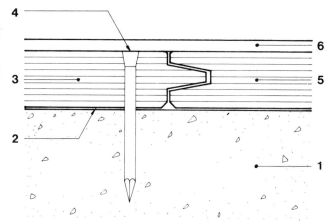

D   Finished plywood panel to insulated concrete floor

When the plywood panels are to be the finished flooring over a
concrete floor slab, the panels can be laid, without fixing, on a
layer of polystyrene 25 mm thick laid on a vapour barrier placed
on top of the concrete. Each panel is tapped home at the tongue
to ensure a tight fit at the joint.

1   Concrete floor slab
2   Vapour barrier
3   Expanded polystyrene 25 mm thick
4   Finished plywood tongued and grooved panel 15 mm thick
5   Finished plywood tongued and grooved panel 15 mm thick

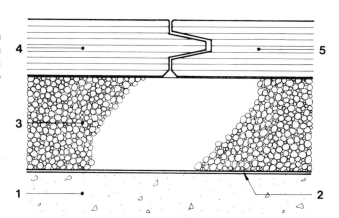

A Bonded monolithic construction

The screed is laid on an in situ concrete base slab before the concrete has set, normally within 3 hours of placing of the concrete. The thickness of the screed is not less than 10 mm and not more than 25 mm. The screed is laid in bays to correspond with those of the structural base. The base and the screed shrink together and separation is unlikely to occur.

1 Concrete base slab
2 Screed—cement:sand 1:4

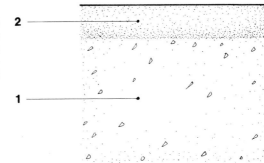

B Bonded separate construction

The concrete base slab is laid and allowed to set and harden. The surface of the concrete is thoroughly hacked, cleaned and dampened to reduce suction. A grout or a bonding agent is then applied to the surface immediately before the screed is laid. The thickness of screed is not less than 40 mm.

1 Concrete base slab
2 Screed—cement:sand 2:9

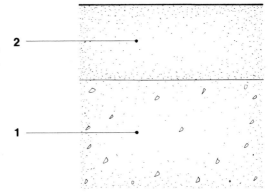

C Unbonded construction on damp-proof membrane

The concrete base slab is laid and allowed to set and harden. The slab is cleaned and covered with a damp-proof membrane. The screed is laid to a thickness of not less than 50 mm. When the screed contains heating cables, the thickness is not less than 60 mm.

1 Concrete base slab
2 Damp-proof membrane
3 Screed—cement:fine aggregate:coarse aggregate 2:3:6

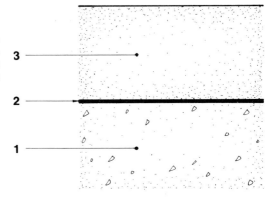

D Unbonded construction on layer of insulation

The concrete base slab is laid and allowed to set, harden and dry out. Expanded polystyrene slabs 25 mm thick are laid and closely butted together. The screed is laid with a thickness of not less than 60 mm.

1 Concrete base slab
2 Expanded polystyrene slab 25 mm thick
3 Screed—cement:fine aggregate:coarse aggregate 2:3:6

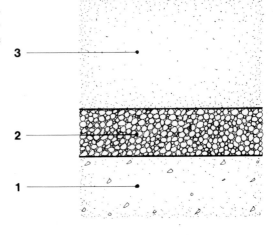

FLOOR FINISHES: Timber flooring

A Softwood board flooring

The timber battens are splayed and bedded on the damp-proof membrane over the concrete base slab. Clout nails, with their heads projecting, are nailed along both sides of the battens to connect to the screed. The screed is laid as dry as possible and level with the top of the battens. The timber flooring is nailed to the batten with lost-head nails. The boards are face-nailed to each batten with two nails for boards up to 175 mm wide, the outer nails being between 15 mm and 20 mm from the edge.

1 Concrete base slab
2 Damp-proof membrane
3 Timber batten treated with preservative
4 Clout nail at 450 mm centres on alternate sides
5 Screed
6 Softwood board flooring
7 Lost-head nail 50 mm long

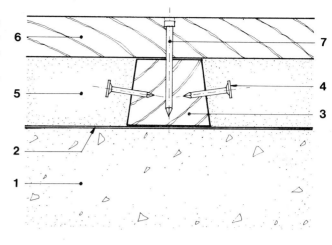

B Softwood board flooring

An alternative method is to use square battens which are fixed with masonry nails to a screed laid over the damp-proof membrane on the concrete slab. The softwood board flooring is nailed to the battens with lost-head nails.

1 Concrete base slab
2 Damp-proof membrane
3 Screed
4 Timber batten 36 mm x 36 mm
5 Masonry nail
6 Softwood board flooring
7 Lost-head nail 50 mm long

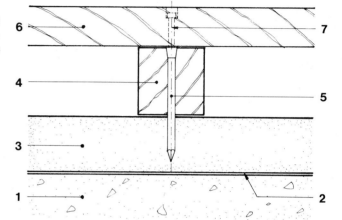

C Softwood strip flooring

An alternative method of laying board flooring is to cover the concrete site slab with a damp-proof membrane and nail square battens directly to the concrete with masonry nails. The flooring is then nailed to the battens with lost-head nails. The flooring is secret-nailed to each batten, the nails being driven into the side of the strip just above the tongue at an angle of about 50 degrees to the vertical.

1 Concrete base slab
2 Damp-proof membrane
3 Timber batten 36 mm x 36 mm
4 Masonry nail
5 Softwood board flooring
6 Lost-head nail 40 mm long

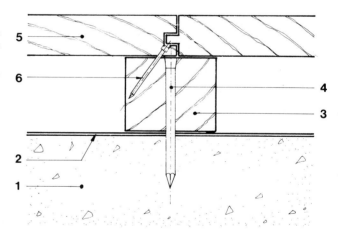

D Interlocking hardwood block flooring

The surface of the screed must be rigid, level, dry, dust-free, without irregularities of the surface, but with a slightly coarsened finish similar to a wood-float finish. The underside of each hardwood block is dipped in the adhesive and then placed immediately into position.

1 Concrete base slab
2 Screed of cement:sand 1:4
3 Adhesive and damp-proof membrane
4 Hardwood block

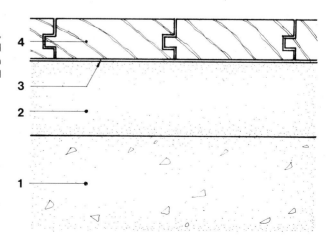

FLOOR FINISHES: Clay floor tile on concrete base

SCALE 1:2

A Unbonded bedding

The concrete base is cleaned and covered with a separating layer of polythene or building paper lapped 100 mm. A stiff cement: sand mix 1 : 4. 15 to 25 mm thick, is levelled to take the tiles. The bedding is dusted with dry cement and lightly trowelled until the cement becomes damp. The tiles are laid immediately with a joint clearance of 3 mm minimum and tamped level. The joints are filled at least 12 hours later. When the floor exceeds 15 m in one direction, a movement joint is provided at the perimeter.

1 Concrete base
2 Polythene or building paper separating layer
3 Cement:sand 1 : 4 bedding, 15 mm to 25 mm thick
4 Clay floor tile
5 Unfilled gap (movement joint)

B Bonded bedding

A stiff cement:sand mix 1 : 4, is laid directly on to the concrete base which may need to be dampened to reduce suction. The bed, 20 mm to 40 mm thick, is tamped and fully compacted. It is dusted with dry cement and lightly trowelled until the cement becomes damp. The tiles are laid immediately with a joint clearance of 3 mm minimum and are tamped level. The joints are filled at least 12 hours later.

1 Concrete base
2 Cement:sand 1 : 4 bedding, 20 mm to 40 mm thick
3 Clay floor tile
4 Unfilled gap (movement joint)

C Joint between tiles

The joint between the clay tiles is filled as a separate operation at least 12 hours after the tiles have been laid. A mix of Portland cement:fine dry sand 1 : 1 with the consistency of a paste forms a grout which is worked well into the gap between the tiles and finished flush with their surface. Surplus grout is cleaned off by brushing with sharp sand.

1 Concrete base
2 Separating layer
3 Unfilled gap (movement joint)
4 Cement:sand 1 : 4 bedding
5 Clay floor tile
6 Portland cement:sand 1 : 1, joint 3 mm thick

D Expansion joint

When the clay floor tiling exceeds 15 m in any direction the tiling may expand and the concrete base may shrink considerably. An expansion joint is incorporated along the perimeter and, if required, across the flooring. When a coved tiled skirting is used, the expansion joint is in the form of an expansion strip positioned between the skirting tiles and the flooring.

1 Concrete base
2 Separating layer
3 Cement:sand 1 : 4 bedding
4 Clay coved skirting tile
5 Expansion strip
6 Cement:sand 1 : 4 bedding
7 Clay floor tile

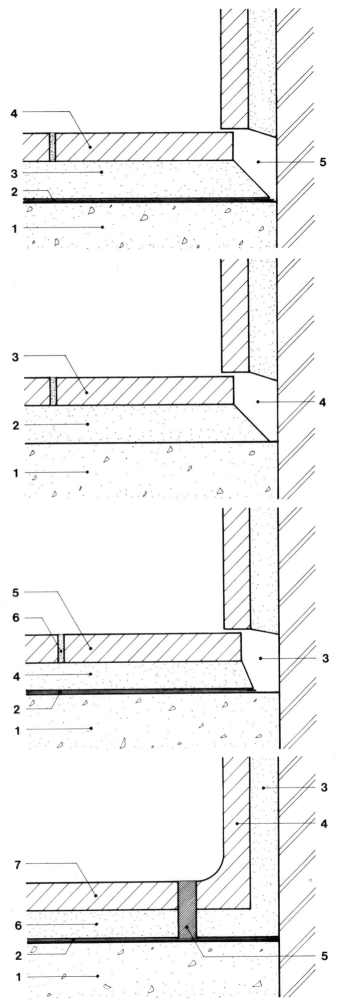

FLOOR FINISHES: Clay floor tiles

A Expansion joint

An expansion joint across floors of clay tiles is recommended when any floor dimension exceeds 15 m. Gaps with a clearance of up to 10 mm are filled with a compressible filler board, a separating strip and a sealant. The depth of sealant is generally not less than 12 mm. The filler must be tightly packed so that no voids remain at the base of the gap.

1 Concrete base
2 Compressible filler board
3 Cement : sand 1 : 4 bed
4 Clay floor tile
5 Separating strip
6 Sealant

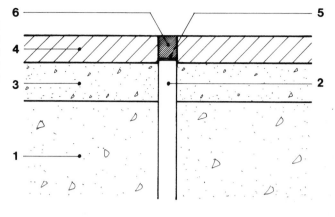

B Compression joint

When the concrete base is likely to contract and the flooring is bonded directly to it, a compression joint is provided to accommodate the movement. The sealant of two-part polysulphide is square in cross-section and adheres to the sides of the floor tiling but is separated from the base slab and supported by a continuous strip of foam polyethylene packed in the gap between the tile bed.

1 Concrete base
2 Cement : sand 1 : 4 bed
3 Clay floor tile
4 Foam polyethylene strip
5 Two-part polysulphide sealant 18 mm x 18 mm

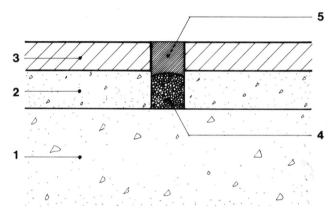

C Supported expansion joint for light loading

When the clearance of an expansion joint exceeds 12 mm, the gap is formed and maintained by two metal angle sections that are fixed firmly into the bed. The gap between the two angles is filled with a compressible filler board, a separating strip and a sealant. The sealant must be able to take up the specified maximum and minimum clearance between the faces of the angle sections. The width : depth ratio varies from 1 : 1 for a clearance of 12 mm up to 2 : 1 for a clearance of 50 mm.

1 Concrete base
2 Compressible filler board
3 Continuous metal angle section
4 Cement : sand 1 : 4 bed
5 Clay floor tile
6 Polythene separating strip
7 Sealant

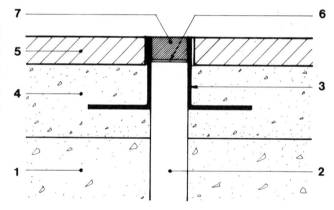

D Supported expansion joint for heavy loading

When traffic is likely to be heavy and the maximum possible movement is to be accommodated by the joint sealant, a depth of sealant of 25 mm is used with a width of 50 mm. The sealant is separated from the compressible filler board by a polythene bond breaker placed in a rebate in the floor screed.

1 Concrete base
2 Compressible filler board
3 Cement : sand 1 : 4 bed
4 Clay floor tile
5 Polythene bond breaker
6 Two-part polysulphide sealant

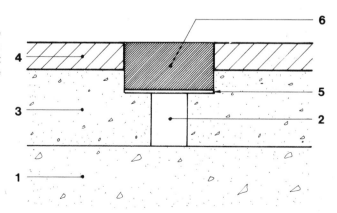

FLOOR FINISHES: Expansion joints

A Expansion joint for floor finish 15 mm thick
A strip of mortar is placed along the edges of the concrete slab to form a level and smooth surface. The aluminium sections are placed on both sides of the gap provided for expansion and temporarily nailed with masonry nails so that the top edge is level with the finished floor level. The screed and floor finish are then placed in position. The joint is closed by inserting the flexible PVC gasket. The maximum permissible clearance is 30 mm and the minimum 20 mm.

1 Concrete slab with gap for expansion
2 Mortar strip
3 Aluminium section
4 Masonry nail
5 Screed
6 Sheet flooring
7 PVC gasket

B Expansion joint for floor finish 35 mm to 50 mm thick
The sequence of construction is similar to that in A above. The aluminium sections are designed as a pair of interlocking sections that may be assembled to suit floor thicknesses that vary between 35 mm and 50 mm. The maximum permissible clearance is 30 mm and the minimum is 20 mm.

1 Concrete slab
2 Mortar strip
3 Aluminium interlocking sections
4 Masonry nail
5 Screed
6 Floor tile
7 PVC gasket

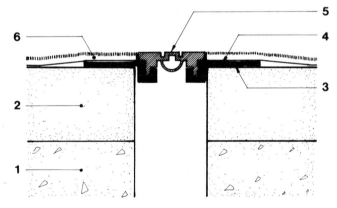

C Expansion joint for carpet floor finish 5 mm thick
A screed is laid with a smooth and level surface. The aluminium section is positioned on both sides of the gap provided for expansion and fixed to the screed with adhesive. The flexible PVC gasket is inserted and the carpet laid to butt closely to the edge of the gasket. The maximum permissible clearance is 40 mm and the minimum 30 mm.

1 Concrete slab
2 Screed
3 Adhesive
4 Aluminium section
5 PVC gasket
6 Carpet 5 mm thick

D Expansion joint between floor and wall
The gap to allow for expansion is provided between the floor slab and wall. Aluminium sections are fixed to the floor and wall with masonry nails. The floor sections are interlocking to suit floor thicknesses between 25 mm and 30 mm. The screed and floor finish are laid and the wall plastered. The flexible PVC gasket is then inserted. The maximum permissible clearance is 40 mm and the minimum is 30 mm.

1 Concrete slab
2 Block wall
3 Aluminium section
4 Masonry nail
5 Screed
6 Sheet flooring
7 Plaster
8 PVC gasket

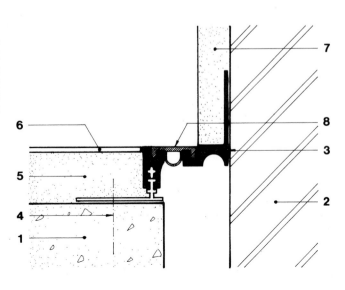

A Joint across screed and floor finish

The concrete structural floor slab is divided into bays and the gap between adjacent slabs, with a clearance of 25 mm, is filled with dry sand. The movement joint strip is placed over the gap between the slabs. The sides of the strip form a permanent shuttering for the floor screed and the top forms a datum for levelling the screed and for the level of the finished floor.

1 Concrete structural floor slab
2 Sand filling
3 Polychloroprene movement joint strip
4 Screed
5 Vinyl floor finish

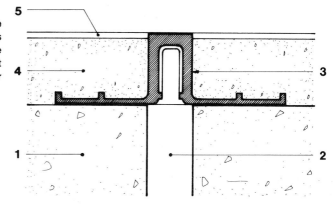

B Joint across granolithic floor

When the thickness of screed or similar flooring is required to be thicker than the depth of the movement joint strip, the strip is bedded and levelled on a semi-dry mortar layer. The strips are laid to suit the required layout of bays and are interconnected by special junction pieces. The flooring over the complete floor area may then be laid as a single operation.

1 Concrete structural floor slab
2 Sand filling
3 Mortar bed
4 Polychloroprene movement joint strip
5 Granolithic flooring

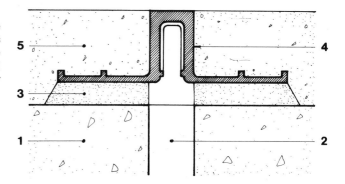

C Typical layout of movement joint gaskets

Four kinds of gasket are used to make up any rectilinear subdivision of the floor. All gaskets are made for a polychloroprene based compound and are formed as a straight extrusion, a moulded T junction, a moulded 4-way junction, and a moulded corner junction. The junction pieces incorporate projections which are designed to interlock with the straight sections. The straight section may be cut to the required length on site or may be joined by means of adhesive to another section.

1 Straight movement joint strip
2 T junction gasket
3 4-way junction gasket
4 Corner junction gasket

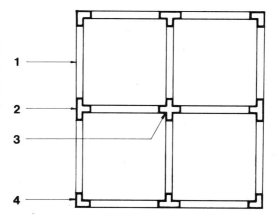

D Joint between gaskets

The joint between a 4-way junction gasket and a straight joint strip is made by means of a channel section that is formed as a projection on each prong of the junction. The corresponding channel of the strip extrusion slides over and interlocks with the projecting channel of the junction. The joint with other junction gaskets is made in the same way.

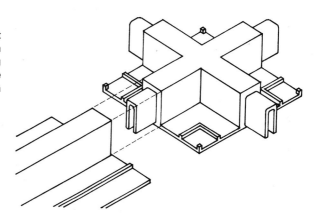

FLOOR FINISHES: Timber flooring on concrete

A Timber flooring on a concrete floor slab

Standard floor clips have twin legs that are bedded at 400 mm centres in the concrete slab before it has set. A damp-proof membrane is spread over the slab. The side ears of the clip are opened, timber battens are placed in position between the ears and two round plain head nails are used in each ear to connect the clip to the batten.

1 Concrete floor slab
2 Damp-proof membrane
3 Sheet steel sherardized standard floor clip 32 mm wide
4 Timber batten 50 mm x 50 mm
5 Sherardized steel round plain head nail: 4 per clip
6 Timber floor

B Timber flooring on a concrete floor slab

Standard single leg floor clips are an alternative form of floor clip with a single central leg that has two shaped hooks designed to bond into the concrete or screed before it is dry. The two ears are opened out to contain the timber floor batten that is nailed to them with plain head nails.

1 Concrete floor slab
2 Damp-proof membrane
3 Sheet steel sherardized single leg floor clip
4 Timber batten 50 mm x 50 mm
5 Sherardized steel round plain head : 4 per clip
3 Sheet steel sherardized single leg floor clip
4 Timber batten 50 mm x 50 mm
5 Sherardized steel round plain head nail: 4 per clip
6 Timber floor

C Timber flooring on a concrete floor slab

Direct fix acoustic floor clips are fixed when the timber flooring is laid and can also be used for existing concrete slabs. The lower plate of the clip is nailed directly to the concrete slab with masonry nails 18 mm long. The clips are 32 mm wide and are spaced at 400 mm centres. The timber battens are carried in the channel between the ears of the clip and are nailed to it with round plain head nails. The acoustic pad that is incorporated in the clip is made of a special type of rubber that will maintain its resilience.

1 Concrete floor slab
2 Damp-proof membrane
3 Sheet steel sherardized direct fix floor clip
4 Sherardized steel masonry nail 18 mm long
5 Timber batten 50 mm x 50 mm
6 Sherardized steel round plain head nail: 4 per clip
7 Timber floor

D Timber flooring on a concrete floor slab

Short leg acoustic floor clips are an alternative form of acoustic clip with a central leg that has two shaped hooks designed to bond into the concrete or screed before it is dry. The clip incorporates a pad made of a special type of rubber that will maintain its resilience. The floor batten is inserted between the two legs of the clip and nailed to them.

1 Concrete floor slab
2 Damp-proof membrane
3 Sheet steel sherardized short leg acoustic floor clip
4 Timber batten 50 mm x 40 mm
5 Sherardized steel round plain head nail: 4 per clip
6 Timber floor

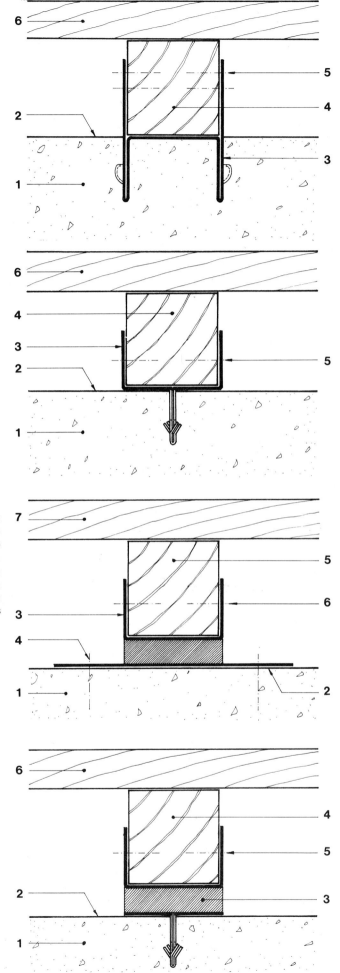

FLOOR FINISHES: Flooring grade chipboard

SCALE 1:2

A Chipboard flooring on timber joists
With joists spaced at 400 mm centres the chipboard boards are
18 mm thick and are nailed at about 300 mm centres to joists
supporting the edges of the boards and at about 500 mm centres
to intermediate joists. Loose tongues are fitted and glued into
the grooves along the edges of adjacent boards. Annular nails
50 mm long are used with the nail heads punched below the
surface of the board and no filling.

1 Timber floor joists
2 Chipboard flooring grade board 18 mm thick
3 Chipboard tongue
4 Adhesive
5 Annular nail 50 mm long

B Chipboard flooring on battens
The concrete slab is covered with polythene sheeting of a similar
vapour barrier. Timber battens are positioned at 600 mm centres
for chipboard 22 mm thick or at 400 mm centres for chipboard
18 mm thick. Tongues of chipboard are fitted and glued in the
grooves along the edges of adjacent boards. The boards are then
nailed to the battens with annular nails 50 mm long.

1 Concrete floor slab
2 Polythene sheeting vapour barrier
3 Timber batten 46 mm x 46 mm
4 Chipboard flooring grade board 18 mm thick
5 Chipboard tongue
6 Adhesive
7 Annular nail 50 mm long

C Chipboard flooring on insulation slab
The concrete slab is covered with a damp-proof sheeting followed by slabs of semi-rigid polystyrene butted closely together.
The chipboard boards, tongued and grooved on all four edges,
are placed on the insulation without fixing. The tongues along
two edges of a board are fitted into the corresponding grooves
of the adjacent board and are glued. A clearance of 10 mm is
left between the edge of the floor and the adjoining wall on all
sides of the flooring to provide for thermal movement.

1 Concrete floor slab
2 Damp-proof sheeting
3 Polystyrene flooring grade 25 mm thick
4 Chipboard flooring grade 18 mm thick
5 Adhesive

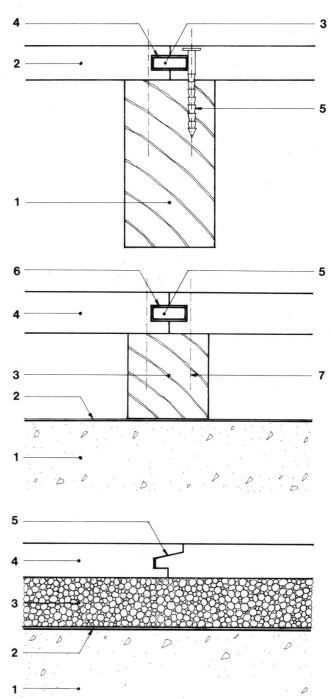

183

A Acoustic insulation with a screeded floating floor
The structural floor which is not less than 100 mm thick is cleaned and covered with Impact Sound Duty, Grade ISD, polystyrene slabs 25 mm thick. The same material is placed against the walls up to finished floor level. All joints are closely butted and taped. The polystyrene is covered with a cement: sand screed 1:4 mix 60 mm thick in areas not exceeding 60 sq m so as to minimise cracking. A PVC floor tile or similar floor finish is then laid.

1 Structural floor 100 mm thick
2 Expanded polystyrene 25 mm thick, Grade ISD
3 Cement and sand screed 60 mm thick
4 PVC floor tile

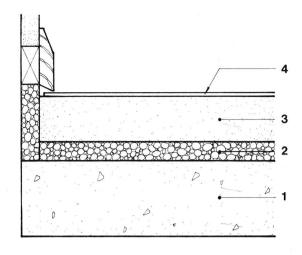

B Acoustic insulation with a chipboard floating floor
An alternative floor consists in covering the concrete structural floor with Impact Sound Duty, Grade ISD, polystyrene slabs and then laying a 1000-gauge polyethylene foil to prevent the passage of moisture. Tongued and grooved chipboard 18 mm thick is laid with a clearance of 15 mm between the edge of the flooring and the face of the wall. The tongued and grooved joints are normally glued.

1 Structural floor 100 mm thick
2 Expanded polystyrene 25 mm thick, Grade ISD
3 Polyethylene foil moisture barrier
4 Chipboard 18 mm tongued and grooved

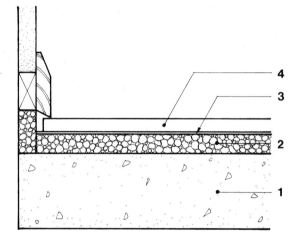

C Thermal insulation with an unheated concrete floor
At ground floor level the downward flow of heat is reduced by first placing a layer of standard duty, Grade SD, polystyrene slabs over a damp-proof membrane on the sand blinding. The slabs are closely butted and the joints taped. The concrete floor slab is then laid and finally covered with PVC floor tiles or a similar floor finish.

1 Hardcore base
2 Sand
3 Polyethylene damp-proof membrane
4 Expanded polystyrene 50 mm thick
5 Concrete slab 100 mm thick
6 PVC floor tile

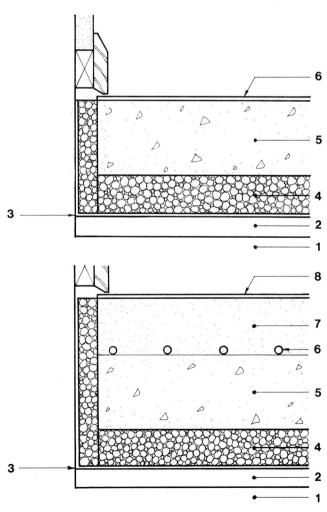

D Thermal insulation with a heated concrete floor
When the ground floor is to be heated by means of underfloor electric cable, the polyethylene film, expanded polystyrene slabs and concrete slab are laid as in C above. The heating cables are then set out and covered with a cement:sand screed 1:4 mix, 75 mm thick. PVC tiles or a similar floor finish is then laid.

1 Hardcore base
2 Sand
3 Polyethylene damp-proof membrane
4 Expanded polystyrene 50 mm thick
5 Concrete slab 100 mm thick
6 Heating cable
7 Cement and sand screed 75 mm thick
8 PVC floor tile

CEILING FINISHES: Plaster on metal lath

A Flat suspended ceiling

The hangers are cast into the support slab during its construction, or fixed afterwards, and carry main bearer channels. Runner channels are fixed at right angles to the bearers at 350 mm centres with wire ties. The expanded metal lath is wired to the runners. A coat of plaster is then applied to the lath followed by two finishing coats to give a total plaster thickness of 16 mm.

1 Hanger 25 mm x 3 m flat
2 Mild steel bearer channel 38 mm x 11 mm
3 Galvanized wire tie
4 Mild steel runner channel 19 mm x 10 mm
5 Galvanized wire tie
6 Expanded metal lath
7 Plaster 16 mm thick in three coats

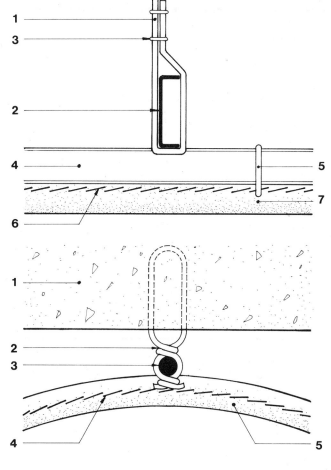

B Curved suspended ceiling

Hairpins, cast into the concrete support slab at 600 mm centres, are twisted around reinforcing rods which are used to support the lath. The preformed curved expanded metal lath is wired to the rods. A coat of plaster is then applied to the lath followed by two finishing coats to give a total plaster thickness of 16 mm.

1 Concrete slab
2 Hairpin 3 mm diameter cast into slab
3 Mild steel rod 10 mm diameter
4 Expanded metal lath
5 Plaster 16 mm thick in three coats

C Ceiling fixed to concrete beams

The concrete beam has a timber fillet cast into and along its underside. The expanded metal lath is nailed to the timber fillet with clout nails at each rib, 89 mm apart. A coat of plaster is then applied to the lath followed by two finishing coats to give a total plaster thickness of 16 mm.

1 Concrete beam
2 Timber fillet cast in beam
3 Expanded metal lath
4 Galvanized clout nail 38 mm long
5 Plaster 16 mm thick in three coats

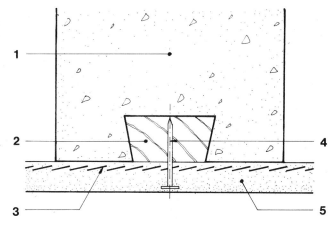

D Ceiling fixed to steel beams

Flat clips are used to attach flat hangers to the lower flange of the steel support joist. Light steel channel runners spaced at 350 mm centres are fixed to the hangers. The expanded metal lath is then wired to the runners. A coat of plaster is then applied to the lath followed by two finishing coats to give a total plaster thickness of 16 mm.

1 RSJ support beam
2 Mild steel clip 25 mm x 3 mm
3 Mild steel hanger 25 mm x 3 mm
4 Mild steel channel runner 38 mm x 10 mm
5 Expanded metal lath
6 Galvanized wire tie 3 mm diameter
7 Plaster

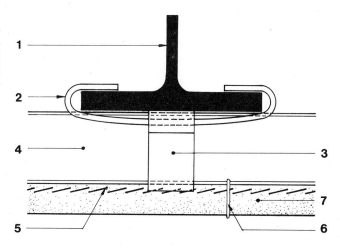

185

A Particle board may be used for ceiling finishes in a number of different ways, four of which are shown on this page. A suspended ceiling may be formed by the use of prefabricated panels grooved to fit the flanges of the standard suspended T section. The grooves are accurately positioned so as to ensure a level ceiling and narrow gaps between the panels, with the T completely concealed.

1 Suspension wire
2 Galvanised T section
3 Particle board 30 mm thick

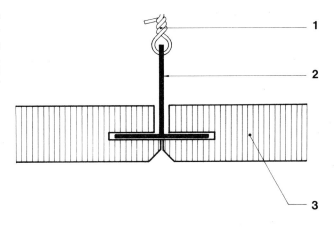

B When the finished ceiling is required close to the supporting structure, wood battens are first fixed and packed out to give a level lower surface. The prefabricated tongued and grooved panels are then nailed to the battens.

1 Structural ceiling
2 Timber batten
3 Particle board ceiling panel 26 mm thick
4 Lost-head steel nail 50 mm long

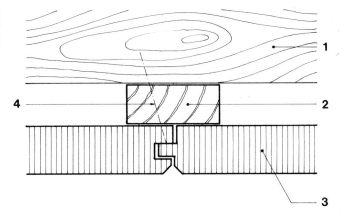

C An alternative method is to use prefabricated ceiling panels which are chamfered on all four edges and grooved on opposite sides to take hardboard tongues. Timber battens are fixed to the supporting structure and packed out as required to give a level lower surface. The panels are then nailed to span between the battens with loose tongues inserted in the grooves along the unsupported edges.

1 Supporting structure
2 Timber battens
3 Ceiling panel 600 mm x 600 mm x 22 mm
4 Lost-head steel nail 50 mm long
5 Hardboard tongue 30 mm x 3.2 mm

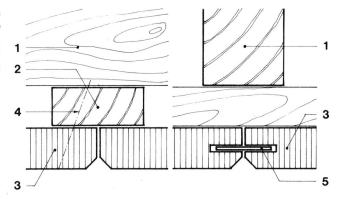

D A decorative ceiling with special acoustic characteristics is obtainable by means of strips nailed below a glass fibre mat. The thickness, width and spacing of the strips can be varied to suit particular requirements. The strips are nailed at right angles to the supporting joists. The mat is placed between the joists and carried on the strips.

1 Timber joists
2 Glass fibre mat
3 Particle board strip 100 mm x 22 mm
4 Lost-head nail 62 mm long

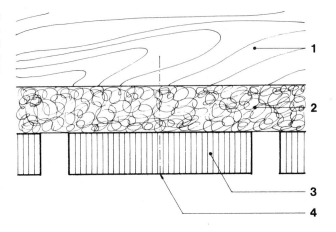

CEILING FINISHES : Timber fibre board

A Longitudinal joint between ceiling sheets

Thicknessed timber battens are shot fired to the structural slab to give a level surface. Battens ex 75 mm x 25 mm are used at the joint on all four sides of each sheet and additional battens ex 50 mm x 25 mm are positioned at 300 mm centres across the sheet. The sheets are secured to the battens with a layer of contact adhesive along the face of the battens and with wire staples fixed into the slots.

1 Structural concrete slab
2 Timber batten ex 75 mm x 25 mm
3 Masonry nail
4 Gap filling contact adhesive
5 Timber fibre board with longitudinal slots
6 Wire staple

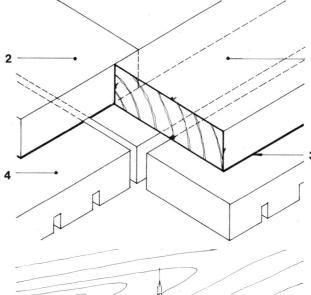

B Junction of ceiling sheets and support battens

The longitudinal joint between sheets is maintained at the same width as the slots. The transverse joint between adjacent sheets is made with a clearance of 6 mm.

1 Transverse batten
2 Longitudinal batten
3 Contact adhesive
4 Ceiling board

C Longitudinal joint between ceiling strips

The timber fibre board strips are tongued along one long and one short edge, and grooved along the other two edges. In this case the battens are nailed at right angles to ceiling joists at 285 mm centres. The long grooved edge of a strip is placed along the centre of a batten and stapled to it at 100 mm centres. The corresponding tongued long edge of an adjacent strip is then inserted into the groove and the strip is lightly tapped home.

1 Timber ceiling joist
2 Timber batten ex 50 mm x 25 mm
3 Round plain head nail
4 Timber fibre board tongued and grooved strip
5 Wire staple 13 mm long
6 Fibre board strip

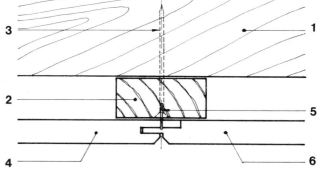

D Junction of ceiling strips

1 Timber ceiling joist
2 Timber batten
3 Timber fibre board grooved edges
4 Timber fibre board tongued edge

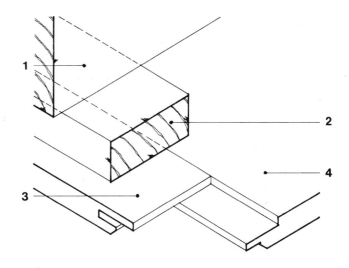

CEILING FINISHES: Sound absorbent panels

A The sound absorbent panels, 20 mm thick, are supplied with the four edges grooved to take fixing clips, mouldings or tees. 50 mm x 25 mm battens are located centrally on the joints between panels at approximately 600 mm centres and are packed out to give a level ceiling. The panels are secret fixed with panel pins. A short length of plastic T moulding is inserted between the panels as assembly proceeds.

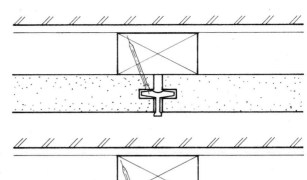

B The panels are positioned with a clearance of 16 mm and the gap is filled with a timber U-shaped moulding that is fitted into the panel grooves during assembly of the panels.

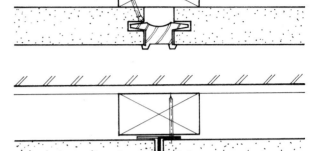

C The panels are positioned with a clearance of not less than 3 mm. A folded metal H-shaped locating clip is nailed to the timber batten. The lower flanges of the clip engage the groove of the panel and a continuous hardboard tongue is inserted below the clip into the same groove.

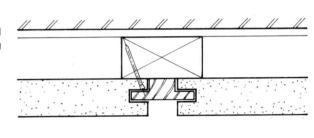

D The panels are positioned with a clearance of 16 mm and and secret nailed to the timber batten. A rebated timber moulding is inserted in the 6 mm wide groove of the panel.

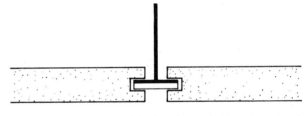

E The panels are supported on suspended metal T sections so as to form a suspended ceiling. The lower flange of the T fits the 6 mm wide groove in the edge of the panel and has a hardboard tongue placed on the underside that engages in the same groove. The clearance between the edges of the panels is 13 mm.

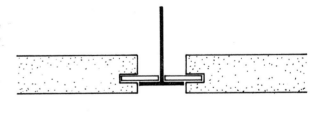

F Each panel is fitted with a hardboard tongue that is supported on the top of the lower flange of the T section. The clearance between the edges of the panels is slightly greater than the width of the flange of the T section.

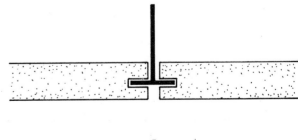

G The lower flange of the T section engages fully into a 4 mm wide groove in the panel so as to give a maximum clearance between the panels of 6 mm.

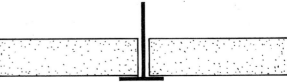

H The panels have a clearance of 6 mm and are supported directly by the lower flanges of the T section.

CEILING FINISHES : Mineral fibre tiles

A   Longitudinal section of suspended ceiling with concealed grid

The main support channels spaced 1200 mm apart are suspended from the supporting structure by means of suspension wire. Z sections are spaced 600 mm apart. The upper flange of a Z section is clipped to the channels and the lower flanges fit into grooves along the edges of the ceiling tiles.

1   Steel main support channel
2   Wire support clip
3   Z section
4   Mineral fibre ceiling tile 600 mm x 600 mm x 22 mm

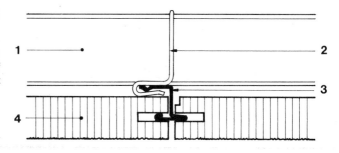

B   Cross section of suspended ceiling with concealed grid

The joint between ceiling tiles at right angles to the Z section supports is formed by means of a splice with flat ends. The ends are carried on the lower flanges of the Z sections and the spline is fitted into the grooves along the edges of adjoining tiles.

1   Steel main support channel
2   Z section
3   Wire support clip
4   Mineral fibre ceiling tile
5   Spline

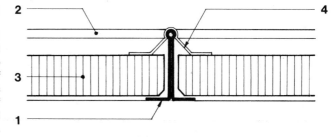

C   Longitudinal section of suspended ceiling with exposed grid

The suspended ceiling with an exposed grid consists of a grid of T sections which interlock and provide support flanges on all four sides of each ceiling tile. The main T section runners are spaced apart the width of a tile and are suspended by means of suspension wire from the supporting structure. Similar sections are fitted at right angles and spaced apart to suit the length of the tile. The tile is placed in position and held down with special clips which clip over the cylindrical top flange of the T sections.

1   Main T section runner
2   Cross T section
3   Mineral fibre ceiling tile
4   Hold down clip

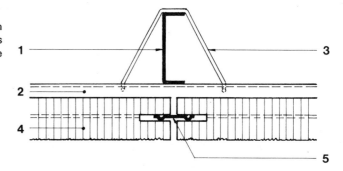

D   Cross section of suspended ceiling with exposed grid

The joint between tiles at right angles to the main T section runners is formed by a short length of cross T which is locked at both ends to the main runner. The ceiling tiles are laid on the flanges and held down by special clips which clip over the cylindrical top flange of the cross T.

1   Main T section runner
2   Cross T section
3   Mineral fibre ceiling tile
4   Hold down clip

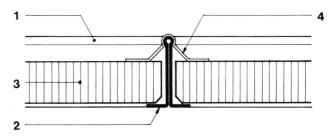

CEILING FINISHES : Finishes to soffits

A Slate soffit

When the soffit lining is slate, slabs of a maximum thickness of
25 mm are recommended to avoid excessive weight. The slab is
bedded to the support structure on mortar dabs and fixed in
position with an expanding bolt and a 6 mm diameter washer.
Holes are drilled in the slate and countersunk to take a slate pellet
or button.

1 Concrete support soffit
2 Mortar dab 12 mm thick bed joint
3 Slate slab 25 mm thick maximum
4 Expanding bolt and 6 mm diameter washer
5 Slate pellet or slate button

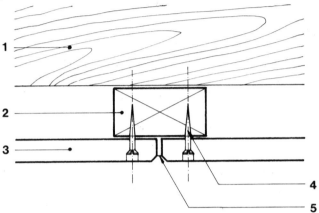

B Asbestos soffit

Soffits made of asbestos composition flat sheets are normally
fixed with wood screws inserted in pre-drilled holes, countersunk and filled. The joints between sheets are placed over the
support battens and are filled, if required, with Swedish putty or
a similar filler.

1 Timber support
2 Timber batten ex 50 mm x 25 mm
3 Asbestos composition sheet 13 mm thick
4 Corrosion-resistant wood screw in pre-drilled holes
5 Swedish putty or other similar filler

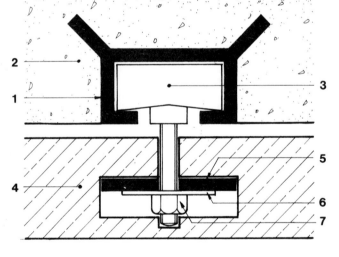

C Stone soffit

A phosphor bronze channel with lower flanges is cast into the
concrete support slab. A boss with a fixed stud and a plate is slid
along the channel so that one side of the plate enters a recess cut
in the edge of the stone soffit slab. A nut and washer are then
attached to retain the plate in position. The adjoining slab, with
a corresponding recess in its edge, is then moved sideways into
position to be supported by the other side of the plate.

1 Phosphor bronze channel
2 Concrete support slab
3 Phosphor bronze boss and stud
4 Stone soffit slab
5 Phosphor bronze plate 75 mm x 50 mm x 6 mm
6 Washer
7 Nut

D Marble soffit

A short length of phosphor bronze dovetail slotted channel is
cast in the concrete support slab in the required position. A
cramp in the form of a plate, dovetail shaped at one end and
with a dowel at the other end is inserted into the channel. The
edge of each marble soffit slab is drilled to take the dowel and
a recess is cut in each slab to take the thickness of the plate.

1 Phosphor bronze dovetail slotted channel
2 Concrete support slab
3 Phosphor bronze cramp with dowel
4 Phosphor bronze dowel 75 mm long, 6 mm diameter
5 Marble soffit slab

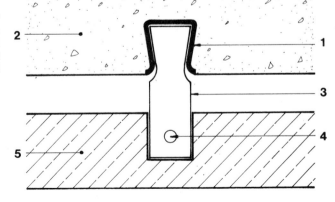

FITTINGS: Driven fixings

A A method of fixing fixtures to low density building blocks is to use a Loden anchor that consists of a tubular sleeve of plated steel flattened at one end to form a head and having an expander pin at the other. The anchor is located by means of a setting tool and driven home with a hammer until the stop on the tool is reached. The tool is then removed and hammering continued so as to spread the sleeves and provide a firm anchorage.

1 Aerated concrete block
2 Timber batten fixture
3 Loden anchor

B Another method of fixing to masonry a wide variety of light fixtures is by means of a special nail that includes a flanged expansion sleeve. A hole of the recommended diameter and depth is first drilled through the fixture into the masonry. The sleeved nail is inserted into the hole. The head of the nail is hammered home flush with the anchor sleeve causing it to expand and make a permanent fixing.

1 Masonry
2 Fixture
3 Sleeved nail

C An alternative method of driven fixing is by means of a masonry nail consisting of a high quality steel specially treated for maximum strength, plated for corrosion resistance and having a special head shape to prevent hammer skid and point shape to prevent splitting of timber. The nail is driven through the timber fixture, using short positive hammer blows. The nail should not be used in a mortar joint.

1 Masonry of brick or concrete block
2 Timber fixture
3 Masonry nail

D Another method for fixing fixtures to low-density masonry is by means of a flush head nail in conjunction with a specially formed tube that guides the nail and diverts it sideways into the masonry. The special tube is hammered through the fixture directly into the masonry. The steel nail is then inserted into the tube and hammered down the tube until it is driven home.

1 Masonry
2 Fixture
3 Seamless solid drawn shaped tube before nailing
4 Shaped tube in position
5 Round plain head nail in final position

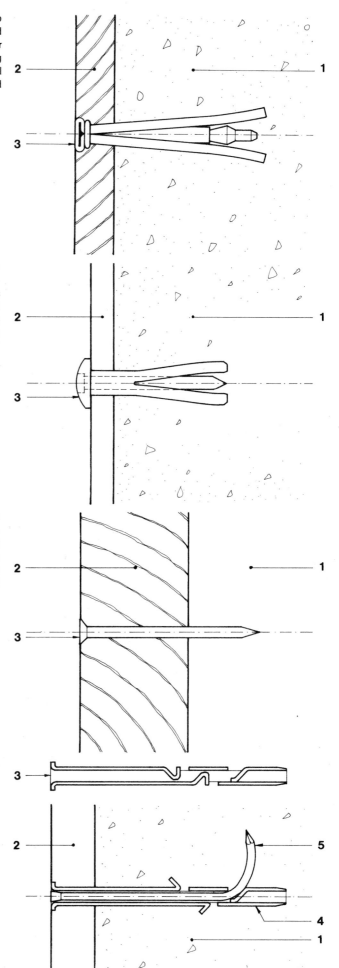

FITTINGS : Screw fixings

A A simple and effective method of fixing fittings to most types of masonry, brickwork and concrete is to use a fibre Rawlplug and wood screw. A hole of recommended diameter and depth is drilled. The screw is inserted one or two turns into the Rawlplug, and that is then pushed into the hole using the screw. The screw is turned to the full extent of the thread only. The screw is then withdrawn, the fixture placed in position, and the screw re-entered and turned until tight.

1 Masonry
2 Plaster
3 Hole pre-drilled to take rawlplug
4 Fibre rawlplug impregnated with a waterproofing binding agent
5 Fixture
6 Wood screw

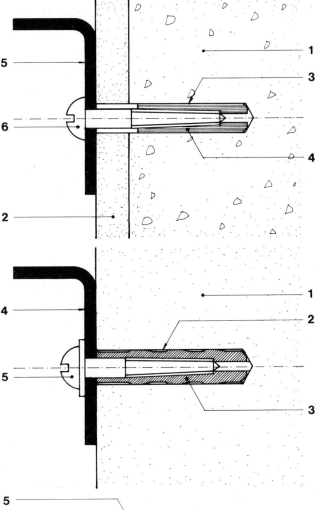

B An alternative method of screw fixing, particularly in soft materials and lightweight building blocks is to use a nylon Rawlplug. A hole of the recommended diameter and depth is drilled to take the rawlplug. The plug is inserted and, if necessary, tapped home with a light hammer. The fixture is placed in position and the wood screw inserted and turned until tight.

1 Lightweight block
2 Hole pre-drilled to take rawlplug
3 Nylon rawlplug
4 Fixture
5 Wood screw

C The handrail bolt, that is also called a handrail screw, is used to join the butt ends of two lengths of timber such as handrails. It consists of a bar threaded at both ends with a square nut at one end and a circular nut with grooves and washer at the other. The square nut is gripped in a square mortise in the end of one handrail. The circular nut is inserted in the mortise of the other handrail and is turned by striking the grooves with a handrail punch. Two or more dowels are inserted in the ends of the handrails to ensure alignment as the ends are brought together.

1 Handrail
2 Square nut positioned in mortise
3 Handrail bolt
4 Handrail
5 Wood dowel
6 Washer
7 Circular nut with 6 grooves

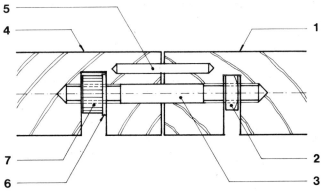

D The coach screw is generally used to connect heavy timber sections. It has a square head and a coarse tapered thread with a gimlet point. Part of the hole is pre-drilled and the head of the screw is turned with a spanner.

1 Timber section
2 Timber section
3 Washer
4 Steel coach screw

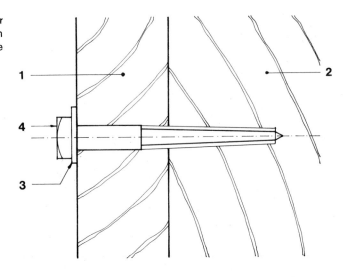

A A method of fixing fittings to a hollow masonry block, hollow wall lining or hollow door is to use a Rawlnut. It consists of a tough natural rubber sleeve with a metal nut bonded in one end and a moulded external flange at the other. A hole of recommended diameter is drilled through the material. The Rawlnut is inserted up to its flange. The screw is passed through the fixture into the Rawlnut and tightened so as to compress the rubber sleeve.

1 Plasterboard wall lining
2 Hole pre-drilled to take Rawlnut
3 Rawlnut
4 Fixture
5 Screw

B An alternative method of fixing fittings to cavity blocks and hollow partitions is by means of a gravity toggle. The material of the wall is drilled through with a hole of the recommended diameter. The fixing screw is passed through the fixture into the toggle and the toggle is passed through the hole into the cavity when it is allowed to drop and rest against the back face of the material. The screw is tightened until tight.

1 Aerated concrete block
2 Pre-drilled hole to take toggle
3 Gravity toggle
4 Fixture
5 Screw

C Another method of making fixings to cavity walls where only one side of the material is accessible is by using a spring toggle. It consists of a plated steel, spring actuated toggle bar pivoted on a swivel nut. A hole of the recommended diameter is drilled through to the cavity. The fixing screw is passed through the fixture so as to allow the toggle wings to spring apart and rest on the back face of the wall material. The screw is tightened until firm.

1 Hollow concrete wall block
2 Hole drilled to take spring toggle
3 Fixture
4 Spring toggle
5 Screw for spring toggle

D Fixing to cavity walls and partitions or sheets of plywood or hardboard with a limited space behind can also be done with an anchor screw. The minimum necessary depth of hollow space is 18 mm. The wall material is drilled through with a hole of the recommended size to take the anchor in its closed position. The screw and anchor are inserted through the fixture and hole. The screw is tightened so as to pull back the flanges of the anchor against the back of the material.

1 Plywood wall
2 Hole drilled to take anchor screw
3 Fixture
5 Anchor screw

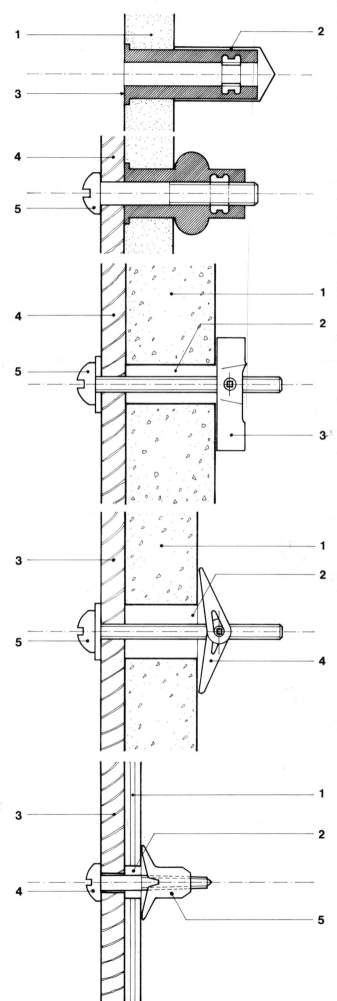

FITTINGS : Expansion anchors : bolt fixings

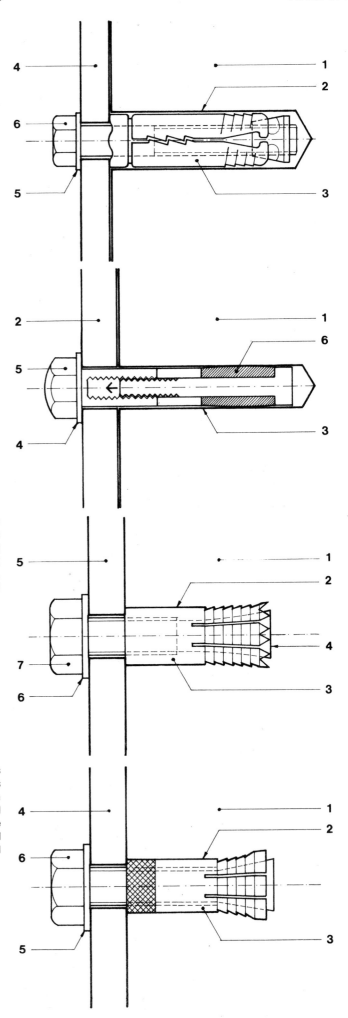

A This type of expansion anchor consists of a shield with a built-in expander nut and a separate bolt. A hole is first drilled of the recommended diameter and depth. The anchor shield is inserted and the fixture positioned over the hole. The bolt is passed through the fixture into the shield and tightened, thus causing the expander nut to rise and force the segments of the shield radially outwards against the side of the hole.

1 Masonry
2 Pre-drilled hole
3 Expansion anchor
4 Fixture
5 Washer
6 Bolt

B This type of anchor bolt that is used for fixing to both hard and soft materials has a PVC sleeve. When the bolt is tightened, the sleeve is compressed in length and expands radially giving a 360 degree full length grip. A hole is drilled in the masonry of a diameter equal to that of the bolt. The holes in the fixture can be used as a template. The bolt is inserted in the hole and the head of the bolt tightened.

1 Masonry
2 Fixture
3 Pre-drilled hole
4 Washer
5 Expansion anchor
6 PVC expansion sleeve

C The self-drill anchor incorporates a core drill that is used to cut a hole in the masonry. The hole is then cleaned out and a conical expander plug inserted in the toothed end. Anchorage is obtained by driving the drill over the plug at the lower end so as to expand the cylindrical walls of the drill against the sides of the hole. The fixture is placed over the anchor and a bolt inserted and tightened.

1 Masonry
2 Pre-drilled hole
3 Self-drill anchor
4 Plug
5 Fixture
6 Washer
7 Bolt

D The toothless anchor is similar in design to the one above, but as the name implies, has no cutting teeth to act as a drill. A hole is drilled with a percussive hammer to the recommended depth and to the same diameter as the anchor. The anchor is inserted and driven home with a few hammer blows on the appropriate setting tool, expanding the dovetail casing over the conical steel plug at the lower end. The fixture is applied and the bolt screwed home.

1 Masonry
2 Pre-drilled hole
3 Toothless anchor
4 Fixture
5 Washer
6 Bolt

FITTINGS : Expansion anchors : stud fixings

SCALE 1 : 1

A The sleeve anchor is a versatile heavy-duty anchor because alternative heads are available for fixing. It consists of a loose metal shield that expands over a conical wedge at the lower end when the head nut is tightened. A hole is drilled to the recommended depth and of the same diameter as the anchor. The anchor is inserted, the fixture placed in position, and the nut tightened so as to expand the ribs of the sleeve radially against the sides of the hole.

1 Masonry
2 Pre-drilled hole
3 Sleeve anchor
4 Fixture
5 Washer
6 Nut

B This type of expansion anchor has tapered wedges at the lower end that are expanded by a plug which is forced upwards when the stud is tightened. A hole is pre-drilled to the recommended depth of a diameter equal to the diameter of the anchor. The stud is inserted in the hole, the fixture offered up, and the washer and dome nut attached. As the dome nut is tightened, the wedges at the lower end are forced against the sides of the hole.

1 Masonry
2 Pre-drilled hole
3 Fixture
4 Stud anchor
5 Washer
6 Dome nut

C This type of expansion anchor has a conical lower end that is partly surrounded by a clip or wedges. A hole is drilled in the masonry of the same diameter as the stud. The fixture is placed in position and the anchor is inserted in the hole. The nut is applied and tightened thereby pulling up the stud and forcing the wedges at the lower end radially outwards.

1 Masonry
2 Pre-drilled hole
3 Fixture
4 Stud anchor
5 Washer
6 Nut

D This type of expansion anchor has an integral projecting stud and a loose metal shield that expands radially over a wedge at the lower end when the nut is tightened. The hole of a recommended diameter and depth is first drilled. The shell and stud are put into the hole as one unit leaving the stud projecting from the hole. The fixture is positioned and the washer and nut are tightened so as to expand the shield parallel to the sides of the hole and secure the anchor.

1 Masonry
2 Pre-drilled hole
3 Stud anchor
4 Fixture
5 Washer
6 Nut

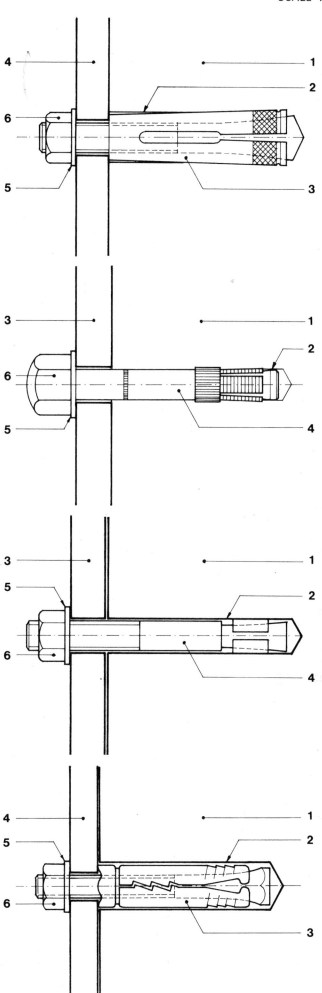

195

FITTINGS : Cast-in fixings

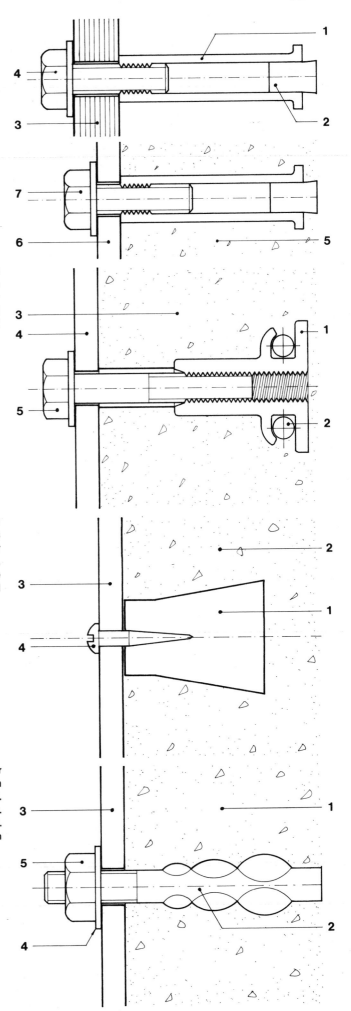

A There are a number of alternative fixings available for casting into concrete. They are placed in position before the concrete is cast round them. One of these fixings is a high-grade malleable iron casting in the form of an internally threaded socket at one end and having a base flange at the other. A bolt is passed through the pre-drilled formwork and the socket is bolted firmly to the inner face of the formwork. When the concrete is cured, bolt and form-work are removed. The fixture is placed in position and the bolt reused.

1 Socket of cast iron or aluminium bronze or stainless steel
2 Cork (in position while concreting)
3 Shuttering
4 Bolt (in position while concreting)
5 Concrete
6 Fixture
7 Bolt

B Another type of cast-in socket is for use in thinner concrete components and has a rectangular base that contains two pro-jections designed to take spreader reinforcing bars. The spreader bars are placed in the socket and tied to reinforcement. A greased bolt is inserted in the socket, the concrete is poured and allowed to set. The bolt is then removed for reuse.

1 Slab type socket
2 Reinforcing bar
3 Concrete
4 Fixture
5 Bolt

C Another form of insert for casting into concrete is a tough composition moulded block that has a dovetail shape. It provides for retention of nails or screws. The block is fixed to the inner face of the shuttering with a nail in a prepared hole in the block. When the concrete is cured, the formwork is removed and the end of the nail cut off. Alternatively, the blocks can be pressed into position in the surface of freshly poured concrete.

1 Moulded composition block
2 Concrete
3 Fixture
4 Fixing screw

D There are two main kinds of simple foundation bolts: rag or lewis bolts and indented bolts. The indented bolt consists of a bar threaded at one end with indentations along the other end. The bolts are normally supplied with ordinary hexagon nuts. The bolt is placed in position and concrete is cast around it. The fixture, drilled to take the screw thread, is placed in position and held firmly in place with nuts and washers.

1 Concrete
2 Steel indented bolt
3 Fixture
4 Steel washer
5 Steel nut

A Standard support

The aluminium alloy support slotted channel is shaped to retain the shelf brackets and slotted to locate them at any interval of 25.4 mm. The support channel is levelled with adjacent support channels. A countersunk wood screw is then inserted through the top hole into a plug and the channel is plumbed. Another wood screw is then inserted at the bottom and intermediate screws are spaced 203 mm apart. Brackets are positioned at the heights determined by the slots in the channel.

1 Structural wall
2 Aluminium alloy slotted support channel
3 Plug
4 Countersunk wood screw at 203 mm centres 25 mm long
5 Aluminium alloy bracket

B Support channel to retain wall panels

An alternative type of slotted aluminium alloy support channel has flanges designed to retain wall panels 12 mm thick against the structural wall. The support channel is levelled with adjacent channels. A countersunk wood screw is inserted through the top hole into a plug and the support is plumbed. A screw is then inserted at the bottom and further intermediate screws are added to suit the loading conditions. Brackets with shaped hooks are then located and held in the support slots to carry the shelves.

1 Structural wall
2 Wall panel 12 mm thick
3 Aluminium alloy slotted support channel with flanges
4 Plug
5 Countersunk wood screw 25 mm long
6 Aluminium alloy bracket

C Support post

A free-standing post may be formed from a hollow square section placed centrally with a support channel section riveted to each of the four sides. The maximum length recommended with top and bottom fixing is 2400 mm. Similar posts may be formed using the central section and one, two, or three sections riveted to it.

1 Aluminium alloy hollow square section
2 Aluminium alloy slotted support channel

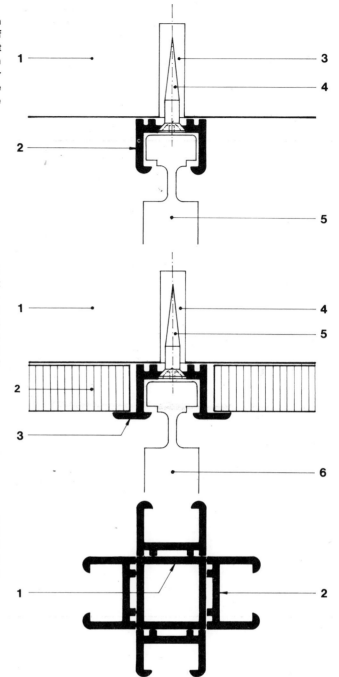

D Support brackets

The support brackets are made of aluminium alloy in lengths ranging from 100 mm to 600 mm in 50 mm steps. There are many different types and finishes, but all brackets are designed to fit the support channel and locate in a support slot. A bracket is positioned by inserting the hooked end into the support channel with the bracket tilted upwards and to one side. It is then twisted upright with the front end upwards and then pressed gently downwards so as to locate in a slot in the support channel at the required height.

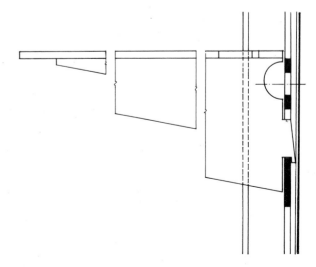

FITTINGS : Chemical fixings

A Chemical adhesives, also known as resin anchor grouts, can be used to make a fixing to concrete, masonry and other materials. They are used in conjunction with a wide range of bars, studs, bolts, and sockets. The recommended diameter of hole to be drilled in the material is between 4 mm and 12 mm larger than the diameter of the bar or bolt. The recommended minimum depth of hole is 100 mm. The hole is best drilled with a rotary percussive air drill using air or water to flush out the hole. A hole drilled with a standard electric drill must be thoroughly cleared of dust and preferably wire brushed and scoured. Holes or pockets that are cast in concrete should be dovetail shaped or have rough sides to give anchorage. A capsule containing polyester resin and quartz granules, with a phial of hardener, is inserted into the hole. The bar is then pressed into the hole, breaking the capsule and mixing the contents to form a resinous mortar that sets in about an hour at normal temperatures. An alternative method is to prepare the mix, pour it into the hole and insert the anchor bar.

1 Masonry
2 Hole
3 Chemical adhesive
4 Dowel of ribbed rolled steel bar

B Ribbed reinforcement bar with threaded end

C Continuously threaded studding

D Indented foundation bolt

E Hexagonal head bolt with head placed downwards

F Socket bolt

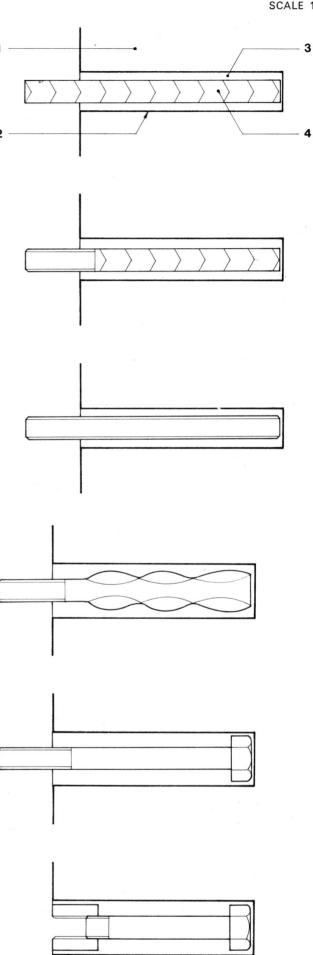

198

A   Frame of solid rectangular sections
The sections are cut to length and cut square. The joint is prepared with V cuts and is then butt welded, using fillet welds which are left as laid.

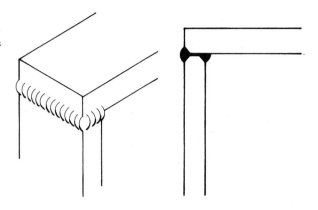

B   Frame of solid rectangular sections
The sections are cut to length and cut square. The joint is prepared with V cuts and is then butt welded with fillet welds which are ground off flush with the faces of the sections.

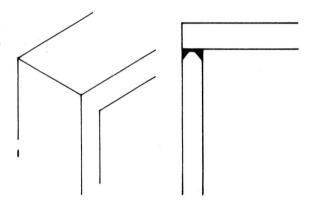

C   Frame of solid square sections
The sections are cut accurately to length and square. The two sections are connected by a steel countersunk machine screw in a drilled and tapped hole.

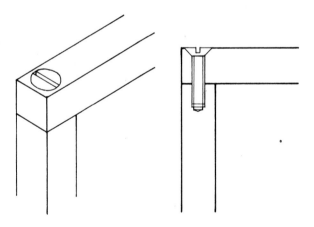

D   Frame of rectangular hollow sections
The two rectangular sections are cut at the end and mitred at 45° to each other. The joint is made with butt weld fillets on all four sides of the section which are left as laid.

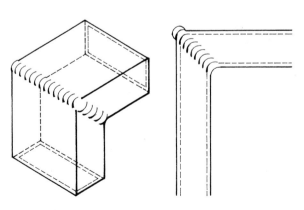

FITTINGS: Steel railings: infilling bars

A Square bars welded

The infilling square bar is cut to length and butted to the hand-rail. Butt fillet welds are used on all four sides and left as laid.

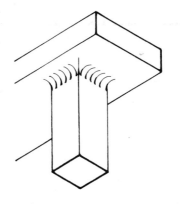
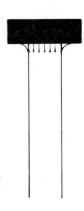

B Round bars welded

The handrail is drilled to take the round infilling bar. The bar is inserted into the hole, but stopped short to provide a recess for weld metal. The bar is plug welded to the rail, the welds being left as laid. For raking work, the holes are drilled at the required angle to the handrail and are reamed so as to give a tight fit.

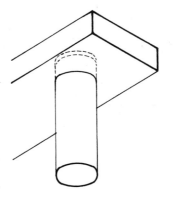
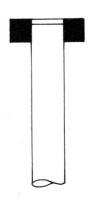

C Round bars screwed

The infilling round bar or standard is cut to length and cut square with the handrail, or at an angle in the case of raking work. The handrail and bar are drilled and tapped. The connection is made with a steel countersunk machine screw which is smoothed off after being screwed home.

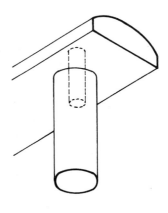
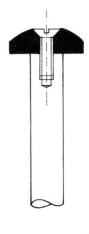

D Rectangular hollow section welded

The infilling section or standard is cut to length and cut square with the handrail. The section is butted against the rail and fillet welds are laid on all four sides. The welds are left as laid.

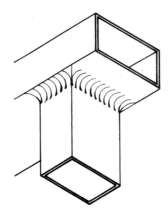
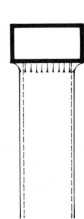

FITTINGS: Railings: jointing of horizontal rails

A Rectangular bars welded

The two rectangular bars are cut square and butted together on site. The ends of the bars are prepared with a V cut to take the weld metal. Butt weld fillets are laid on all four sides of the joint and left as laid. The weld metal may be ground flush with the faces of the bars if a smooth finish is required.

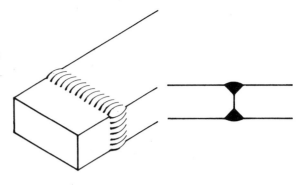

B Round tubes welded

The two round tubes are connected on site with a short tube inserted internally to serve as a dowel, help lining up and assist the welding. The adjacent tubes are kept slightly apart and a fillet weld is laid round the joint and left as laid.

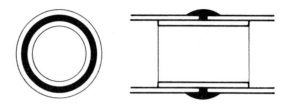

C Rectangular bars screwed

When a rustproofing treatment has been carried out on the bars after manufacture, welding on site is not recommended. The joint between two bars is made by means of a machine halved joint connected with a minimum of two steel countersunk machine screws which are smoothed down after screwing home.

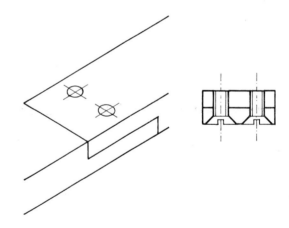

D Rectangular hollow sections welded

The two rectangular hollow sections are connected on site by means of short plates welded to the inside surfaces at the end of one tube. The ends of the sections are prepared with a V cut to take the weld metal. Butt weld fillets are laid on all four sides of the joint and are left as laid

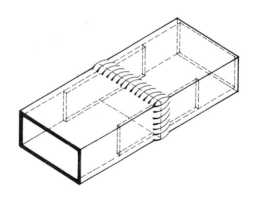

A Lead to lead
When a lead pipe is to be joined to another lead pipe, the joint is made with a wiped soldered joint, or burned joint or fused joint. The end of one pipe is belled out in the form of a socket into which the other pipe is fitted. Molten plumber's solder is then poured on and as it cools it is wiped around the pipe with a pad of special cloth to give the shape and thickness required for the strength of the joint. A lead pipe is connected to a copper pipe in the same way.

1 Lead pipe
2 Lead pipe
3 Wiped soldered joint

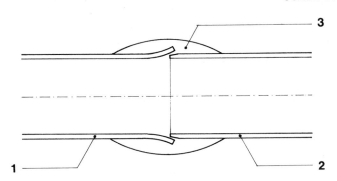

B Lead to copper
When a lead pipe is to be joined to a sanitary fitting, a brass sleeve piece is used between the two. One end of the sleeve piece is joined to the lead pipe with a wiped soldered joint, as described in A above, and the other end is connected to the fitting with a brass coupling nut.

1 Lead pipe
2 Brass sleeve piece
3 Wiped soldered joint
4 Brass coupling nut

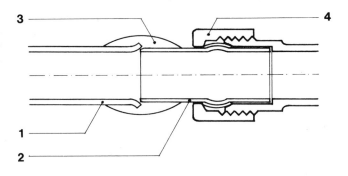

C Lead to cast iron
When a lead pipe is to be joined to the socketed end of a cast iron pipe, a brass or copper sleeve piece is used between the two. The lead pipe is passed through the sleeve piece and turned over at the end. The sleeve piece is joined to the lead pipe by means of a soldered wiped joint. The gap between the sleeve and the socket is packed with a gasket of hemp or yarn and caulked with molten lead.

1 Lead pipe
2 Brass or copper sleeve piece
3 Cast iron pipe
4 Hemp or yarn gasket
5 Lead

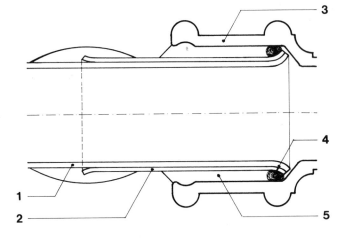

D Lead to stoneware
When a lead pipe is to be joined to the socketed end of a stoneware pipe, a brass or copper sleeve piece is used between the two. The lead pipe is passed through the sleeve piece and turned over at the end. The sleeve piece is joined to the lead pipe by means of a soldered wiped joint. The gap between the sleeve and the stoneware socket is first fitted with a gasket of hemp or yarn and then caulked with a mixture of equal parts of Portland cement and sand.

1 Lead pipe
2 Brass or copper sleeve
3 Wiped soldered joint
4 Stoneware pipe
5 Hemp or yarn gasket
6 Portland cement and sand mixture 1 : 1

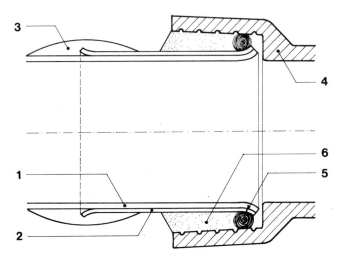

A Blown joint, also, cup-and-cone joint or copper-bit joint
The blown joint is made between lead pipes as an alternative to a wiped joint. The end of one pipe is filed on the outside to a taper. The end of the second pipe is opened out and fitted over the tapered portion of the first pipe. The joint is filled with fine solder, an alloy of two thirds tin and one third lead, which is poured in while molten.

1 Lead pipe
2 Lead pipe
3 Fine solder

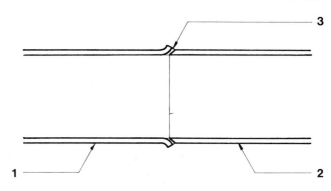

B Silver brazed joint
The silver brazed joint is made between two light-gauge copper tubes. The end of one tube is opened out to form a socket to fit over the other tube. The ends of the two tubes are heated to a dull red, the joint is touched with a strip of silver solder, which melts and is drawn into the gap between the tubes by capillary attraction. Silver solder is an alloy of copper, silver and phosphorus and has a low melting point.

1 Copper light-gauge tube
2 Copper light-gauge tube with socket end
3 Silver solder

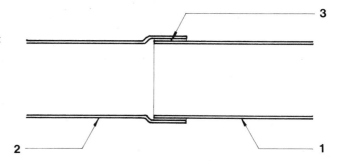

C Solvent welded joint
The solvent welded joint is made between pipes of acrylonitrile-butadiene-styrene (ABS). The end of one pipe is opened out to form a socket which fits over the second pipe. Both interfaces are cleaned with a diluted form of solvent so as to destroy the release agent used in manufacture of the pipe. Solvent welding cement of tetrachloride is applied to both interfaces. One pipe is inserted into the other and given a half turn. The joint is then left for 24 hours to set.

1 ABS pipe with socket
2 ABS pipe
3 Solvent welding cement

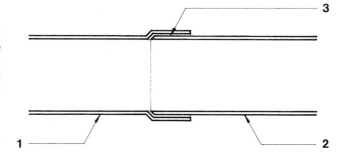

D Socket fusion joint
The socket fusion joint is made between pipes of polypropylene. The sockets and pipes are sized to give an interference fit. The inner surface of the socket and the outer surface of the end of the pipe are heated by means of special tools to a controlled temperature above the melt temperature and the two parts are then carefully pressed together. Maximum joint strength is achieved immediately on cooling. The joint is best made under workshop conditions.

1 Polypropylene socket
2 Polypropylene pipe
3 Fused interface

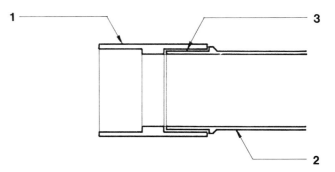

A Vitrified clay pipes for underground drainage

The joint is made between vitrified clay pipes by means of a push-fit polypropylene flexible coupling. The end of one pipe is cleaned and painted with lubricant. The coupling is pushed down over the end of the pipe until the internal separating flange touches the pipe end. The second pipe is then fitted in the same way into the other end of the coupling. The coupling is designed to accept pipe movement of 20 mm linear draw per joint, 5 degree angular movement per joint and 10 mm line displacement per joint.

1 Vitrified clay pipe
2 Lubricant
3 Polypropylene push-fit flexible coupling with sealing gaskets
4 Lubricant
5 Vitrified clay pipe

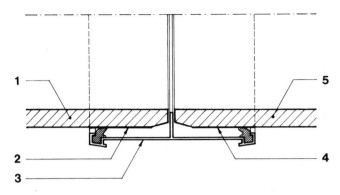

B Perforated vitrified clay pipes for subsoil drainage

The joint is made between perforated vitrified clay plain ended pipes by means of a dry push-fit flexible integral polyethylene sleeve. Each pipe is delivered to the site with the sleeve fixed on one end. The sleeve of the first pipe, and the spigot of the second pipe are cleaned. The spigot is then pushed fully home into the sleeve of the first pipe.

1 Perforated vitrified clay plain ended pipe
2 Polyethylene sleeve piece
3 Perforated vitrified clay plain ended pipe

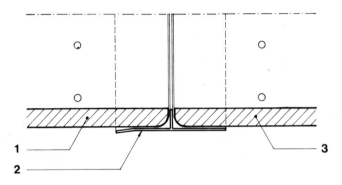

C Vinyl pipes for soil and waste

The joint between vinyl pipes for soil and waste water disposal is by means of a special vinyl socket that incorporates an accurately moulded rectangular groove to take a D-shaped ring seal. The spigot of the pipe is lubricated, inserted into the socket and pushed home. It is then marked at the point of entry and withdrawn a distance of 10 mm to permit movement due to temperature change.

1 Vinyl pipe
2 Vinyl socket
3 D-shaped ring seal
4 Vinyl pipe

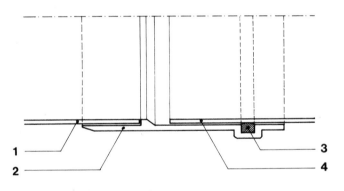

D Polypropylene pipes for waste

The joint between polypropylene pipes for waste water disposal is made with a polypropylene coupling that incorporates collars containing grooves to take ring seals. The end of the pipe is lubricated with silicone grease or liquid detergent or graphite grease or other similar grease and is then inserted into the coupling and pushed home. The push fit allows for thermal expansion and contraction of the pipe.

1 Polypropylene pipe 38 mm diameter nominal bore
2 Lubricant
3 Collar with ring seals

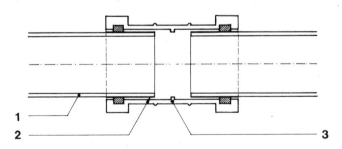

SERVICES : Compression joints for pipes

A Non-manipulative compression joint for copper tube or stainless steel

The end of the copper tube is cut square and the edges made smooth. The tube is then inserted into the compression fitting, without removing the cap and ring, and pushed home so that the end of the tube touches the tube stop inside the body of the fitting. The capnut is tightened by hand followed by a recommended minimum number of turns with a spanner. Alternatively, the cap and ring can be removed, slid onto the tube in sequence, and the tube then inserted fully into the fitting. The ring and nut are then positioned and the nut tightened as with the first method.

1 Brass compression fitting
2 Hand drawn copper tube
3 Spherical compression ring
4 Brass capnut

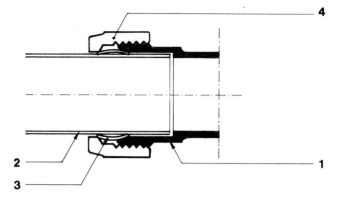

B Manipulative compression joint for copper tube

The capnut and ring are removed from the compression fitting and slid in sequence over the end of the tube which is then expanded with an expanding or flaring tool. The sleeve piece is then inserted into the flared end of the tube and positioned in the compression fitting. The capnut and anti-friction ring are then tightened by hand followed by a recommended minimum number of turns with a spanner.

1 Brass compression fitting
2 Sleeve piece
3 Half-hard copper tube
4 Anti-friction ring
5 Brass capnut

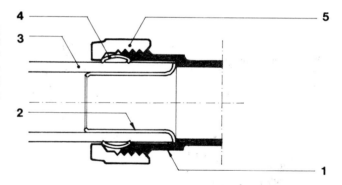

C Compression joint for polythene tube

The capnut and ring are removed from the compression fitting and slid over the end of the polythene tube. The flanged insert is pushed into the end of the tube and the tube inserted fully into the compression fitting until contact is made with the tube stop inside the body of the fitting. The capnut is then tightened by hand followed by a further one-and-a-half turns with a spanner.

1 Brass compression fitting
2 Brass flanged insert
3 Polythene tube
4 Spherical compression ring
5 Brass capnut

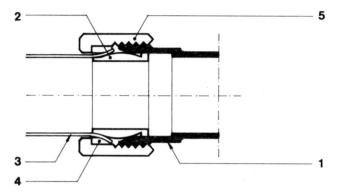

D Compression joints with coupler

A straight coupler compression fitting is used to form a joint between tubes of different materials. Each type of material is fitted with its appropriate compression ring which is retained against the wall of the tube by the tightening of the capnut. Other compression fittings include elbows, bends, T's and crosses.

1 Brass coupler fitting
2 Ferrule
3 Flanged insert
4 Polythene tube
5 Spherical compression ring
6 Capnut
7 Copper tube
8 Anti-friction ring
9 Capnut

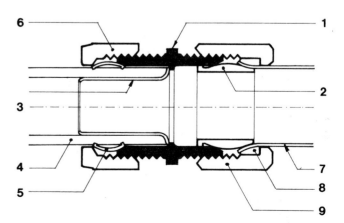

SERVICES : Spigot and socket drainpipes

A Vitrified clay pipes for sewers and drains
The joint between vitrified clay pipes is made by means of a push-fit spigot and socket containing a rubber ring. The end of the socket is cleaned and a layer of lubricant is spread over the polyester moulding inside the socket. A rubber ring is fitted into the groove in the polyester. The spigot is then pushed home into the socket by hand, using a slight side-to-side movement. The material of the jointing ring is made to suit particular effluents.

1 Vitrified clay pipe socket end
2 Natural rubber ring or butyl rubber or chloroprene rubber
3 Lubricant
4 Vitrified clay pipe spigot end

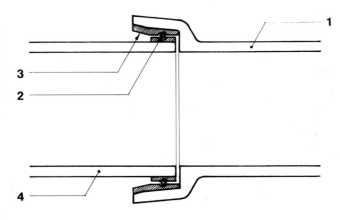

B Vitrified clay half-section channels for drains
The joint between vitrified clay half-section channels is made with a spigot and socket. The ends of the pipes are thoroughly wetted before jointing. The angle of the socket is filled with a tarred gasket. The gap between the socket and spigot is filled with 1 : 3 cement:sand mortar and a 45 degree fillet is formed around the outside of the end of the socket. The joint is left for 48 hours before pressure testing.

1 Vitrified clay half-channel section socket end
2 Vitrified clay half-channel section spigot end
3 Tarred gasket
4 Cement:sand mortar 1 : 3

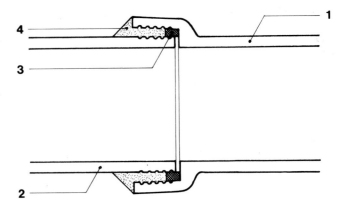

C Vitrified clay pipes for drains
The joint between vitrified clay drainpipes is made with a spigot and socket. The ends of the pipes are thoroughly wetted immediately before jointing. The corner of the socket is filled with yarn to two-thirds of the depth of the socket and the caulking compound is then packed into place with a hammer and wet caulking tool. The surface of the compound is then soaked with water and allowed to set.

1 Vitrified clay pipe socket end
2 Vitrified clay pipe spigot end
3 Yarn gasket
4 Cold caulking compound of asbestos and special cement products

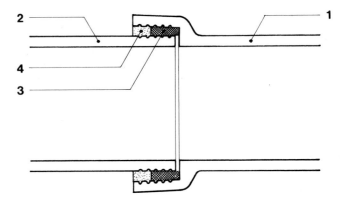

D Cast iron pipes for drains
The joint between cast iron pipes is made with a spigot and socket. The spigot is inserted into the socket and the gap is packed with a gasket of hemp or yarn to half the depth of the socket. Molten lead is then caulked to fill the joint.

1 Cast iron pipe socket end
2 Cast iron pipe spigot end
3 Hemp or yarn gasket
4 Molten lead

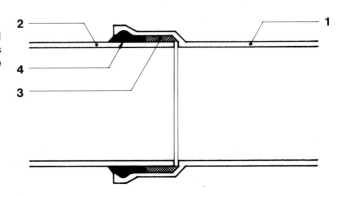

A Rainwater outlet in asphalt roof finish
The roof outlet, together with its insert for an asphalt roof finish, is placed in position in the concrete roof slab. The first layer of asphalt is applied around the rim of the outlet. The second layer of asphalt is then dressed around and up to the stop of the insert. The grating is finally fixed to the insert with self-tapping screws.

1 Polypropylene roof outlet
2 Polypropylene insert for asphalt roof finish
3 Concrete roof slab
4 Cement screed
5 Asphalt
6 Polypropylene domical grating
7 Self-tapping screw

B Rainwater outlet in roofing felt finish
The roof outlet is placed in position in the concrete roof slab. The first layer of roofing felt is dressed around the edge of the outlet. The second layer is dressed over the flange and to the edge of the bowl. The third layer is then dressed into the bowl, cut radially to fit, and bedded in hot bitumen. The insert is then located and locked into position with self-tapping screws fixed to the outlet. The grating is finally fixed to the insert with self-tapping screws.

1 Polypropylene roof outlet
1 Concrete roof slab
3 Cement screed
4 Roofing felt
5 Polypropylene insert roofing felt finish
6 Roofing felt
7 Polypropylene domical grating
8 Self-tapping screw

C Rainwater outlet to polypropylene rainwater pipe
The joint between the rainwater outlet and a polypropylene rainwater pipe is made by applying an adhesive to the circular aperture slot which is formed at the base of the outlet, inserting the pipe into the slot and pushing it home.

1 Polypropylene roof outlet
2 Adhesive
3 Polypropylene rainwater pipe

D Rainwater outlet to cast iron rainwater pipe
The joint between the rainwater outlet and a cast iron rainwater pipe is made by means of a short length of connecting pipe. The circular aperture slot in the base of the outlet is lined with an adhesive and the upper end of the connecting pipe is pushed into the slot. The lower end of the pipe is inserted into the socket of the rainwater pipe and connected to it with a caulking compound.

1 Polypropylene roof outlet
2 Adhesive
3 Polypropylene connecting pipe
4 Cast iron rainwater pipe
5 Caulking compound

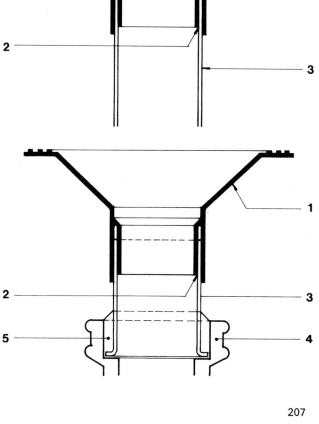

A **Insert channel 3.05 kg/m**
The galvanized cold rolled steel insert channel is pre-filled with expanded plastic foam and is firmly fixed to the shuttering in the required position before the concrete is poured. After the concrete has been poured and has set, the plastic filler is removed so as to leave a channel clean and free from grout and cement and ready to take the standard self-locating nut assemblies, clamps, brackets and other attachments at any point along the length of the channel where required.

1 Galvanized steel insert channel
2 Expanded foam plastic filler
3 Concrete slab

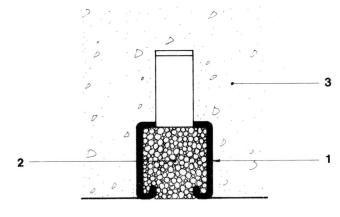

B **Insert channel 1.94 kg/m**
The supporting capacity of the insert channel depends mainly on the strength of the concrete. The channel may be used in continuous lengths or in short lengths placed in the required positions. The standard length of channel is 6096 mm and the lugs are spaced at 102 mm centres.

1 Galvanized steel insert channel
2 Expanded foam plastic filler
3 Concrete slab

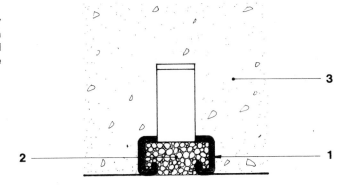

C **Insert channel 1.30 kg/m**
The light section insert channel is cold rolled from a light gauge steel sheet to the same sizes as those used for the channel in B above.

1 Galvanized steel insert channel light gauge
2 Expanded foam plastic filler
3 Concrete slab

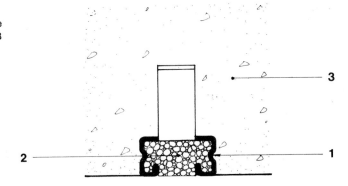

D **Insert channel 0.73 kg/m**
The very light section is rolled to give an overall cross-section that measures 25 mm x 12.5 mm. The section is designed to accommodate 6 mm clamping nuts with M6 x 13 mm diameter high tensile screws. Lugs are spaced alternately at 61 mm and 39 mm centres thus allowing 3000 mm standard lengths to be cut at 100 mm modular intervals.

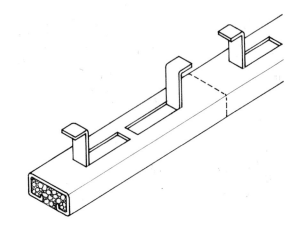

SERVICES : Fixings for pipes

A Single fixing with the one-piece pipe clamp

The pipe is placed at the required position and at right angles to the support channel. The self-locating nut assembly is inserted in the channel and held in place by the spring. The clamp is fitted round the pipe, the shaped end is retained in the channel and the drilled flat is bolted to the nut. Clamps are available for all sizes of pipe from 21 mm diameter to 219 mm diameter.

1 Steel support channel
2 Pipe
3 Galvanized steel strip pipe clamp
4 Self-locating nut assembly

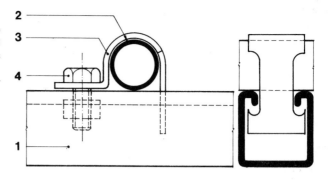

B Fixing with two-piece pipe clamp

The pipe is placed at the required position and at right angles to the support channel. The two half clamps are inserted to grip the flanges of the channel on both sides of the pipe and are bolted together through the hole in the flat flange of each clamp. Clamps are available for all sizes of pipe from 9 mm diameter to 320 mm diameter.

1 Steel support channel
2 Pipe
3 Galvanized steel strip pipe clamp
4 Nut and bolt

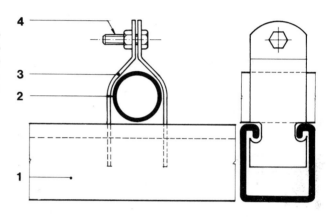

C Double fixing with one-piece pipe clamp

The pipe is placed at the required position and at right angles to the support channel. The U-shaped pipe clamp is positioned over the pipe, the two nut assemblies are located inside the support channel and the two bolts are tightened so that the serrated grooves in the nut grip the flanges of the channel. Clamps are available for all sizes of pipe from 21 mm diameter to 219 mm diameter.

1 Steel support channel
2 Pipe
3 Galvanized steel pipe clamp 5 mm thick
4 Self-locating nut assembly and bolt

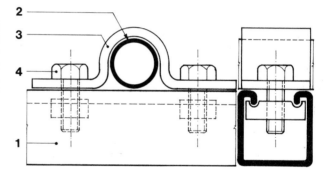

D Support on pipe roller

Heavy pipes, which do not need to be fixed or require to be allowed to move longitudinally, may be supported on rollers which are carried on chairs bolted to the support channel with one self-locating nut assembly and bolt.

1 Steel support channel
2 Chair for pipe roller
3 Self-locating nut assembly and bolt
4 Manganese bronze roller
5 Pipe

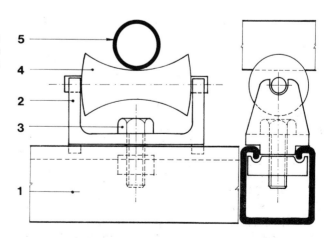

Source Material

BOOKS

Books listed in Library Bibliography 207, *Joints and Jointing*, Building Research Station (1968)

Brunskill, R. W., *Illustrated Handbook of Vernacular Architecture*, Faber and Faber (1970)

Launching, B., *Handbook of Fixings and Fastenings*, The Architectural Press (1971)

Scott, J. S., *Dictionary of Building*, Newnes-Butterworth (1974)

ARTICLES

Articles listed in Library Bibliography 207, *Joints and Jointing*, Building Research Station (1968)

Day, A. G., 'The Inverted Roof', *The Architects' Journal*, 1047-1052 (May 1975)

Eglit, V. I. and Yakub, O., 'Classification of Joints and Sealants', *Build International*, 19-22 (Nov. 1969)

Garrido, Michael J., 'An Examination of Elastomeric Sealants', *Industrialised Building*, **4**, No. 9, 25-28 (Sept. 1967)

Garrido, Michael J. 'Sealants, Joint Failure', *New Building*, 8, No. 10, 15-17 (Oct. 1967)

Gjelsvik, Toré, 'Glazing Design in Norway', *Build International*, 10-11 (June 1969)

Gjelsvik, Toré, 'Classification of Jointing Materials', *Build International*, 111-116 (April 1970)

Grey, G., 'Jointing of Service Pipes', *The Architects' Journal*, 1279-1283 (May 1970)

Groeger, R. G., 'Mastics for External Jointing' *The Architects' Journal*, Information Sheet 1520 (Aug. 1967)

Groeger, R. G., 'A Guide to the Use of Sealants and Mastics', *The Architects' Journal*, Information Sheet 1603.

Harrison, H. W., 'Joints in External Cladding—a Quantitative Study', *Industrialised Building Systems and Components*, 42, 44, 46, 48 (Sept. 1970)

Heinicke, Dr. Ing. Gottfried, 'Arbeitsgrundlagen zu Genauigkeitsuntersuchungen und Passungsberechnungen', *Deutsche Architektur*, (1966, 1967: 8 issues)

Keay, Bernard T., 'Interchangeability and Jointing', *Building*, (Feb. 1967)

Koppes, Wayne F., 'Joint Seals—Fundamental Requirements, Standards, and Tests', *Build International*, 31-35 (Sept.-Oct. 1968)

Meikle, T. A. V., 'A Guide to the Use of Sealants', *Architecture and Building News*, **7**, No. 3 (Oct. 1970)

Murphy, W. E., 'Jointing Between Precast Concrete Facade Panels', *The Architects' Journal*, 146, No. 20 1231-1234 (Nov. 1967)

O'Brien, M., 'Structural Fastening', *Building*, 167-187 (July 1969)

Sliwa, Jan, 'Accuracy in Building', *The Architects' Journal*, **146**, No. 20, 1235-1238 (Nov. 1967)

Sliwa, Jan, 'Introduction to the Design of Joints', *The Architects' Journal*, 1125-1128 (April 1969)

Volbeda, A.,' Tolerances and Fits', *Build International*, 19-21 (April 1969)

Wallis, R. J., 'The Use of Gaskets in Buildings', *R.I.B.A. Journal*, 389-392 (Sept. 1969)

Walters, Roger, 'A National Strategy', *The Modular Quarterly* 1967) No. 4, Transactions 62/30, 15-18.

PAPERS

1948-1966. Papers listed in Library Bibliography 207, *Joints and Jointing*, Building Research Station, 1968

Bonshor, R. B. and Harrison H. W., '*The Relationship Between Component Size and Joint Dimension*', Building Research Station, Current Paper 5/71.

Building Research Station, '*Joints Between Concrete Wall Panels; Open Drained Joints*', Digest 85, 2nd Series (1967)

Building Research Station, '*Joint Movements*', BRS News, 4-5 (Winter 1968)

Burhouse, P., '*Connections (Joints) in Structural Concrete*', Min. of Public Buildings and Works, Building Research Station, Engineering Papers 46/47, 13 (BRS 1967)

Chaddock, D. H., '*Introduction to Fastening Systems*' Engineering Design Guides 0I, Design Council, Oxford University Press (1974)

CIB, '*Symposium on Weather-tight Joints for Walls*' Proceeding Papers, Oslo: Norges Byggforsknings-institutt (1968)

Copper Development Association, '*Copper and Alloy Fixings for Buildings*', Copper Development Association, Technical Note TN21, (1975)

Eden, F. J. and Seymour-Walker, '*Joints in the Context of an Assembly Process*', Building Research Station, Current Paper 2/71

Glover, T. and Tower, D. E., '*Long Strip Copper Roofing*', Copper Development Association, Technical Note TN 17 (1973)

Harrison, H. W., '*Joints and Component Interchange*', Min. of Technology, Building Research Station, Current Papers, Design Series 56, BRS (1967)

Harrison, H. W. and Bonshor, R. B., '*Weatherproofing of Joints: a Systematic Approach to Design*', Building Research Station, Current Paper 29/70

Herbert, M. R. M., '*Open-jointed Rain Screen Claddings*', Building Research Station, Current Paper 89/74

Kirkbride, T. W., '*Building Facing Blockwork*', Cement and Concrete Association (1972)

Paterson, W. S., '*Fixings in Concrete and Masonry: an Appraisal of Present Knowledge*', Construction Industry Research and Information Association, Technical Note 51 (1973)

Ryder, J. F. and Baxter, T. A., '*The Extent and Rate of Joint Movements in Modern Buildings*', Building Research Station, Current Paper 2/71

Shields, J., '*Adhesive Bonding*', Engineering Design Guides 02, Design Council, Oxford University Press (1974)

Taylor, K. H., '*Joints in Cladding*', Rubber and Plastics Research Association of Great Britain, Research Report 176, (May 1969)

The Sealant Manufacturers Conference '*A Manual for Application for Two-part Polysulphide Sealants*' (1967)

BRITISH STANDARDS

BS 65 & 540; Part 1 : 1971	Clay Drain and Sewer Pipes Including Surface Water Pipes and Fittings. Part 1. Pipes and Fittings.
BS 65 & 540; Part 2 : 1972	Clay Drain and Sewer Pipes Including Surface Water Pipes and Fittings. Part 2. Flexible Mechanical Joints.
BS 66 & 99 : 1970	Cast Copper Alloy Pipe Fittings for Use with Screwed Copper Tubes.
BS 1204 : 1964	Synthetic Resin Adhesives. Gap Filling (Phenolic and Aminoplastic) for Constructional Work in Wood.
BS 1210 : 1963	Wood Screws.
BS 1236-40 : 1956	Sills and Lintels (Clayware, Cast Concrete and Natural Stone)
BS 1243 : 1964	Metal Ties for Cavity Wall Construction.
BS 1281 : 1966	Glazed Ceramic Tiles and Tile Fittings for Internal Walls.
BS 1494 : Part 1 : 1964	Fixings for Sheet, Roof and Wall Coverings.
BS 1494 : Part 2 : 1967	Sundry Fixings.
BS 1579 : 1960	Connectors for Timber.
BS 2494 : Part 2 : 1967	Rubber Joint Rings for Gas Mains, Water Mains and Drainage Purposes. Part 2. Rubber Joint Rings for Drainage Purposes.
BS 2847 : 1957	Glossary of Terms for Stone Used in Building.
BS 2900 : 1970	Recommendations for the Co-ordination of Dimensions in Building. Glossary of Terms.
BS 3049 : 1958	Pedestrian Guard Rails (metal).
BS 3669 : 1963	Recommendations for the Selection, Formation and Definition of Technical Terms.
BS 3798 : 1964	Coping units (of Clayware, Unreinforced Cast Concrete, Unreinforced Cast Stone, Natural Stone and Slate).
BS 3921 : 1974	Clay Bricks and Blocks.
BS 4118 : 1967	Glossary of Sanitation Terms.
BS 4127 : 1967	Light Gauge Stainless Steel Tubes.
BS 4374 : 1968	Sills of Clayware, Cast Concrete, Cast Stone and Natural Stone.
BS 4643 : 1970	Glossary of Terms Relating to Joints and Jointing in Building.

BRITISH STANDARD CODES OF PRACTICE

CP 102 : 1963	Protection of Buildings Against Water from the Ground.
CP 112 : 1967	The Structural Use of Timber.
CP 112 : Part 2 : 1971	The Structural Use of Timber. Metric Units.
CP 112 : Part 3 : 1973	The Structural Use of Timber. Trussed Rafters for Roofs of Dwellings.
CP 116	The Structural Use of Pre-cast Concrete.
CP 121 : Part 1 : 1973	Walling. Part 1 : Brick and Block Masonry.
CP 121.201 (1951)	Masonry Walls.
CP 121.202 (1951)	Masonry—Rubble Walls.
CP 122 : 1952	Walls and Partitions of Blocks and of Slabs.
CP 123.101 (1951)	Dense Concrete Walls.
CP 143	Sheet Roof Coverings.
CP 144	Roof Coverings.
CP 151 : Part 1 : 1957	Doors and Windows Including Frames and Linings. Part 1 : Wooden Doors.
CP 152 : 1966	Glazing and Fixing of Glass for Buildings.
CP 201 : Part 2 : 1972	Flooring of Wood and Wood Products. Part 2. Wood Flooring.
CP 204 : 1965	In-situ Floor Finishes.
CP 212 : Part 1 : 1963	Wall Tiling. Part 1 : Internal Ceramic Wall Tiling Under Normal Conditions.
CP 221 : 1960	External Rendered Finishes.
CP 297 : 1972	Precast Concrete Cladding (Non-loadbearing).
CP 298 : 1972	Natural Stone Cladding (Non-loadbearing).
CP 308 : 1974	Drainage of Roofs and Paved Areas.

MANUFACTURERS' TRADE AND TECHNICAL LITERATURE

From the manufacturers and trade associations listed on page 212.

Manufacturers and associations

The author and publisher wish to thank the manufacturers and associations listed below for their co-operation in supplying technical information which was of help in the compilation of details in the following sections of Part II.

Whilst the provision of technical information has been essential for the compilation of this work, the responsibility for the selection, arrangement and presentation of material is solely that of the author.

Addresses of these manufacturers and associations can be found on page 213.

Foundations (*pages 46-55*)

Adshead Ratcliffe & Co Ltd
Burt Bolton (Timber) Ltd
Conder Group Services Ltd
Council of Forest Industries of British Columbia
Expandite Ltd

Frames (*pages 56-70*)

Automated Building Components Europe SA
Automatic Pressings Ltd
Cape Boards and Panels Ltd
Concrete Ltd
Conder Group Services Ltd
Cooper & Turner Ltd
MacAndrews & Forbes Ltd
National Research Council of Canada

Stairs (*page 71*)

Altro Ltd

Roofs (*pages 72-98*)

Briggs Amasco Ltd
British Gypsum Ltd
The British Screw Co Ltd
British Uralite Ltd
Cape Universal Claddings Ltd
Copper Development Association
Expanded Polystyrene Product Manufacturers
  Association
Hills Glass and Windows Ltd
Lead Development Association
Nutrim
Profilit Glass Ltd
Redland Roof Tiles Ltd
Torvale Building Products Ltd (Woodcemair Division)
The Velux Co Ltd
Zinc Development Association

Walls (*pages 99-130*)

Adshead Ratcliffe & Co Ltd
Birtley Manufacturing (Sales) Ltd

Bostik Ltd
British Uralite Ltd
Cement & Concrete Association
Council of Forest Industries of British Columbia
Farmiloe Sealants Division
Finnish Plywood Development Association
Forticrete Ltd
GKN Steelstock Ltd
Gränges Essem (UK) Ltd
Harris & Edgar Ltd
Hills Glass and Windows Ltd
Langley London Ltd
Profilit Glass Ltd
Redland Claddings Ltd
Ruberoid Ltd
Seaboard International (Timber & Plywood) Ltd
Servicised
Wincilate Ltd

Windows (*pages 131-142*)

Adshead Ratcliffe & Co Ltd
Blacknell Buildings Ltd
Clark-Eaton Ltd
Expandite Ltd
John Carr (Doncaster) Ltd
Leyland & Birmingham Rubber Co Ltd
The Standard Patent Glazing Co Ltd
Steel Window Association
Tremco Ltd

External Doors (*pages 143-145*)

Chamberlain Weatherstrips Ltd

Internal Doors (*pages 146-152*)

Applied Acoustics
Cape Boards and Panels Ltd
Crosby & Co Ltd
Schauman (UK) Ltd
Sealmaster Ltd

Partitions (*pages 153-165*)

C. F. Anderson & Son Ltd
Bakelite Zylonite Ltd
British Gypsum Ltd
Council of Forest Industries of British Columbia
Dexion Ltd
Gliksten Plywood Ltd
GTE Unistrut Ltd
Hatmet Contracts Ltd
Unilock-Tenon International Ltd

Internal Wall Finishes (*pages 166-174*)

Applied Acoustics
British Gypsum Ltd
Eternit Building Products Ltd
Expamet Building Products Ltd
Finnish Plywood Development Association

Floor Finishes (*pages 175-184*)

Adshead Ratcliffe & Co Ltd
Altro Ltd
C. F. Anderson & Son Ltd
Chipboard Promotion Association Ltd
Compribrand (Gt. Britain) Ltd
Expanded Polystyrene Product Manufacturers
  Association
Expandite Ltd
Finnish Plywood Development Association

Fittings (*pages 191-201*)

Artur Fischer (UK) Ltd
Chemical Building Products Ltd
FEB (Great Britain) Ltd
Hilti (Gt. Britain) Ltd
Phillips Drill Co (UK) Ltd
The Rawlplug Co Ltd
Society of Railing and Balustrade Makers
Tebrax Ltd

Ceiling Finishes (*pages 185-190*)

Applied Acoustics
Cape Boards & Panels Ltd
Expamet Building Products Ltd
Gliksten Plywood Ltd
Treetex Acoustics Ltd
Wincilate Ltd

Services (*pages 202-209*)

Chemical Pipe and Vessel Co Ltd
Conex Sanbra Ltd
Expandite Ltd
GTE Unistrut Ltd
The Hepworth Iron Co Ltd
Ruberoid Ltd

Addresses of manufacturers and associations

For the convenience of readers, the names and addresses of manufacturers and associations who have supplied technical information are given below.

Where UK manufacturers have supplied details of their US and Canadian company or distributor, these have been given. Similarly US and Canadian 'sister' organisations have been listed where British associations have provided the details.

Adshead Ratcliffe & Co Ltd
Derby Road
Belper
Derby DE5 1WJ

Altro Ltd
Caxton Hill
Hertford SG13 7NB

Compass Commercial Enterprises
51 Glengowan Road
Toronto
Ontario
Canada

C. F. Anderson & Son Ltd
7-9 Islington Green
London N1 2XJ

Applied Acoustics
8 Manchester Square
London W1M 5AB

Artur Fischer (UK) Ltd
25 Newtown Road
Marlow
Bucks SL7 1JY

Fischer of America Inc
151 Forest Street
Montclair
NJ 07042
USA

Automated Building Components Europe SA
A.B.C. (UK) Ltd
No 2 Site Trading Estate
Farnham
Surrey

Automated Building Components Inc
PO Box 59-2037
AMF Miami
Florida 33159
USA

Automatic Pressings Ltd
Halesfield Industrial Estate
Telford
Shropshire TF7 4LD

Bakelite Zylonite Ltd
Enford House
139 Marylebone Road
London NW1 5QE

Birtley Manufacturing (Sales) Ltd
Mary Avenue
Birtley
Tyne and Wear DH3 1JF

Blacknell Buildings Ltd
25 Westmead
Farnborough
Hampshire GU14 7LB

Bostik Ltd
Leicester
LE4 6BW

Bostik Division
USM Corporation
Boston Street
Middleton
Massachusetts
USA

Briggs Amasco Ltd
Goodwyns Place
Towerl Hill Road
Dorking
Surrey RH4 2AW

British Gypsum Ltd
Ferguson House
15 Marylebone
London NW1 5JE

Westroc Industries Ltd
2650 Lakeshore Highway
Clarkson
Ontario
Canada

The British Screw Co Ltd
153 Kirkstall Road
Leeds LS4 2AT

British Uralite Ltd
Higham
Rochester
Kent

Burt Bolton (Timber) Ltd
Ariel Chambers
52 King Edward Street
Hull HU1 3EQ

Cape Boards and Panels Ltd
Iver Lane
Uxbridge UB8 2JQ

Cape Universal Claddings Ltd
PO Box 165
Tolpits
Watford WD1 8QZ

Cement and Concrete Association
Wexham Springs
Slough SL3 6PL

Prestressed Concrete Institute
20 North Wacker Drive
Chicago
Illinois 6060
USA

American Concrete Institute
22400 West Seven Mile Road
PO Box 19150
Redford Station
Detroit
Michigan 48219
USA

Chamberlain Weatherstrips Ltd
262 Hook Road
Chessington
Surrey

Chemical Building Products Ltd
Cleveland Road
Hemel Hempstead
Herts HP2 7DL

Celtite Inc
PO Box 33024
13670 York Road
Cleveland
Ohio 44133
USA

Chemical Pipe and Vessel Co Ltd
Frimley Road
Camberley
Surrey GU15 2QQ

Polytech Plastic Industries
964 E. Swedesford Road
Box Q
Exton
Pa 19341
USA

Chipboard Promotion Association Ltd
7a Church Street
Esher
Surrey

Clark-Eaton Ltd
Southern Industrial Area
Bracknell
Berkshire RG12 4UU

Compribrand (Gt. Britain) Ltd
Towerfield Road
Shoeburyness
Essex SS3 9QQ

Concrete Ltd
399 Strand
London WC2R 0NB

Conder Group Services Ltd
Kings Worthy
Winchester
Hampshire SO23 7SJ

Conex Sanbra Ltd
Whitehall Road
Tipton
West Midlands DY4 7JU

Cooper & Turner Ltd
Vulcan Works
Vulcan Road
Sheffield S9 2FW

Cooper & Turner Inc
33 North Hazel Street
Youngstown
Ohio 44503
USA

Copper Development Association
Orchard House
Mutton Lane
Potters Bar
Hertfordshire EN6 3AP

Council of Forest Industries of British Columbia
Templar House
81 High Holborn
London WC1

Crosby & Co Ltd
Craven House
The Hart
Farnham
Surrey GU9 7HB

Dexion Ltd
Dexion House
PO Box 7
Wembley
Middlesex HA9 0JW

Eternit Building Products Ltd
56-70 High Street
Putney
London SW15 1SF

Expamet Building Products Ltd
16 Caxton Street
London SW1H 0RA

The Expanded Metal Corporation
1080 Expamet Drive SE
Smyrna
Georgia 30080
USA

Expanded Polystyrene Product Manufacturers
   Association
1 Keymer Road
Hassocks
Sussex BN6 8AE

Expandite Ltd
1-9 Chase Road
London NW10 6PS

Farmiloe Sealants Division
Key Terrain House
Larkfield
Maidstone ME20 7PJ

FEB (Great Britain) Ltd
Albany House
Swinton Hall Road
Swinton
Manchester M27 1DT

Finnish Plywood Development Association
Broadmead House
21 Panron Street
London SW1Y D4R

Finnish Plywood Development Association
210 East Broad Street
Falls Church
22046 Virginia
USA

Forticrete Ltd
The Mill Lane
Glenfield
Leicester LE3 8DX

GKN Steelstock Ltd
PO Box 25
Stourvale Works
Clensmore Street
Kidderminster
Worcs DY10 2JU

Gliksten Plywood Ltd
PO Box 118
Carpenters Road
London E15 2DY

Gränges Essem (UK) Ltd
Leon House
223 High Street
Croydon CR0 9XT

GTE Unistrut Ltd
Unistrut House
Edison Road
Elms Industrial Estate
Bedford MK4 10HU

GTE Unistrut International Inc
Wayne
Michigan
USA

Harris & Edgar Ltd
Progress Works
222 Purley Way
Croydon CR9 4JH

Hatmet Contracts Ltd
70 Salusbury Road
London NW6

The Hepworth Iron Co Ltd
Hazelhead
Stocksbridge
Sheffield S30 5HG

Hills Glass and Windows Ltd
Glass Works
Chester Street
Birmingham B6 4AG

Hilti (Gt. Britain) Ltd
Hilti House
Chester Road
Manchester M16 0GW

Hilti Inc
360 Fairfield Avenue
PO Box 809
Stamford
Connecticut 06904
USA

John Carr (Doncaster) Ltd
Watch House Lane
Doncaster

Langley London Ltd
163/5/7 Borough High Street
London SE1

Lead Development Association
34 Berkeley Square
London W1X 6AJ

The Leyland & Birmingham Rubber Co Ltd
Leyland
Preston PR5 1UB

MacAndrews & Forbes Ltd
Pembroke House
44 Wellesley Road
Croydon CR9 3QE

National Research Council of Canada
Science & Technology Division
Canadian High Commission
1 Grosvenor Square
London W1X 0AB

National Research Council of Canada
Division of Building Research
Montreal Road
Ottawa K1A 0R6
Ontario
Canada

Nutrim
WP Metals Ltd
Aldridge
Staffordshire

Phillips Drill Co (UK) Ltd
Queenslie Industrial Estate
Glasgow G33 4BL

Profilit Glass Ltd
Pembroke House
44 Wellesley Road
Croydon CR9 3PD

The Rawlplug Co Ltd
Rawlplug House
London Road
Kingston upon Thames
Surrey KT2 6NR

Redland Claddings Ltd
Redland House
Reigate
Surrey RH2 0SJ

Redland Roof Tiles Ltd
Redland House
Reigate
Surrey RH2 0SJ

Monier Raymond Co
PO Box 158
Corona
California 91720
USA

Ruberoid Ltd
1 New Oxford Street
London WC1A 1PE

Schauman (UK) Ltd
76-80 College Road
Harrow
Middlesex HA1 1JN

Seaboard International (Timber & Plywood) Ltd
British Columbia House
3 Regent Street
London SW1Y 4NY

Seaboard International Lumber & Plywood Inc
3000 Marcus Avenue
Lake Success
NY 11040
USA

Sealmaster Ltd
Pampisford
Cambridge

Servicised
2 Caxton St
London SW1

Society of Railing and Balustrade Makers
Glen House
Stag Place
London SW1

The Standard Patent Glazing Co Ltd
Forge Lane
Dewsbury
West Yorkshire WF12 9EL

Steel Window Association
26 Store Street
London WC1E 7RJ

Steel Window Institute
2130 Keith Building
Cleveland
Ohio 44115
USA

Tebrax Ltd
63 Borough High Street
London SE1 1NG

Treetex Acoustics Ltd
Swinton House
324 Grays Inn Road
London WC1

Tremco Ltd
27 St Georges Road
London SW19 4DY

Tremco Ltd
1071 Shaker Boulevard
Cleveland
Ohio 44104
USA

Tremco (Canada) Ltd
220 Wicksteed Avenue
Toronto
Ontario MH4 1G7
Canada

Unilock-Tenon International Ltd
176-184 Vauxhall Bridge Road
London SW1V 1DX

The Velux Co Ltd
Gunnels Wood Road
Stevenage
Hertfordshire SG1 2BN

Wincilate Ltd
The Town Hall
Bow Road
London E3 2SD

Woodcemair
Division of Torvale Building Products Ltd
The Limes
Dudley Road
Sedgley
Dudley
West Midlands DY3 1SU

Zinc Development Association
34 Berkeley Square
London W1X 6AJ

Index